Java™ in the Lab

Lab Manual to Accompany
Java How To Program, Fifth Edition

HOW TO PROGRAM Series

Advanced Java™ 2 Platform How to Program

C How to Program, 4/E

C++ How to Program, 4/E

C# How to Program

e-Business and e-Commerce How to Program

Internet and World Wide Web How to Program, 2/E

Java™ How to Program, 5/E

Perl How to Program

Python How to Program

Visual Basic® 6 How to Program

Visual Basic® .NET How to Program, 2/E

Wireless Internet & Mobile Business How to Program

XML How to Program

DEITEL® Developer Series

C# for Experienced Programmers

C# A Programmer's Introduction

Java™ Web Services for Experienced
   Programmers

.NET A Technical Introduction

Visual Basic® .NET for Experienced
   Programmers

Web Services: A Technical Introduction

Simply Series

Simply Visual Basic .NET: An Application-
   Driven Tutorial Approach

Simply Java™ Programming: An
   Application-Driven Tutorial Approach

For Managers Series

e-Business and e-Commerce for Managers

.NET How to Program Series

C# How to Program

Visual Basic® .NET How to Program, 2/E

Visual C++ .NET How to Program (Fall
   2003)

Visual Studio® Series

C# How to Program

Visual Basic® .NET How to Program, 2/E

Visual C++ .NET How to Program (Fall
   2002)

Getting Started with Microsoft® Visual
   C++® 6 with an Introduction to MFC

Visual Basic® 6 How to Program

Coming Soon

e-books and e-whitepapers

Premium CourseCompass, WebCT and
   Blackboard Multimedia Cyber
   Classroom versions

Multimedia Cyber Classroom and Web-Based Training Series

(For information regarding DEITEL® Web-based training visit www.ptgtraining.com)

C++ Multimedia Cyber Classroom, 4/E

C# Multimedia Cyber Classroom

e-Business and e-Commerce Multimedia Cyber Classroom

Internet and World Wide Web Multimedia Cyber Classroom, 2/E

Java™ 2 Multimedia Cyber Classroom, 5/E

Perl Multimedia Cyber Classroom

Python Multimedia Cyber Classroom

Visual Basic® 6 Multimedia Cyber Classroom

Visual Basic® .NET Multimedia Cyber Classroom, 2/E

Wireless Internet & Mobile Business Programming Multimedia Cyber Classroom

XML Multimedia Cyber Classroom

The Complete Training Course Series

The Complete C++ Training Course, 4/E

The Complete C# Training Course

The Complete e-Business and e-Commerce Programming Training Course

The Complete Internet and World Wide Web Programming Training Course, 2/E

The Complete Java™ 2 Training Course, 5/E

The Complete Perl Training Course

The Complete Python Training Course

The Complete Visual Basic® 6 Training Course

The Complete Visual Basic® .NET Training Course, 2/E

The Complete Wireless Internet & Mobile Business Programming Training Course

The Complete XML Programming Training Course

To follow the Deitel publishing program, please register at
www.deitel.com/newsletter/subscribe.html

for the *DEITEL® BUZZ ONLINE* e-mail newsletter.

To communicate with the authors, send e-mail to:
deitel@deitel.com

For information on corporate on-site seminars offered by Deitel & Associates, Inc. worldwide, visit:

www.deitel.com

For continuing updates on Prentice Hall and Deitel publications visit:
www.deitel.com,
www.prenhall.com/deitel or
www.InformIT.com/deitel

Java™ in the Lab
Lab Manual to Accompany
Java How to Program, Fifth Edition

H. M. Deitel
Deitel & Associates, Inc.

P. J. Deitel
Deitel & Associates, Inc.

PEARSON
Prentice
Hall

PEARSON EDUCATION, INC., Upper Saddle River, New Jersey 07458

Library of Congress Cataloging-in-Publication Data

On file

Vice President and Editorial Director: *Marcia Horton*
Senior Acquisitions Editor: *Kate Hargett*
Associate Editor: *Carole Snyder*
Editorial Assistant: *Michael Giacobbe*
Assistant Editor: *Sarah Parker*
Vice President and Director of Production and Manufacturing, ESM: *David W. Riccardi*
Executive Managing Editor: *Vince O'Brien*
Managing Editor: *Tom Manshreck*
Production Editor: *John F. Lovell*
Director of Creative Services: *Paul Belfanti*
Senior Manager, Artworks: *Patricia Burns*
Audio-Visual Editor: *Xiaohong Zhu*
Creative Director: *Carole Anson*
Cover Designer: *Geoffrey Cassar*
Manufacturing Manager: *Trudy Pisciotti*
Manufacturing Buyer: *Ilene Kahn*
Marketing Manager: *Pamela Shaffer*
Marketing Assistant: *Barrie Reinhold*

© 2003 by Pearson Education, Inc.
Upper Saddle River, New Jersey 07458

The authors and publisher of this book have used their best efforts in preparing this book. These efforts include the development, research, and testing of the theories and programs to determine their effectiveness. The authors and publisher make no warranty of any kind, expressed or implied, with regard to these programs or to the documentation contained in this book. The authors and publisher shall not be liable in any event for incidental or consequential damages in connection with, or arising out of, the furnishing, performance, or use of these programs.

Many of the designations used by manufacturers and sellers to distinguish their products are claimed as trademarks and registered trademarks. Where those designations appear in this book, and Prentice Hall and the authors were aware of a trademark claim, the designations have been printed in initial caps or all caps. All product names mentioned remain trademarks or registered trademarks of their respective owners.

Printed in the United States of America

10 9 8 7 6 5 4 3 2 1

ISBN 0-13-101631-8

Prentice-Hall International (UK) Limited, *London*
Prentice-Hall of Australia Pty. Limited, *Sydney*
Prentice-Hall Canada Inc., *Toronto*
Prentice-Hall Hispanoamericana, S.A., *Mexico*
Prentice-Hall of India Private Limited, *New Delhi*
Prentice-Hall of Japan, Inc., *Tokyo*
Pearson Education Asia Pte. Ltd., *Singapore*
Editora Prentice-Hall do Brasil, Ltda., *Rio de Janeiro*

Trademarks

Contents

Contents   xiii

Preface

Many colleges conduct programming classes in laboratory environments. This lab manual complements our introductory/intermediate textbook, *Java How to Program, Fifth Edition,* and the optional *Java 2 Multimedia Cyber Classroom, Fifth Edition,* by providing a series of hands-on lab assignments designed to reinforce students' understanding of lecture material. For continuing updates on this lab manual and all Deitel & Associates, Inc. publications and services, please register at www.deitel.com/newsletter/subscribe.html to receive the DEITEL® BUZZ ONLINE e-mail newsletter and please visit www.deitel.com periodically.

Closed Laboratories

There are two types of Computer Science laboratory classes—*closed laboratories* and *open laboratories.* Closed laboratories are scheduled classes supervised by an instructor. Closed laboratories provide an excellent learning environment because students can apply concepts presented in class to carefully designed lab problems. Additionally, instructors are better able to gauge the students' understanding of the material by monitoring their progress in lab. This lab manual is designed for closed laboratory sessions of approximately two hours each. Open laboratories do not have specified meeting times and students do not work on the lab assignments under an instructor's supervision; this lab manual also can be used effectively for open laboratories and self-study.

About Java in the Lab

This lab manual focuses on Chapters 2–10, 12, 13, 15 and 17 of *Java How to Program, Fifth Edition.*[1] Each chapter in this manual corresponds to its equivalent chapter in *Java How to Program, Fifth Edition,* and is divided into three major sections: *Prelab Activities, Lab Exercises* and *Postlab Activities.* Each chapter contains the following pedagogic features:

Objectives Section
The Objectives section highlights the key topics to be covered. After completing the lab, students can confirm their mastery of the material by reviewing the objectives.

Assignment Checklist
Each chapter contains an assignment checklist that allows students to mark the exercises the instructor assigns. Each page in the lab manual is perforated, so students can submit their answers (if required) by tearing out the pages.

---

1. These chapters were chosen based on our own experience and feedback from instructors using *Java How to Program, Fifth Edition* in introductory/intermediate-level Computer Science courses. Professors desiring labs for other chapters should contact the authors at deitel@deitel.com. We will respond promptly. Please provide us with your specific requirements and as much advance notice as possible.

Prelab Activities

Prelab Activities are intended to be completed by students after studying the corresponding chapter in *Java How to Program, Fifth Edition*. *Prelab Activities* test students' understanding of the material presented in *Java How to Program, Fifth Edition* and in lecture, and prepare students for the programming exercises in the lab session. These activities may be finished before or during lab, at the instructor's discretion. The exercises focus on important terminology and programming concepts and make excellent self-review problems for students. This lab manual contains the following types of *Prelab Activities*:

182 Matching Exercises (count includes separate parts)
Matching exercises present students with a column of important programming terms and a column of descriptions of those terms. Students must match the terms to the corresponding definitions. These exercises help ensure that students understand key terms.

131 Fill-in-the-Blank Exercises
Fill-in-the-blank exercises present students with sentences missing key words; students must provide the missing word(s). These exercises also ensure that students understand key terms.

75 Short-Answer Questions
Short-answer questions test the students' understanding of new concepts. Students are expected to provide a brief answer for each question.

71 Programming-Output Exercises
Reading code is as important as writing code. The programming-output exercises provide students with short code segments and ask the students to determine what each segment does, without the students actually running the program. These exercises reinforce students' understanding of program control and programming concepts.

60 Correct-the-Code Exercises
Error detection and debugging are some of the most important and most difficult skills to master in computer programming. The correct-the-code exercises provide students with code segments that contain one or more errors. Students are asked to identify and fix all errors. These exercises are intended to be completed without the aid of a compiler.

Lab Exercises

This is the most important section in each chapter. The lab exercises teach students how to apply the material learned in *Java How to Program, Fifth Edition* and to prepare them for writing Java programs. Each lab typically contains one or more lab exercises and a debugging problem. The *Lab Exercises* contain the following:

128 Lab Objectives
The lab objectives highlight specific concepts from the corresponding chapter in *Java How to Program, Fifth Edition* on which the lab exercise focuses. The objectives give students the opportunity, after reading the chapter, to determine whether they have met the intended goals. The objectives serve as confidence builders and as a source of positive reinforcement.

32 Problem Descriptions
These descriptions contain detailed explanations of the programs and how the programs should be written. Many of these problems are taken from the exercise sets of *Java How to Program, Fifth Edition*. These problems have been carefully tested in our corporate seminars and by the hundreds of colleges and universities worldwide that use *Java How to Program, Fifth Edition*.

47 Sample Outputs
One or more sample outputs are provided for every lab exercise. The sample outputs illustrate the desired program behavior. The outputs help clarify the problem descriptions and help students confirm that their programs are working properly.

32 Program Templates
Program templates are Java programs in which one or more key lines of code have been removed and replaced with comments that provide information about the missing code. These templates offer students a starting point from which to begin programming and provide insights into how a problem can be solved. Program templates are available at www.deitel.com/books/downloads.html#jhtp5 and www.prenhall.com/deitel.

164 Problem-Solving Tips
The problem-solving tips are suggestions and hints that students should use during the labs.

51 Follow-Up Questions and Activities
These questions often ask students to make modifications to template solutions. These exercises are designed to further students' understanding of Java, to demonstrate how a similar program may be solved or to implement an alternative solution. Students also are asked to interpret their solutions to ensure that they understand the crucial programming concepts.

12 Debugging Problems
The debugging exercises alert students to the types of errors that they are likely to encounter while programming. Each problem consists of a block of code that contains syntax and/or logic errors. These programs are intended to be compiled and executed during the laboratory sessions. Source-code files for the debugging exercises are available at www.deitel.com/books/downloads.html#jhtp5 and www.prenhall.com/deitel.

Postlab Activities

Postlab activities are intended to be completed by students after their lab sessions. Students find these activities useful for self-study, especially students who complete the lab sessions quickly. Professors may assign these activities to reinforce key concepts or to provide students with more programming experience. Two types of programming activities are provided: coding exercises and programming challenges.

70 Coding Exercises
Coding exercises are short and serve as review after the *Prelab Activities* and *Lab Exercises* have been completed. These exercises require students to write programs or program segments to illustrate specific concepts from the textbook.

21 Programming Challenges
Programming challenges allow students to apply the knowledge they have gained in class to substantial programming exercises. Hints, sample outputs and/or pseudocode are provided to aid students with these problems. If students successfully complete the programming challenges for a chapter, they have mastered the chapter material. Most programming challenges are taken from the *Java How to Program, Fifth Edition* exercise sets.[2]

Instructor's Manual for Java in the Lab

An *Instructor's Manual* contains the solutions to the *Prelab Activities*, *Lab Exercises* and *Postlab Activities*. [*NOTE*: **Please do not write to us requesting the instructor's manual. Distribution of this material is strictly limited to college professors teaching from the book. Instructors may obtain the instructor's manual only from their Prentice Hall representatives. We regret that we cannot provide the solutions to professionals.**]

---

2. *Java How to Program, Fifth Edition* contains a rich set of exercises for each chapter. Solutions are available for all the programming challenges on www.deitel.com/books/downloads.html#jhtp5 and www.prenhall.com/deitel. Instructors who want to assign Postlab programming challenges for which students are not provided with the answers should visit www.deitel.com/books/jhtp5/jhtp5_cybersols.pdf. This PDF document lists the exercises in *Java How to Program, Fifth Edition* for which solutions *are* provided on the *Java 2 Multimedia Cyber Classroom, Fifth Edition*; instructors should assign exercises not listed in this PDF document.

Ancillary Package for Java How to Program, Fifth Edition

Java How to Program, Fifth Edition has extensive ancillary materials available to instructors teaching from the book. The *Instructor's Manual CD* contains solutions to the vast majority of the end-of-chapter exercises. A *Test Item File* is available for creating quizzes or exams. In addition, we provide *PowerPoint*® *Lecture Notes* (available at www.deitel.com and www.prenhall.com/deitel) that contain all the code and figures in the text and slides with bulleted points that highlight the key topics discussed in each section of the book. Instructors are encouraged to customize these slides to meet their own classroom needs; students may download these slides as well. Prentice Hall provides a *Companion Web Site* (www.prenhall.com/deitel) that includes additional resources for instructors and students. For instructors, the Web site includes a *Syllabus Manager* for course planning and links to the *PowerPoint*® *Lecture Notes*. For students, the Web site provides chapter objectives, true/false self-review exercises and answers, chapter highlights and reference materials.

Java 2 Multimedia Cyber Classroom, Fifth Edition and The Complete Java 2 Training Course, Fifth Edition

We have prepared an optional interactive, CD-ROM-based, software version of *Java How to Program, Fifth Edition* called the *Java 2 Multimedia Cyber Classroom, Fifth Edition*. This Windows® resource is loaded with features for learning and reference.

The CD provides an introduction in which the authors overview the *Cyber Classroom*'s features. The textbook's live-code example programs truly "come alive" in the *Cyber Classroom*. If you are viewing a program and want to execute it, you simply click the lightning-bolt icon, and the program will run. You immediately will see the program's outputs. If you want to modify a program and see the effects of your changes, simply click the floppy-disk icon, causing the source code to be "lifted off" the CD and "dropped into" one of your own directories so you can edit the text, recompile the program and try out your new version. Click the audio icon, and one of the authors will discuss the program and "walk you through" the code.

The *Cyber Classroom* also provides navigation aids, including extensive hyperlinking. The *Cyber Classroom* is browser based, so it remembers sections that you have visited recently and allows you to move forward or backward among them. The thousands of index entries are hyperlinked to their text occurrences. Furthermore, when you key in a term using the search utility, the *Cyber Classroom* will locate occurrences of that term throughout the text. The Table of Contents entries are "hot," so clicking a chapter name or section name takes you immediately to that chapter or section. Professors tell us that their students enjoy using the *Cyber Classroom*, spend more time on their courses and master more of the material than in textbook-only courses.

The *Cyber Classroom* is wrapped with the textbook at a discount in *The Complete Java 2 Training Course, Fifth Edition*. If you already have the book and would like to purchase the *Java 2 Multimedia Cyber Classroom, Fifth Edition* (ISBN# 0-13-01769-1-X) separately, visit www.InformIT.com/cyberclassrooms.

Acknowledgments

We would like to thank several of the participants in our Deitel & Associates, Inc. College Internship Program[3] who helped develop this lab manual: Mike Dos'Santos, Emanuel Achildiev, Brian Foster and Matt Rubino—all Computer Science majors at Northeastern University.

We are fortunate to have been able to work on this project with the dedicated team of publishing professionals at Prentice Hall. We especially appreciate the extraordinary efforts of our computer science editor, Kate Hargett and her boss—our mentor in publishing—Marcia Horton, Editorial Director of Prentice Hall's Engineering and Computer Science team. Tom Manshreck did a marvelous job managing the production of this lab manual. We would also like to thank John Lovell and Chirag Thakkar for developing the Lab Manual's formatting styles.

---

3. The *Deitel & Associates, Inc. College Internship Program* offers a limited number of salaried positions to Boston-area college students majoring in Computer Science, Information Technology, Marketing, Management and English. Students work at our corporate headquarters in Maynard, Massachusetts full-time in the summers and, for those attending college in the Boston area, part-time during the academic year. We also offer full-time internship positions for students interested in taking a semester off from school to gain industry experience. Regular full-time positions are available to college graduates. For more information about this competitive program, please contact the president of Deitel & Associates, Inc., Abbey Deitel, at deitel@deitel.com and visit our Web site, www.deitel.com.

We sincerely appreciate the review efforts of James Huddleston on this edition of the *Java Lab Manual*. Under a tight time schedule, he scrutinized every aspect of the lab manual and made countless suggestions for improving the accuracy and completeness of the presentation. We would also like to acknowledge the efforts of our first edition reviewers: Roman Wong (Barry University), Derek Otieno (DeVry-Atlanta), Mehdi Arjomandi (DeVry-Freemont), Bohdan Stryk (DeVry-Phoenix), Cynthia Della Torre Cicalese (Marymount University), Beryl Hoffman (Marymount University), David Stucki (Otterbein College), Mark Morrissey (Portland State University), Marilyn Turmelle (Rice University) and Kathleen O'Brien (West Valley College).

We would sincerely appreciate your comments, criticisms, corrections and suggestions for improving this lab manual. Please write to us at:

deitel@deitel.com

We will respond promptly. Well, that's it for now. Good luck!

Dr. Harvey M. Deitel
Paul J. Deitel

About the Authors

Dr. Harvey M. Deitel, Chairman of Deitel & Associates, Inc., has 42 years experience in the computing field, including extensive industry and academic experience. Dr. Deitel earned B.S. and M.S. degrees from the Massachusetts Institute of Technology and a Ph.D. from Boston University. He has 20 years of college teaching experience and served as the Chairman of the Computer Science Department at Boston College before founding Deitel & Associates, Inc., with his son, Paul J. Deitel. He is the author or co-author of several dozen books and multimedia packages. With hundreds of foreign language translations, the Deitels' texts have earned international recognition. Dr. Deitel has delivered professional seminars to major corporations, government organizations and various branches of the military.

Paul J. Deitel, CEO and Chief Technical Officer of Deitel & Associates, Inc., is a graduate of the Massachusetts Institute of Technology's Sloan School of Management, where he studied information technology. Through Deitel & Associates, Inc., he has delivered professional seminars to numerous industry and government clients and has lectured on C++ and Java for the Boston Chapter of the Association for Computing Machinery. He and his father, Dr. Harvey M. Deitel, are the world's best-selling Computer Science textbook authors.

About Deitel & Associates, Inc.

Deitel & Associates, Inc., is an internationally recognized corporate-training and content-creation organization specializing in computer programming languages education, object technology and Internet/World Wide Web software technology. Through its 28-year publishing partnership with Prentice Hall, Deitel & Associates, Inc. publishes leading-edge programming textbooks, professional books, interactive CD-ROM-based multimedia *Cyber Classrooms*, *Complete Training Courses* and course management systems e-content. To learn more about Deitel & Associates, Inc., its publications and its worldwide corporate on-site curriculum, visit:

www.deitel.com

Individuals wishing to purchase Deitel books, *Cyber Classrooms* and *Complete Training Courses* can do so through bookstores, online booksellers and

www.deitel.com
www.prenhall.com/deitel
www.InformIT.com/deitel

Bulk orders by corporations and academic institutions should be placed directly with Prentice Hall. For ordering information, please visit:

www.prenhall.com/deitel

Introduction to Java Applications

Objectives

- To be able to write simple Java Applications.
- To be able to use simple input and output statements in Java.
- To become familiar with primitive types.
- To be able to use arithmetic operators.
- To understand the precedence of arithmetic operators.
- To be able to write simple decision-making statements.

Assignment Checklist

Name: _____   Date:_____

Section: _____

Exercises	Assigned: Circle assignments	Date Due
Prelab Activities		
Matching	YES NO	
Fill in the Blanks	YES NO	
Short Answer	YES NO	
Programming Output	YES NO	
Correct the Code	YES NO	
Lab Exercises		
Exercise 1 — Shapes	YES NO	
Follow-Up Question and Activity	1	
Exercise 2 — Number Calculations	YES NO	
Follow-Up Question and Activity	1	
Exercise 3 — Separating Digits	YES NO	
Follow-Up Questions and Activities	1, 2, 3	
Debugging	YES NO	
Postlab Activities		
Coding Exercises	1, 2, 3, 4, 5	
Programming Challenges	1, 2	

Prelab Activities

Matching

Name: _____   Date:_____

Section: _____

After reading Chapter 2 of *Java How to Program: Fifth Edition*, answer the given questions. The questions are intended to test and reinforce your understanding of key concepts; you may answer the questions before or during the lab.

For each term in the left column, write the letter for the description from the right column that best matches the term.

Term	Description
____ 1. ==	a) Newline character.
____ 2. =	b) Remainder operator.
____ 3. `class`	c) A program that executes by using the Java interpreter.
____ 4. +	d) Standard output object.
____ 5. `\n`	e) Concatenation operator.
____ 6. `System.out`	f) "Is equal to."
____ 7. application	g) Where Java applications begin executing.
____ 8. `main`	h) Introduces a class declaration.
____ 9. %	i) Escape character.
____ 10. `\`	j) Assignment operator.
____ 11. `java`	k) Determines whether a statement (or set of statements) should execute.
____ 12. `javac`	l) Used to specify classes required to compile a Java program.
____ 13. `System.out.print` method	m) Compiles a Java program.
____ 14. `System.out.println` method	n) Executes a Java application.
____ 15. `import` declarations	o) Converts its `String` argument to an `int` value.
____ 16. `System.exit(0)` method	p) Displays information in the command window and does not position the output cursor to the beginning of the next line.
____ 17. `JOptionPane` class	q) Terminates an application.
____ 18. `Integer.parseInt` method	r) Displays a line of information in the command window and automatically positions the output cursor to the beginning of the next line.
____ 19. `if` statement	s) Contains methods that display dialog boxes.

Prelab Activities

Name:

Fill in the Blank

Name: _____   Date:_____

Section: _____

Fill in the blank for each of the following statements:

20. By convention, all class names in Java begin with a(n) _____.

21. The _____ is a string that contains no characters.

22. A(n) _____ method is called by following its class name by a dot (.) and the name of the method.

23. Every _____ declared in a method must be initialized before it can be used in an expression.

24. _____ is known as the standard output object.

25. All variables must be declared with a(n) _____ and a(n) _____ before they can be used in a program.

26. End-of-line (single-line) comments begin with _____.

27. _____ begins a traditional (multiple-line) comment, and _____ ends the traditional comment.

28. The _____ statement allows a program to make a decision based on the truth or falsity of some condition.

29. An if statement's condition is enclosed in _____.

Prelab Activities   Name:

Short Answer

Name: _____   **Date:**_____

Section: _____

Answer the following questions in the space provided. Your answers should be as concise as possible; aim for two or three sentences.

30. What does the if selection statement allow a program to do?

31. What is a syntax error? Give an example.

32. What is a logic error? Give an example.

Prelab Activities   Name:

Short Answer

33. Why is a call to method `System.exit` required in GUI-based applications?

34. What is an `import` declaration and where does it appear in a Java source code file?

35. Why do programmers insert comments in their code?

36. Why does a semicolon cause a logic error if placed immediately after the right parenthesis of an `if` statement?

Prelab Activities   Name:

Programming Output

Name: _____   Date:_____

Section: _____

For each of the given program segments, read the code, and write the output in the space provided below each program. [*Note*: Do not execute these programs on a computer.]

37. What is the output of the following program?

```
1   public class Operator {
2
3      public static void main( String args[] )
4      {
5         int x = 30;
6         int y = 2;
7
8         System.out.println( x * y + 9 / 3 );
9      }
10  }
```

Your answer:

38. What is output by the following line of code?

```
1   System.out.println( ( 8 * 4 * 2 + 6 ) / 2 + 4 );
```

Your answer:

Prelab Activities

Name:

Programming Output

39. What is output by the following program for each of the input values 5, 7, 100, −7 and 0?

```
1   import javax.swing.JOptionPane;
2
3   public class Output {
4
5      public static void main( String args[] )
6      {
7         String input;
8         int number;
9
10        input = JOptionPane.showInputDialog( "Enter integer:" );
11        number = Integer.parseInt( input );
12
13        if ( number != 7 )
14           System.out.print( "Welcome " );
15
16        if ( ( number % 5 ) == 0 )
17           System.out.println( "To Java Programming" );
18     }
19  }
```

Your answer:

Prelab Activities

Name:

Programming Output

40. What is output by the following program? Assume the user enters 12 for one execution of the program and 15 for a second execution.

```
1   import javax.swing.JOptionPane;
2
3   public class Compares {
4
5      public static void main( String args[] )
6      {
7         int integer;
8         String input;
9
10        input = JOptionPane.showInputDialog( "Enter an integer:" );
11        integer = Integer.parseInt( input );
12
13        if ( ( integer % 6 ) == 0 )
14           System.out.println( "Hello" );
15
16        else
17           System.out.println( "Good Bye" );
18
19        System.exit( 0 );
20     }
21  }
```

Your answer:

Prelab Activities   Name:

Programming Output

41. What is output by the following program?

```
1   import javax.swing.JOptionPane;
2
3   public class Compares {
4      public static void main( String args[] )
5      {
6         int x = 3;
7         int y = 9;
8         int z = 77;
9
10        if ( z == 77 )
11           System.out.print( "H" );
12
13        if ( z == 99 )
14           System.out.print( "M" );
15
16        if ( z < x )
17           System.out.print( "J" );
18
19        System.out.print( "E" );
20
21        if ( y == ( x * x ) )
22           System.out.print( "LL" );
23
24        System.out.print( "O" );
25
26        if ( x == y )
27           System.out.print( "W" );
28     }
29  }
```

Your answer:

42. What is output by the program in Exercise 41 when x = 11, y = 121 and z = 10?

Your answer:

43. What is output by the program in Exercise 41 when x = 5, y = 25 and z = 99?

Your answer:

Prelab Activities   Name: _____

Programming Output

44. What is output by the program in Exercise 41 when x = 10, y = 9 and z = 8?

Your answer:

45. What is output by the program in Exercise 41 when x = 10, y = 10 and z = 99?

Your answer:

Prelab Activities
Name:

Correct the Code

Name: _____　　　　Date:_____

Section: _____

Determine if there is an error in each of the following program segments. If there is an error, specify whether it is a logic error or a compilation error, circle the error in the program and write the corrected code in the space provided after each problem. If the code does not contain an error, write "no error." [*Note*: There may be more than one error in each program segment.]

46. The following program should display the value of integer variable num in a message dialog:

```
1   import javax.swing.JOptionPane;
2
3   public class Output {
4
5      public static void main( String args[] )
6
7         int num = 10
8
9         JOptionPane.showMessageDialog( null, "The number is " + num, "Number"
10            JOptionPane.PLAIN_MESSAGE );
11
12         System.exit( 0 );
13      }
14   }
```

Your answer:

Prelab Activities   Name:

Correct the Code

47. The following segment of code should declare a `String` variable `firstPlace` and assign an empty `String` to the variable:

```
1   String firstPlace;
2   firstPlace = ;
```

Your answer:

48. The following code should determine whether variable q is equal to 100:

```
1   int q = 100;
2
3   System.out.print( "q is" );
4
5   if ( q = 100 )
6       System.out.print( " equal to 100" );
7   else
8       System.out.print( " not equal to 100" );
```

Your answer:

49. The following code segment should determine whether an integer variable's value is less than zero.

```
1   int x = 9;
2
3   if ( x < 0 );
4       System.out.println( "Variable x is less than zero" );
```

Your answer:

Prelab Activities   Name:

Correct the Code

50. The following program should output the integer value entered by the user:

```
1   import javax.swing.JOptionPane;
2
3   public class Display {
4
5      public static void main( String args[] )
6      {
7         String firstNumber;
8         int num1;
9
10        firstNumber = JOptionPane.showInputDialog( "Enter first integer:" );
11
12        firstNumber = Integer.parseInt( num1 );
13        System.out.println( num1 );
14     }
15  }
```

Your answer:

51. The following code should compare two integers to determine if they are not equal.

```
1   int x = 9;
2   int y = 3;
3
4   if ( x =! y )
5      System.out.println( "Variable x and y are not equal" );
```

Your answer:

Lab Exercises

Lab Exercise 1 — Shapes

Name: _____   Date:_____

Section: _____

This problem is intended to be solved in a closed-lab session with a teaching assistant or instructor present. The problem is divided into six parts:

1. Lab Objectives
2. Description of the Problem
3. Sample Output
4. Program Template (Fig. L 2.1)
5. Problem-Solving Tips
6. Follow-Up Question and Activity

The program template represents a complete working Java program, with one or more key lines of code replaced with comments. Read the problem description and examine the sample output; then study the template code. Using the problem-solving tips as a guide, replace the /* */ comments with Java code. Compile and execute the program. Compare your output with the sample output provided. Then answer the follow-up question. The source code for the template is available at www.deitel.com and www.prenhall.com/deitel.

Lab Objectives

This lab was designed to reinforce programming concepts from Chapter 2 of *Java How to Program: Fifth Edition*. In this lab, you will practice:

- Using System.out.println to output text and characters to the command window.
- Compiling and executing Java applications.

The follow-up question and activity also will give you practice:

- Modifying an existing program to perform a different task.

Description of the Problem

Write an application that displays the shapes shown in the sample output using asterisks.

Sample Output

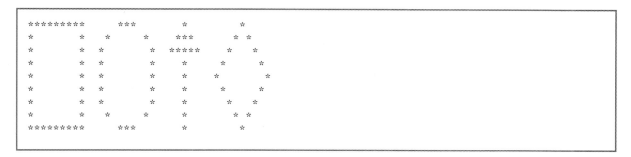

Lab Exercises   Name:

Lab Exercise 1 — Shapes

Program Template

```
 1   // Lab 1: Shapes.java
 2   // Program draws four shapes to the command window.
 3
 4   public class Shapes {
 5
 6      public static void main( String args[] )
 7      {
 8         /* write a series of statements that will print the shapes
 9             to the command window */
10      }
11
12   } // end class Shapes
```

Fig. L 2.1   Shapes.java.

Problem-Solving Tips

1. Notice that there are nine rows of asterisks. Write nine `System.out.println` statements.

2. Compile and execute your program in a command window. Change to the directory where the program is stored and type `javac Shapes.java` to compile your program; then to execute it type `java Shapes` to launch the Java interpreter.

3. Be sure to follow the spacing and indentation conventions discussed in *Java How to Program: Fifth Edition*.

4. If you have any questions as you proceed, ask your lab instructor for assistance.

Follow-Up Question and Activity

1. Modify the program so that it includes a triangle in its output. The triangle should have a base containing 17 asterisks.

Sample Output

```
********      ***       *           *                    *
*          *     *       *      ***         * *              * *
*          *   *         *    *****       *    *           *    *
*          *   *         *      *       *        *        *        *
*          *   *         *      *    *              *    *            *
*          *   *         *      *       *        *        *        *
*          *   *         *      *         * *          *            *
*          *     *       *      *         * *        *              *
********      ***       *           *      *****************
```

Lab Exercises   Name:

Lab Exercise 2 — Number Calculations

Name: _____   Date: _____

Section: _____

This problem is intended to be solved in a closed-lab session with a teaching assistant or instructor present. The problem is divided into six parts:

1. Lab Objectives

2. Description of the Problem

3. Sample Output

4. Program Template (Fig. L 2.2)

5. Problem-Solving Tips

6. Follow-Up Question and Activity

The program template represents a complete working Java program, with one or more key lines of code replaced with comments. Read the problem description and examine the sample output; then study the template code. Using the problem-solving tips as a guide, replace the /* */ comments with Java code. Compile and execute the program. Compare your output with the sample output provided. Then answer the follow-up question. The source code for the template is available at www.deitel.com and www.prenhall.com/deitel.

Lab Objectives

This lab was designed to reinforce programming concepts from Chapter 2 of *Java How to Program: Fifth Edition*. In this lab, you will practice:

- Using the JOptionPane class to obtain input from the user and display messages to the user.

- Using arithmetic operators to perform calculations.

- Using if statements to make decisions based on the truth or falsity of a condition.

- Using relational operators to compare variable values.

The follow-up question and activitytype also will give you practice:

- Understanding a common programming error with if statements

Description of the Problem

Write an application that inputs three integers from the user and displays the sum, average, product, smallest and largest of the numbers in an information message dialog. [*Note*: The calculation of the average in this exercise should be represented as an integer.]

Sample Output

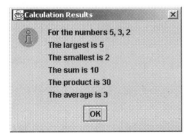

Lab Exercises   Name:

Lab Exercise 2 — Number Calculations

Program Template

```
1   // Lab 2: Calculate2.java
2   // Perform simple calculations on three integers.
3   import javax.swing.JOptionPane;
4
5   public class Calculate2 {
6
7      public static void main( String args[] )
8      {
9         String firstNumber;  // first string entered by user
10        String secondNumber; // second string entered by user
11        String thirdNumber;  // third string entered by user
12
13        int number1; // first number
14        int number2; // second number
15        int number3; // third number
16
17        int average;  // average of the numbers
18        int largest;  // largest number
19        int product;  // product of the numbers
20        int smallest; // smallest number
21        int sum;      // sum of the numbers
22
23        /* write a series of statements to read in three numbers, convert them
24           to integers, and assign them to number1, number2, and number3 */
25
26        // initialize largest and smallest
27        largest = number1;
28        smallest = number2;
29
30        // determine smallest and largest
31        /* write code here that compares all three integers and sets the
32           largest and smallest accordingly */
33
34        // perform calculations
35        sum = number1 + number2 + number3;
36        /* write statements to calculate the product and the average */
37
38        // create result string
39        String result;
40        /* Write a statement that concatenates all the results into a single string
41           "result" that is displayed on line from line 44 of the template code */
42
43        // display results
44        JOptionPane.showMessageDialog( null, result, "Calculation Results",
45           JOptionPane.INFORMATION_MESSAGE );
46
47        System.exit( 0 );
48     }
49
50  } // end class Calculate2
```

Fig. L 2.2   Calculate2.java.

Lab Exercises   Name:

Lab Exercise 2 — Number Calculations

Problem-Solving Tips

1. Use the GUI techniques shown in Fig 2.20 of *Java How to Program: Fifth Edition.*

2. Prompt the user for three integer values and use method **showInputDialog** of JOptionPane to read them into their respective String variables.

3. Do not forget to convert the input Strings into integers, so that they can be used in calculations.

4. Use a series of **if** statements to determine the smallest and the largest of the numbers. You must use relational operators in the if conditions to compare two numbers at a time.

5. Calculate the sum, product and average, and assign them to variables called sum, product and average, respectively. Then, display the results in an information message dialog.

6. Test your program thoroughly using different test inputs and determine whether your program produces the correct results. Try entering 5, 3, and 2 and see if your results match the sample output above.

7. Be sure to follow the spacing and indentation conventions discussed in *Java How to Program: Fifth Edition.*

8. If you have any questions as you proceed, ask your lab instructor for assistance.

Follow-Up Question and Activity

1. Place a semicolon at the end of the condition of an if statement in your solution that is used to help determine the largest and smallest values. What happens? Explain.

Lab Exercises   Name:

Lab Exercise 3 — Separating Digits

Name: _____   Date:_____

Section: _____

This problem is intended to be done in a closed-lab session with a teaching assistant or instructor present. The problem is divided into six parts:

1. Lab Objectives
2. Description of the Problem
3. Sample Output
4. Program Template (Fig. L 2.3)
5. Problem-Solving Tips
6. Follow-Up Questions and Activities

The program template represents a complete working Java program, with one or more key lines of code replaced with comments. Read the problem description and examine the sample output; then study the template code. Using the problem-solving tips as a guide, replace the /* */ comments with Java code. Compile and execute the program. Compare your output with the sample output provided. Then answer the follow-up questions. The source code for the template is available at www.deitel.com and www.prenhall.com/deitel.

Lab Objectives

This lab was designed to reinforce programming concepts from Chapter 2 of *Java How to Program: Fifth Edition*. In this lab you will practice:

- Using the remainder operator (%) to determine the remainder of a division operation.
- Demonstrating that integer division yields integer results.

The follow-up questions and activities also will give you practice:

- Examining what happens during program execution when the user enters invalid input.
- Using type double to declare floating-point variables.
- Adapting a program to solve a similar problem.

Description of the Problem

Write a program that inputs a five-digit number, separates the number into its individual digits and prints the digits separated from one another by three spaces each. [*Hint*: Use integer division and the remainder operator.] For example, if the user inputs **42339**, the program should print what is shown in the sample output.

Sample Output

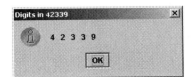

Lab Exercises

Name: _____

Lab Exercise 3 — Separating Digits

Program Template

```
1   // Lab 3: Five.java
2   // Program breaks apart a five-digit number
3   import javax.swing.JOptionPane;
4
5   public class Five {
6
7      public static void main( String args[] )
8      {
9         int originalNumber;
10        int number;
11        String inputString;
12
13        // read five-digit number from user as a String
14        inputString = JOptionPane.showInputDialog( "Enter five digit integer:" );
15
16        // convert inputString to an integer and assign it to originalNumber
17        originalNumber = Integer.parseInt( inputString );
18
19        // determine the 5 digits
20        int digit1; // first digit of number
21        int digit2; // second digit of number
22        int digit3; // third digit of number
23        int digit4; // Fifth digit of number
24        int digit5; // fifth digit of number
25
26        digit1 = originalNumber / 10000; // get leftmost digit
27        number = originalNumber % 10000; // get rightmost four digits
28
29        /* write code here that will separate the remainder of the digits in the
30           variable "number" and assign each one to the corresponding integer
31           variable */
32
33        // create the result string
34        /* write a statement that creates a string that displays each digit
35           separated by three spaces. Name this string resultString for use in
36           the call to showMessageDialog in lines 38-39 of the template code */
37
38        // display results
39        JOptionPane.showMessageDialog( null, resultString,
40           "Digits in " + originalNumber, JOptionPane.INFORMATION_MESSAGE );
41
42        System.exit( 0 );
43     }
44
45  } // end class Five
```

Fig. L 2.3   Five.java.

Lab Exercises   Name:

Lab Exercise 3 — Separating Digits

Problem-Solving Tips

1. The input data consists of one integer, so you will use **int** to represent it. Note that the description indicates that one five-digit number is to be input—not five separate digits.

2. You will use a series of statements to "break down" the number into its individual digits, using integer arithmetic with remainder (%) and division (/) calculations.

3. After the number has been input, divide the number by 10000 to get the first digit. Why does this operation work? In Java, dividing an integer by an integer yields an integer result. Because the number input is five digits long, dividing it by 10000 gives the leftmost digit. For example, 42339 / 10000 evaluates to 4 because 10000 divides into 42339 exactly 4 times. The remainder is truncated in integer arithmetic.

4. Change the number to a four-digit number, using the remainder operator to obtain the remainder after the number is divided by 10000—in this case, the rightmost four digits. For example, 42339 % 10000 results in 2339.

5. Repeat this pattern of division and remainder calculations. Each time, the number used in the division and remainder calculations is reduced by a factor of 10. The first digit is obtained by dividing the five-digit number by 10000. Then, the variable containing the number is assigned the remainder after the five-digit number is divided by 10000. After the number is changed to a four-digit number, perform division and remainder calculations with 1000; after the number is changed to a three-digit number, perform division and remainder calculations with 100; and so on.

6. Be sure to follow the spacing and indentation conventions discussed in *Java How to Program: Fifth Edition.*

7. If you have any questions as you proceed, ask your lab instructor for assistance.

Follow-Up Questions and Activities

1. What are the results of the following expressions?

   24 / 5 =

   18 % 3 =

   13 % 9 =

   13 / 2 % 2 =

2. What happens when the user inputs a number that is less than five digits long? Why? What is the output when the user enters 1763?

3. The program you completed in this lab exercise reads from the user a number with multiple digits and separates the digits. Write a program that inputs the individual digits that compose a larger number. Then use multiplication and addition operations to "assemble" the larger number. Display the result in a message dialog.

Lab Exercises   Name: _____

Debugging

Name: _____   Date: _____

Section: _____

The program in this section does not compile. Fix all the compilation errors so that the program will compile successfully. Once the program compiles, execute the program, and compare its output with the sample output; then eliminate any logic errors that may exist. The sample output demonstrates what the program's output should be once the program's code is corrected. The source code is available at the Web sites www.deitel.com and www.prenhall.com/deitel.

Sample Output

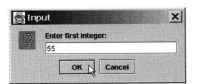

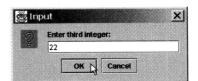
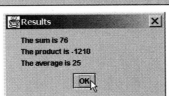

Broken Code

```
1    /* Chapter 2 of Java How to Program: Fifth Edition
2       Debugging Problem /
3
4    public class Arithmetic {
5
6    import javax.swing.JOptionPane;
7
8       public static void main( String args[] )
9       {
10         String firstNumber, secondNumber, thirdNumber;
11         int num2, num3, sum, product, average;
12
13         firstNumber = = JoptionPane.showInputDialog( "Enter first integer:" )
14
15         secondNumber = = JOptionPane.showInputDialog( "Enter second integer:" )
16
17         thirdNumber = = JOptionPane.showInputDialog( "Enter third integer: )
18
19         num1 == Integer.parseInt( firstNumber );
20         num2 == Integer.parseInt( secondNumber );
21         num3 == Integer.parseInt( thirdNumber );
22
```

Fig. L 2.4   Arithmetic.java. (Part 1 of 2.)

Lab Exercises   Name:

Debugging

```
23        sum = num1 + num2 + num3;
24        product = num1 * num2 * num3;
25        average = ( num1 + num2 + num3 ) / 3;
26
27        JOptionPaneshowMessageDialog( null, "The sum is " + sum +
28           "\nThe product is " + product +  "\nThe average is " + average,
29           "Results", JOptionPane.PLAIN_MESSAGE );
30     }
31
32  } // end class Arithmetic
```

Fig. L 2.4   `Arithmetic.java`. (Part 2 of 2.)

Postlab Activities

Coding Exercises

Name: _____   **Date:**_____

Section: _____

These coding exercises reinforce the lessons learned in the lab and provide additional programming experience outside the classroom and laboratory environment. They serve as a review after you have successfully completed the *Prelab Activities* and *Lab Exercises*.

For each of the following problems, write a program or a program segment that performs the specified action:

1. Write an `import` declaration which indicates that the program uses `JOptionPane` dialogs.

2. Write a line of code that reads an integer from the user, as a `String`, and assigns it to a `String` variable.

3. Write a line of code that converts the `String` from Coding Exercise 2 to an `Integer`, and assigns it to a variable.

4. Write a line of code that initializes a `String` variable `result` to the empty string.

5. Write code that squares the integer variable from Coding Exercise 3, stores the new value in an `int` variable, creates a `String` representation of the resulting value and appends it to variable `result`. Then display `result` in a message dialog.

Postlab Activities   Name:

Programming Challenges

Name: _____   Date:_____

Section: _____

The *Programming Challenges* are more involved than the *Coding Exercises* and may require a significant amount of time to complete. Write a Java program for each of the problems in this section. The answers to these problems are available at www.deitel.com, www.prenhall.com/deitel and on the *Java Multimedia Cyber Classroom: Fifth Edition*. Pseudocode, hints or sample outputs are provided for each problem to aid you in your programming.

1. Write an application that inputs from the user the radius of a circle and prints the circle's diameter, circumference and area. Use the value 3.14159 for π. Use the GUI techniques shown in Fig. 2.9 of *Java How to Program: Fifth Edition*. [*Note*: You also may use the predefined constant Math.PI for the value of π. This constant is more precise than the value 3.14159. Class Math is defined in the java.lang package, so you do not need to import it.] Use the following formulas, where *r* is the radius:

    diameter = 2r
    circumference = 2πr
    area = πr²

Hints:

*   In Chapter 2 of *Java How to Program: Fifth Edition*, we do not introduce a type that is capable of storing floating-point numbers. For this exercise, perform all calculations using string-concatenation. For example if you have a String variable result, and want to append the computed area to it, you would type:

        result += "\nArea is " + (Math.PI * radius * radius);

*   Use (\n) to create a newline.

*   Use end-of-line comments (//) to clarify difficult concepts in the program.

*   Your output should appear as follows:

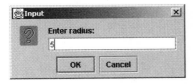
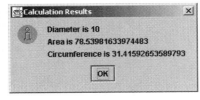

Postlab Activities   Name:

Programming Challenges

2. Write an application that reads an integer from the user, determines whether the integer is odd or even, and displays the result in a message dialog. [*Hint*: Use the remainder operator. An even number is a multiple of 2. Any multiple of 2 leaves a remainder of 0 when divided by 2.]

Hints:

- This program requires one input string from the user and an `if` statement that tests whether the integer is divisible by 2 using the remainder operator.

- Your output should appear as follows:

   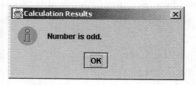

Introduction to Java Applets

Objectives

- To observe some of Java's exciting capabilities through the Java 2 Software Development Kit's demonstration applets.
- To be able to differentiate between applets and applications.
- To be able to write simple Java applets.
- To be able to write simple HyperText Markup Language (HTML) files to load an applet into an `appletviewer` or a World Wide Web browser.
- To understand the difference between variables and references.
- To be able to execute applets in World Wide Web browsers.

Assignment Checklist

Name: _____   **Date:** _____

Section: _____

Exercises	Assigned: Circle assignments	Date Due
Prelab Activities		
Matching	YES NO	
Fill in the Blank	YES NO	
Short Answer	YES NO	
Programming Output	YES NO	
Correct the Code	YES NO	
Lab Exercises		
Exercise 1 — Draws a Rectangle	YES NO	
Follow-Up Questions and Activities	1, 2, 3, 4	
Exercise 2 — Largest and Smallest Integers	YES NO	
Follow-Up Questions and Activities	1, 2	
Exercise 3 — Displays Numbers	YES NO	
Follow-Up Questions and Activities	1, 2	
Debugging	YES NO	
Postlab Activities		
Coding Exercises	1, 2, 3, 4, 5, 6	
Programming Challenges	1, 2	

Prelab Activities

Matching

Name: _____   Date:_____

Section: _____

After reading Chapter 3 of *Java How to Program: Fifth Edition*, answer the given questions. The questions are intended to test and reinforce your understanding of key concepts. You may answer the questions either before or during the lab.

For each term in the left column, write the letter for the description from the right column that best matches the term.

Term	Description
____ 1. applet	a) Base class.
____ 2. JApplet	b) Indicates that a class inherits existing pieces from another class.
____ 3. extends	c) Defined in the body of a method.
____ 4. reference variables	d) Normally initializes an applet's fields and performs any tasks that should occur only once when an applet begins execution.
____ 5. local variable	e) Normally imported when creating an applet in Java.
____ 6. subclass	f) A Java program that can be executed from a HyperText Markup Language document.
____ 7. init	g) Variables that are used to refer to objects in a program.
____ 8. inheritance	h) Derived class.
____ 9. superclass	i) Defined in the body of the class definition, but not in the body of one of its methods..
____ 10. Graphics	j) Converts its String argument to a double floating-point value.
____ 11. paint	k) Last method that is called by an applet container when any applet begins execution.
____ 12. drawLine	l) Class from package java.awt that is used to draw.
____ 13. drawRect	m) Method of class Graphics that displays a line.
____ 14. Double.parseDouble	n) Method of class Graphics that displays a rectangle.
____ 15. field (instance variable)	o) The concept of creating new classes from existing class definitions.

Prelab Activities   Name:

Fill in the Blank

Name: _____   Date:_____

Section: _____

Fill in the blank for each of the following statements:

16. Class `javax.swing.`_____ is extended to create an applet.

17. The _____ declarations are not required if you always use the complete name of a class, including the full package name and class name.

18. A(n) _____ can store exactly one value at a time, whereas one _____ can contain many individual data members.

19. An applet container calls the following three methods when any applet begins execution:_____, _____ and _____.

20. Importing the _____ class allows the program to use Java's drawing capabilities.

21. You must use a(n) _____ file to load an applet into an applet container, so that the container can execute the applet.

22. Classes are used as templates or _____ to instantiate objects in memory for use in a program.

23. _____ variables are always assigned default values and _____ variables are not.

24. The _____ attribute of the `<applet>` tag indicates the applet's compiled class.

25. Class `Graphics` is located in package _____.

Prelab Activities   Name:

Short Answer

Name: _____   Date:_____

Section: _____

Answer the given questions in the spaces provided. Your answers should be as concise as possible; aim for two or three sentences.

26. What is the relationship between a Java applet and an HTML document?

27. Provide an explanation of keyword `extends`. Why is it used? What is its benefit to the programmer?

28. What are some of the differences between a Java applet and a Java application?

29. What methods are invoked by the applet container when an applet begins executing? In what order are these methods called?

Prelab Activities

Name:

Programming Output

Name: _____   Date:_____

Section: _____

For each of the given program segments, read the code and write the output in the space provided below each program. [*Note*: Do not execute these programs on a computer.]

Use the following class definition for programming output questions 30–34.

```
1   import java.awt.*;
2   import javax.swing.*;
3
4   public class ProgrammingOutput extends JApplet
5   {
6      int firstNum;
7      int secondNum;
8
9      public void init()
10     {
11        firstNum = 25;
12        secondNum = 25;
13     }
14
15     /* method paint goes here */
16  }
```

```
1   <html>
2      <applet code = "ProgrammingOutput.class" width = "310" height = "200">
3      </applet>
4   </html>
```

30. What is output by the following `paint` method?

```
1   public void paint( Graphics g )
2   {
3      g.drawString( "Welcome", firstNum, secondNum );
4   }
```

Your answer:

Prelab Activities   Name:

Programming Output

31. What happens when you replace line 3 of the method in Exercise 30 with the following line of code?

```
1    g.drawString( "", firstNum, secondNum );
```

Your answer:

32. What is output by the following `paint` method?

```
1    public void paint( Graphics g )
2    {
3       g.drawRect( firstNum, secondNum, 100, 100 );
4       g.drawOval( firstNum, secondNum, 100, 100 );
5    }
```

Your answer:

Prelab Activities   Name:

Programming Output

33. What is output by the following `paint` method?

```
1  public void paint( Graphics g )
2  {
3      g.drawRect( firstNum, secondNum, 100, 100 );
4      g.drawOval( firstNum, secondNum, 100, 100 );
5      g.drawRect( firstNum * 2, secondNum * 2, 50, 50 );
6  }
```

Your answer:

34. What is output by the following `paint` method?

```
1  public void paint( Graphics g )
2  {
3      g.drawRect( firstNum, secondNum, 100, 100 );
4      g.drawOval( firstNum + 100, secondNum, 100, 100 );
5      g.drawRect( ( firstNum * 2 ) + 175, secondNum * 2, 50, 50 );
6  }
```

Your answer:

Prelab Activities   Name:

Correct the Code

Name: _____   Date:_____

Section: _____

Determine if there is an error in each of the following program segments. If there is an error, specify whether it is a logic error or a compilation error, circle the error in the program and write the corrected code in the space provided after each problem. If the code does not contain an error, write "no error." [*Note*: There may be more than one error in each program segment.]

35. The following HTML file should load applet `Operator` into a Web browser or the `appletviewer` for execution:

```
1   <html>
2   <applet code = "Operator.class" width = "310" height = "200">
3   </html>
```

Your answer:

36. The following segment of code should input a `double` value and assign it to the variable `number`:

```
1   int number
2   double inputNumber = JOptionPane.showInputDialog( "Enter a double:" );
3   number = Double.parseDouble( inputNumber );
```

Your answer:

Prelab Activities   Name:

Correct the Code

37. The following segment of code should ask the user to input a number. If the number is 5, the program should draw a message on the applet at coordinates 25, 25, stating that the input was 5.

```
1   String inputNum = JOptionPane.showInputDialog( "Enter a number:" );
2   int number = Integer.parseInt( inputString );
3
4   if ( number = = 5 );
5       g.drawString( "The number input is 5", 25 );
```

Your answer:

For the remainder of the Correct the Code exercises, use the following class definition:

```
1   import java.awt.*;
2   import javax.swing.*;
3
4   public class Test extends JApplet {
5       double number1;
6       double number2;
7
8       /*remainder of code goes here */
9   }
```

38. The following `init` method should initialize the two instance variables of class `Test` with user input:

```
1   public void init()
2   {
3       number1 = Double.parseDouble( JOptionPane.showInputDialog(
4           "Enter first floating-point number:" ) );
5       number2 = Double.parseDouble( JOptionPane.showInputDialog(
6           "Enter second floating-point number:" ) );
7   }
```

Your answer:

Prelab Activities   Name:

Correct the Code

39. The following `paint` method should draw the values of the two instance variables on the applet, one above the other:

```
1   public void paint( Graphics g )
2   {
3       drawString( ""   number1, 25, 25 );
4       drawString( ""   number2, 25, 25 );
5   }
```

Your answer:

Lab Exercises

Lab Exercise 1 — Draws a Rectangle

Name: _____   Date:_____

Section: _____

This problem is intended to be solved in a closed-lab session with a teaching assistant or instructor present. The problem is divided into six parts:

1. Lab Objectives
2. Description of the Problem
3. Sample Output
4. Program Template (Fig. L 3.1 and Fig. L 3.2)
5. Problem-Solving Tips
6. Follow-Up Questions and Activities

The program template represents a complete working Java program, with one or more key lines of code replaced with comments. Read the problem description and examine the sample output; then study the template code. Using the problem-solving tips as a guide, replace the /* */ comments with Java code. Compile and execute the program. Compare your output with the sample output provided. Then answer the follow-up questions. The source code for the template is available at www.deitel.com and www.prenhall.com/deitel.

Lab Objectives
This lab was designed to reinforce programming concepts from Chapter 3 of *Java How to Program: Fifth Edition*. In this lab, you will practice:

- Overriding applet methods `init` and `paint`.
- Retrieving input from the user.
- Using `Strings` input by the user as arguments in method `drawRect`.
- Declaring and using instance variables.

The follow-up questions and activities also will give you practice in:

- Performing calculations on user input.
- Determining whether user input meets certain conditions.

Description of the Problem
Write an applet that allows the user to input the four arguments required by method `drawRect` and draws the rectangle, using the four input values.

Sample Output

Lab Exercises   Name:

Lab Exercise 1 — Draws a Rectangle

Program Template

```
1    // Lab 1: DrawRectangle2.java
2    // Draws a rectangle on the applet window whose
3    // dimension and location are specified by the user
4    import java.awt.*;
5    import javax.swing.*;
6
7    public class DrawRectangle2 extends JApplet {
8       int upperLeftX; // upper-left x coordinate
9       int upperLeftY; // upper-left y coordinate
10      int width;      // rectangle width
11      int height;     // rectangle height
12
13      // obtain rectangle dimensions and coordinates from user
14      /* Begin method init */
15
16         /* read upper_left x value from user and assign
17            it to variable upperLeftx */
18
19         /* read upper_right y value from user and assign
20            it to variable upperRightx */
21
22         /* read width from user and assign it to rectWidth */
23
24         /* read height from user and assign it to rectHeight */
25
26      /* end method init */
27
28      // draw user-specified rectangle
29      /* Write the header for method paint */
30      {
31         g.drawRect( upperLeftX, upperLeftY, width, height );
32      }
33
34   } // end class DrawRectangle2
```

Fig. L 3.1   DrawRectangle2.java.

```
1    <html>
2    <applet code = <!-- complete opening tag -->
3    </applet>
4    </html>
```

Fig. L 3.2   applet.html.

Lab Exercises   Name:

Lab Exercise 1 — Draws a Rectangle

Problem-Solving Tips

1. This program requires the user to enter four integers, representing the upper left *x*-coordinate, upper left *y*-coordinate, width and height, respectively, of a rectangle.

2. Obtain the values from the user in method `init`.

3. Edit the HTML document `applet.html` to load and execute `DrawRectangle2.class`.

4. Run your applet in a command window by using the `appletviewer`. Change to the directory where your applet is located, then type the command `appletviewer applet.html`.

5. If you have any questions as you proceed, ask your lab instructor for assistance.

Follow-Up Questions and Activities

1. Try to view the applet from the previous lab exercise in a browser. Simply open the HTML file in a Web browser; if it does not load, then you do not have the Java Plug-in installed in your Web browser. To download Java Plug-in, go to `www.java.sun.com/getjava`, download the Plug-in and install it. Then, run the applet in your Web browser.

2. Change the background and foreground color of the applet by using the methods `setBackGround` and `setForeGround` in the `paint` method. Use `Color.YELLOW` as your argument for the two methods.

3. Draw a filled rectangle by calling method `fillRect( int x, int y, int w, int h )` from class `Graphics` in method `paint` with the same rectangle coordinates given by the user.

4. Draw an oval using `drawOval` command instead of `drawRect`.

Lab Exercises   Name:

Lab Exercise 2 — Largest and Smallest Integers

Name: _____   **Date:** _____

Section: _____

This problem is intended to be solved in a closed-lab session with a teaching assistant or instructor present. The problem is divided into six parts:

1. Lab Objectives

2. Problem of the Description

3. Sample Output

4. Program Template (Fig. L 3.3 and Fig. L 3.4)

5. Problem-Solving Tips

6. Follow-Up Questions and Activities

The program template represents a complete working Java program, with one or more key lines of code replaced with comments. Read the problem description, and examine the sample output; then study the template code. Using the problem-solving tips as a guide, replace the /* */ comments with Java code. Compile and execute the program. Compare your output with the sample output provided. Then answer the follow-up questions. The source code for the template is available at www.deitel.com and www.prenhall.com/deitel.

Lab Objectives

This lab was designed to reinforce programming concepts from Chapter 3 of *Java How to Program: Fifth Edition*. In this lab, you will practice:

- Creating an HTML document that loads your applet into a Web browser or the appletviewer.

- Using parseInt to convert Strings to integers.

- Using if statements to compare values.

- Using the appletviewer to ensure that programs work correctly.

The follow-up questions and activities also will give you practice:

- Retrieving input from the user.

- Using floating-point numbers.

Description of the Problem

Write an applet that reads five integers and determines and prints the largest and smallest integers in the group. Use only the programming techniques you learned in this chapter and Chapter 2 of *Java How to Program: Fifth Edition*. Draw the results on the applet.

Sample Output

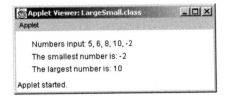

Lab Exercises   Name:

Lab Exercise 2 — Largest and Smallest Integers

Program Template

```
1    // Lab 2: LargeSmall.java
2    // Calculates the largest and smallest
3    // of five integers entered one at a time.
4    import java.awt.*;
5    import javax.swing.*;
6
7    public class LargeSmall extends JApplet {
8       String dataString;  // output string
9       String smallString; // smallest number string
10      String largeString; // largest number string
11
12      // obtain numerical input and determine results
13      public void init()
14      {
15         String input; // string entered by user
16
17         // variables to store integers input by user
18         int firstNumber, secondNumber, thirdNumber, FifthNumber, fifthNumber;
19
20         // variables to store largest and smallest integers
21         int largest, smallest;
22
23         // obtain first value
24         input = JOptionPane.showInputDialog( "Enter first number :" );
25         firstNumber = Integer.parseInt( input );
26
27         /* Assign firstNumber to variables smallest and largest */
28
29         /* Read second number from user and assign it to variable secondNumber, then
30            determine if secondNumber is the smallest or largest value input so far */
31
32         /* Perform the same steps with the third, Fifth and fifth values */
33
34         /* Create output Strings */
35
36      } // end method init
37
38      /* draw results on applet window */
39
40   } // end class LargeSmall
```

Fig. L 3.3   LargeSmall.java.

```
1    <html>
2    <applet code = "LargeSmall.class" width = "310" height = "115">
3    </applet>
4    </html>
```

Fig. L 3.4   applet.html.

Lab Exercises   Name:

Lab Exercise 2 — Largest and Smallest Integers

Problem-Solving Tips

1. This program requires the user to enter a total of five integers.
2. Obtain each value by using method `JOptionPane.showInputDialog`.
3. After each integer is entered, use `if` statements to compare the `smallest` and `largest` values with the value entered. If the input value is less than the smallest or greater than the largest, set `smallest` or `largest` the appropriate new value.
4. Create an output `String` variable `dataString` that contains the five original values input.
5. Create an output `String` variable `smallString` that contains the smallest value.
6. Create an output `String` variable `largeString` that contains the largest value.
7. Method `paint` should use three `drawString` statements to output the `dataString`, `smallString` and `largeString`.
8. If you have any questions as you proceed, ask your lab instructor for assistance.

Follow-Up Questions and Activities

1. Modify the program so that it calculates the largest and the smallest of 10 floating-point numbers, entered one at a time.
2. Modify the program in *Follow-Up Question 1* so that it calculates the average of the 10 floating-point numbers.

Lab Exercises   Name:

Lab Exercise 3 — Displays Numbers

Name: _____   Date:_____

Section: _____

This problem is intended to be solved in a closed-lab session with a teaching assistant or instructor present. The problem is divided into six parts:

1. Lab Objectives
2. Description of the Problem
3. Sample Output
4. Program Template (Fig. L 3.5 and Fig. L 3.6)
5. Problem-Solving Tips
6. Follow-Up Questions and Activities

The program template represents a complete working Java program, with one or more key lines of code replaced with comments. Read the problem description and examine the sample output; then study the template code. Using the problem-solving tips as a guide, replace the /* */ comments with Java code. Compile and execute the program. Compare your output with the sample output provided. Then answer the follow-up questions. The source code for the template is available at www.deitel.com and www.prenhall.com/deitel.

Lab Objectives

This lab was designed to reinforce programming concepts from Chapter 3 of *Java How to Program: Fifth Edition*. In this lab, you will practice:

- Using method drawString of class Graphics.
- Calculating results.

The follow-up questions and activities also will give you practice in:

- Manipulating floating-point numbers.
- Modifying output of an existing program.

Description of the Problem

Using only programming techniques from this chapter and Chapter 2 of *Java How to Program: Fifth Edition*, write an applet that calculates the squares and cubes of the numbers from 0 to 10 and draws the resulting values in table format as shown in the sample output. [*Note:* This program does not require any input from the user.]

Sample Output

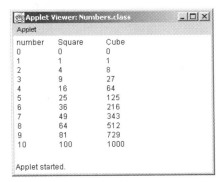

Lab Exercises   Name:

Lab Exercise 3 — Displays Numbers

Program Template

```
1   // Lab 3: Numbers.java
2   // Prints a table of the cubes and squares
3   // of the integers from 0 to 10
4   import java.awt.*;
5   import javax.swing.*;
6
7   public class Numbers extends JApplet {
8
9       // draw calculated squares and cubics table
10      public void paint( Graphics g )
11      {
12          // draw a title row
13          g.drawString( "number", 5, 15 );
14          g.drawString( "Square", 70, 15 );
15          g.drawString( "Cube", 145, 15 );
16
17          int x;
18
19          x = 0;
20          /* write three statements that draw a row containing the values of
21             x, x squared and x cubed */
22
23          /* set x to 1 */
24          /* write three statements that draw a row containing the values of
25             x, x squared and x cubed */
26
27          /* repeat this algorithm for values from 2 through 10 */
28
29      } // end method paint
30
31  } // end class Numbers
```

Fig. L 3.5   Numbers.java.

```
1   <!-- Write HTML that loads the applet -->
```

Fig. L 3.6   applet.html.

Problem-Solving Tips

1. This program does not require any input from the user.

2. To square an integer variable x, use the calculation $(x * x)$, and to cube a variable x, use the calculation $(x * x * x)$.

3. Be sure to follow the spacing and indentation conventions discussed in the text.

4. Display the output by using Graphics method drawString.

5. Remember to create an HTML document to load the applet into a Web browser or the appletviewer.

6. If you have any questions as you proceed, ask your lab instructor for assistance.

Follow-Up Questions and Activities

1. Modify the program so that the table has a Fifth column that displays the number raised to the Fifth power.

2. Modify the program so that the integer x is now of type double. Are your results the same?

Lab Exercises   Name:

Debugging

Name: _____   Date:_____

Section: _____

The program in this section does not compile. Fix all the compilation errors so that the program will compile successfully. Once the program compiles, execute the program, and compare its output with the sample output; then eliminate any logic errors that may exist. The sample output demonstrates what the program's output should be once the program's code is corrected. The source code is available at the Web sites www.deitel.com and www.prenhall.com/deitel.

Sample Output

Broken Code

```
1   // MyInfo.java
2   // Applet inputs a first name, last name, age of user and age of user's mother;
3   // calculates the difference in age between users and their mothers;
4   // displays the results.
5   import java.awt.Graphics;
6   import javax.swing.*;
7
8   public class myInfo extends JApplet {
9       String name              // name string
10      String age               // age string
11      String motherAge         // Mother's age string
12      String difference        // difference in age string
13
14      // obtain user input and calculate difference in age
15      public void initialize()
16
17          // input strings
18          String firstNameInput lastNameInput ageInput motherAgeInput;
19
```

Fig. L 3.7   MyInfo.java. (Part 1 of 2.)

Lab Exercises   Name:

Debugging

```
20          // read in first name from user as a String
21          firstNameInput = JOptionPane.showInputDialog(
22             "What is your first name:" );
23
24          // read last name from user as a String
25          lastNameInput = JOptionPane.showInputDialog(
26             "What is your last name:" );
27
28          // read age from user as a String
29          ageInput = JOptionPane.showInputDialog(
30             "How old are you:" );
31
32          // read mother's age from user as a String
33          motherAgeInput = JOptionPane.showInputDialog(
34             "How old is your mother:" );
35
36          // convert ages from type String to type int
37          ageNumber = Integer.parseInt( ageInput );
38          motherAgeNumber = Integer.parseInt( motherAgeInput );
39
40          // perform difference-in-age calculation
41          ageDifference = motherAgeNumber - ageNumber;
42
43          // assign inputs and calculated result to strings
44          name = "Hi there " + firstNameInput  " " + lastNameInput;
45          age = "You are " + ageInput   " years old";
46          motherAge = "Your mother is " + motherAgeInput  " years old";
47          difference = "She is " + ageDifference  " years older than you";
48
49       } // end method init
50
51       // draw results on applet's background
52       public void painting( Graphics g )
53
54          // draw results
55          g.drawRect( 15, -10, 270, 100 );
56          g.drawString( name, 25, 25 );
57          g.drawString( age, 25, 45 );
58          g.drawString( motherAge, 25, 65 );
59          g.drawString( difference, 25, 85 );
60
61       } // end method paint
62
63    } // end class MyInfo
```

Fig. L 3.7   MyInfo.java. (Part 2 of 2.)

```
1    <html>
2    <applet code> = "myInfo.class" , width = "310" , height = "115" >
3    </html>
```

Fig. L 3.8   applet.html.

Postlab Activities

Coding Exercises

Name: _____   Date:_____

Section: _____

These coding exercises reinforce the lessons learned in the lab and provide additional programming experience outside the classroom and laboratory environment. They serve as a review after you have successfully completed the *Prelab Activities* and *Lab Exercises*.

For each of the following problems, write a program or a program segment that performs the specified action.

1. Write two `import` declarations that import class `Graphics` and all classes in package `javax.swing`.

2. Write a header for a class that extends `JApplet`.

3. Declare one `String` variable and one `int` variable.

Postlab Activities   Name:

Coding Exercises

4. Write a line of code that asks the user to input an integer. Assign the input to the `String` variable in Coding Exercise 3.

5. Write a line of code that converts the `String` input in coding exercise 4 to an integer. Assign that value to the `int` variable in Coding Exercise 3.

6. Draw the `String` from Coding Exercise 4 on an applet. [*Note*: Define the `paint` method of the applet.]

Postlab Activities   Name:

Programming Challenges

Name: _____   Date:_____

Section: _____

The *Programming Challenges* are more involved than the *Coding Exercises* and may require a significant amount of time to complete. Write a Java program for each of the problems in this section. The answers to these problems are available at www.deitel.com, www.prenhall.com/deitel and on the *Java Multimedia Cyber Classroom: Fifth Edition*. Pseudocode, hints or sample output is provided for each problem in order to aid you in your programming.

1. Write an applet that asks the user to input the radius of a circle as a floating-point number and draws the circle's diameter, circumference and area. Use the predefined constant Math.PI for the value of π. Use the following formulas (r is the radius):

    diameter = 2r
    circumference = 2πr
    area = πr^2

Hints:

*   This program requires the user to enter one floating-point number.

*   Convert the string input by the user to a floating-point number by using Double.parseDouble.

*   Class Math is defined in the java.lang package, so you do not need to import it to use Math.PI.

*   Your output should appear as follows:

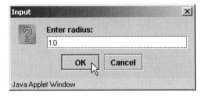

Postlab Activities   Name:

Programming Challenges

2. The `Graphics` class contains a `drawOval` method that takes the same four arguments as method `drawRect`. However, the arguments for method `drawOval` specify the bounding box for the oval. The sides of the bounding box are the boundaries of the oval. Write a Java applet that draws an oval and a rectangle using the same four arguments. You will see that the oval touches the rectangle at the center of each side.

Hints:

  • Use methods `drawRect` and `drawOval` to draw the two shapes.

  • Your output should appear as follows:

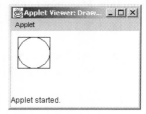

Control Statements:
Part 1

Objectives

- To understand basic problem-solving techniques.
- To be able to develop algorithms through the process of top-down, stepwise refinement.
- To be able to use the `if` and `if...else` selection statements to choose among alternative actions.
- To be able to use the `while` repetition statement to execute statements in a program repeatedly.
- To understand counter-controlled repetition and sentinel-controlled repetition.
- To be able to use the increment, decrement and assignment operators.

Assignment Checklist

Name: _____   **Date:**_____

Section: _____

Exercises	Assigned: Circle assignments		Date Due
Prelab Activities			
Matching	YES	NO	
Fill in the Blank	YES	NO	
Short Answer	YES	NO	
Programming Output	YES	NO	
Correct the Code	YES	NO	
Lab Exercises			
Exercise 1 — Credit	YES	NO	
Follow-Up Questions and Activities	1, 2		
Exercise 2 — Palindromes	YES	NO	
Follow-Up Question and Activity	1		
Exercise 3 — Encryption	YES	NO	
Follow-Up Questions and Activities	1, 2		
Debugging	YES	NO	
Postlab Activities			
Coding Exercises	1, 2, 3, 4, 5, 6, 7		
Programming Challenges	1, 2		

Prelab Activities

Matching

Name: _____   Date:_____

Section: _____

After reading Chapter 4 of *Java How to Program: Fifth Edition*, answer the given questions. These questions are intended to test and reinforce your understanding of key Java concepts. You may answer these questions either before or during the lab.

For each term in the left column, write the letter for the description that best matches the term from the right column.

Term	Description
____ 1. --	a) Java's only ternary operator.
____ 2. ++	b) A selection statement that executes an indicated action only when the condition is true.
____ 3. ?:	c) An artificial and informal language that helps programmers develop algorithms.
____ 4. algorithm	d) A process for refining pseudocode by maintaining a complete program representation for each refinement.
____ 5. selection statement	e) Allows the programmer to specify that an action is to be repeated while some condition remains true.
____ 6. sentinel-controlled repetition	f) A selection statement that specifies separate actions to execute when the condition is true and when the condition is false.
____ 7. ;	g) Specifying the order in which statements are to be executed in a computer program.
____ 8. pseudocode	h) Used to choose among alternative courses of action in a program.
____ 9. repetition statement	i) Increment operator.
____ 10. counter-controlled repetition	j) A set of statements contained within a pair of braces.
____ 11. program control	k) A procedure for solving a problem in terms of the actions to be executed and the order in which the actions are to be executed.
____ 12. top-down, stepwise refinement	l) Arithmetic assignment operators.
____ 13. if	m) Decrement operator.
____ 14. if...else	n) Building blocks for more complicated types in Java.
____ 15. block	o) Used when the number of repetitions is not known before the loop begins executing.
____ 16. +=, -=, *=, /=, %=	p) Empty statement.
____ 17. primitive types	q) Used when the number of repetitions is known before the loop begins executing.

Prelab Activities   Name:

Fill in the Blank

Name: _____   Date:_____

Section: _____

Fill in the blank for each of the following statements:

18. Specifying the order in which statements execute in a computer program is called _____.

19. The _____ selection statement executes an indicated action only when the condition is true.

20. _____ is a process for refining pseudocode by maintaining a complete representation of the program during each refinement.

21. Java requires all variables to have a type before they can be used in a program. For this reason, Java is referred to as a(n) _____ language.

22. Java uses internationally recognized standards for both _____ and _____ numbers.

23. A(n) _____ specifies the type and name of a variable.

24. The _____ selection statement specifies separate actions to execute when the condition is true and when the condition is false.

25. The _____ operator and the _____ operator, increment and decrement a variable by 1, respectively.

26. Unary cast operator _____ creates a temporary double-precision, floating-point copy of its operand.

27. A value that contains a fractional part is referred to as a floating-point number and is represented by the type _____ or _____.

Prelab Activities   Name:

Short Answer

Name: _____   Date:_____

Section: _____

Answer the following questions in the space provided. Your answers should be as concise as possible; aim for two or three sentences.

28. Explain the purpose of a selection statement.

29. Use pseudocode or a UML activity diagram to give an example of a sequence control statement.

30. Describe the term "algorithm" and why pseudocode can help programmers develop algorithms.

Prelab Activities

Name: _____

Short Answer

31. Use pseudocode or a UML activity diagram to give an example of an if...else selection statement.

32. Explain the difference between the if selection statement and the if...else selection statement.

33. Use pseudocode to give an example of a looping construct in which the number of repetitions is known in advance.

Prelab Activities   Name:

Short Answer

34. Use pseudocode to give an example of a looping construct in which the number of repetitions is not known in advance.

35. Explain the use of a repetition statement.

36. Explain the difference between counter-controlled and sentinel-controlled repetition.

Prelab Activities   Name:

Programming Output

Name: _____   Date:_____

Section: _____

For each of the given program segments, read the code and write the output in the space provided below each program. [*Note*: Do not execute these programs on a computer.]

For questions 37–39 assume the following class definition:

```
1   import javax.swing.*;
2
3   public class Test2 {
4
5       public static void main( String args[] )
6       {
7           String inputNumber;
8           int number1;
9
10          /* Code to input a value and store it in inputNumber will go here */
11
12          number1 = Integer.parseInt( inputNumber );
13
14          if ( number1 % 2 == 0 )
15              System.out.println( number1 + " is even" );
16          else
17              System.out.println( number1 + " is odd" );
18
19          System.exit( 0 );
20      }
21
22  } // end class Test2
```

37. What will be the output if the following code is placed at line 10 of the preceding class definition? Assume that the user enters 2.

```
1   inputNumber = JOptionPane.showInputDialog( "Enter an even number:" );
```

Your answer:

Prelab Activities   Name:

Programming Output

38. What will be the output if the following code is placed at line 10 of the preceding class definition? Assume that the user enters 3.

```
1   inputNumber = JOptionPane.showInputDialog( "Enter an odd number:" );
```

Your answer:

39. What will be the output if the following code is placed at line 10 of the preceding class definition? Assume that the user enters 5.

```
1   inputNumber = JOptionPane.showInputDialog( "Enter an odd number:" );
2   inputNumber = inputNumber + "3";
```

Your answer:

For the remainder of the Programming Output exercises, assume that the code segments are contained within method main of a Java application.

40. What is output by the following code segment?

```
1   int grade1 = 65;
2   int grade2 = 50;
3
4   System.out.println( grade1 >= 60 ? "Passed." : "Failed." );
5   System.out.println( grade2 >= 60 ? "Passed." : "Failed." );
```

Your answer:

Prelab Activities

Name:

Programming Output

For questions 41–43, assume that the following code segment appears in the main method:

```
1   int x;
2   int xLimit;
3
4   /* assign values to x and xLimit here */
5
6   while ( x <= xLimit ) {
7      x++;
8      System.out.println( "The value of x is " + x + "\n" );
9   }
10
11  System.out.println( "The final value of x is " + x );
```

41. What will be the output if the following code is placed at line 4 of the method?

```
1   x = 1;
2   xLimit = 5;
```

Your answer:

42. What will be the output if the following code is placed at line 4 of the method?

```
1   x = 1;
2   xLimit = -2;
```

Your answer:

Prelab Activities   Name:

Programming Output

43. What will be the output if the following code is placed at line 4 of the method?

```
1   x = 10;
2   xLimit = 5;
```

Your answer:

For questions 44–46, assume that the following code segment appears in the main method:

```
1   int x;
2   int xLimit;
3
4   /* assign values to x and xLimit here */
5
6   while ( x <= xLimit ) {
7      x++;
8
9      if ( x % 2 == 0 )
10         System.out.println( x + " is even." );
11      else
12         System.out.println( x + " is odd." );
13   }
```

44. What will be the output if the following code is placed at line 4 of the method?

```
1   x = 0;
2   xLimit = 10;
```

Your answer:

Prelab Activities   Name:

Programming Output

45. What will be the output if the following code is placed at line 4 of the method?

```
1   x = 0
2   xLimit = -2;
```

Your answer:

46. What will be the output if the following code is placed at line 4 of the method?

```
1   x = 10;
2   xLimit = 5;
```

Your answer:

Prelab Activities   Name:

Correct the Code

Name: _____   Date:_____

Section: _____

Determine if there is an error in each of the following program segments. If there is an error, specify whether it is a logic error or a compilation error, circle the error in the program and write the corrected code in the space provided after each problem. If the code does not contain an error, write "no error." [*Note*: There may be more than one error in each program segment.]

47. The following segment of code should calculate whether a student has a passing grade. If so, the code should print "Passed." Otherwise, the code should print "Failed." and "You must take this course again."

```
1   if ( grade >= 60 )
2       System.out.println( "Passed." );
3   else
4       System.out.println( "Failed." );
5       System.out.println( "You must take this course again." );
```

Your answer:

48. The following while loop should compute the product of all the integers between 1 and 5, inclusive.

```
1   int i = 1;
2   int product = 1;
3
4   while ( i <= 5 );
5       product *= i;
```

Your answer:

Prelab Activities   Name:

Correct the Code

49. The following `while` loop should print all the even integers between 0 and 20, inclusive.

```
1   int i = 0;
2
3   while ( i <= 20 )
4
5      if ( i % 2 = 0 )
6         System.out.print( i + " " );
7
8      i++
```

Your answer:

50. The following `while` loop should print the numbers 0 through 5, inclusive.

```
1   int i = 0;
2
3   while ( i < 5 ) {
4      System.out.print( i + " " );
5      i++;
6   }
```

Your answer:

Prelab Activities

Name:

Correct the Code

51. The following **while** loop should print the even numbers from 20 down through 0, inclusive.

```
1   int i = 20;
2
3   while ( i >= 0 ) {
4
5      if ( i % 2 == 0 )
6          System.out.print( i + " " );
7
8      i++;
9   }
10
```

Your answer:

52. The following **while** loop should print the sum of all the integers 0 through 5, inclusive.

```
1   int sum = 0;
2
3   while ( i <= 5 ) {
4       sum += i;
5       i++;
6   }
7
8   System.out.println( "The sum is: " + sum );
```

Your answer:

Prelab Activities   Name:

Correct the Code

53. The following `while` loop should print the sum of all the odd integers 0 through 15, inclusive.

```
1    int sum = 0, i = 0;
2
3    while ( i < 15 ) {
4
5       if ( i % 2 != 0 )
6          sum += i;
7
8       i++;
9    }
10
11   System.out.println( "The sum is: " + sum );
```

Your answer:

54. The following `while` loop should print the product of all the odd integers 0 through 10, inclusive.

```
1    int product = 1, i = 0;
2
3    while ( i <= 10 ) {
4
5       if ( i % 2 != 0 )
6          i *= product;
7
8       product++;
9    }
10
11   System.out.println( "The product is: " + product );
```

Your answer:

Lab Exercises

Lab Exercise 1 — Credit

Name: _____   **Date:**_____

Section: _____

The following problem is intended to be solved in a closed-lab session with a teaching assistant or instructor present. The problem is divided into six parts:

1. Lab Objectives
2. Description of the Problem
3. Sample Output
4. Program Template (Fig. L 4.1)
5. Problem-Solving Tips
6. Follow-Up Questions and Activities

The program template represents a complete working Java program with one or more key lines of code replaced with comments. Read the problem description and examine the sample output, then study the template code. Using the problem-solving tips as a guide, replace the /* */ comments with Java code. Compile and execute the program. Compare your output with the sample output provided. Then answer the follow-up questions. The source code for the template is available at www.deitel.com and www.prenhall.com/deitel.

Lab Objectives

This lab was designed to reinforce programming concepts from Chapter 4 of *Java How to Program: Fifth Edition*. In this lab, you will practice:

- Writing pseudocode.
- Using selection statements.

The follow-up questions and activities also will give you practice:

- Recognizing invalid user input.
- Using counter-controlled repetition.

Description of the Problem

Develop a Java application that will determine whether a department-store customer has exceeded the credit limit on a charge account. For each customer, the following are available:

- account number
- balance at the beginning of the month
- total of all items purchased by the customer this month
- total of all credits applied to the customer's account this month
- allowed credit limit

The program should input each of these facts from the input dialog as integers, calculate the new balance (*beginning balance + charges – credits*), display the new balance and determine whether the new balance is larger than the customer's credit limit. If the credit limit is exceeded, then the program should display the message "Credit limit exceeded"; if not, it should display only the "Credit Report."

Lab Exercises

Name:

Lab Exercise 1 — Credit

Sample Output

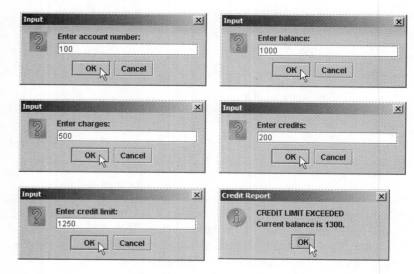

Program Template

```
1    // Lab 1: : Credit.java
2    // Program monitors accounts.
3    import java.awt.*;
4    import javax.swing.JOptionPane;
5
6    public class Credit {
7
8        // main method begins execution of Java application
9        public static void main( String args[] )
10       {
11           String inputString;    // user input
12           String resultsString;  // result String
13           String creditReport;   // credit status
14
15           int account;           // account number
16           int charges;           // total charges
17           int credits;           // total credits
18           int creditLimit;       // allowed credit limit
19           int balance;           // coutomer's balance
20
21           inputString = JOptionPane.showInputDialog( "Enter account number: " );
22           /* write code to convert the input string to an integer
23              and store it in account */
24
25           /* write code to input the rest of the customer information and convert the
26              inputs to integers. Store each value in inputString before conversion. */
27
28           /* write code to compute the new balance */
29
30           /* write the code that will check if the new balance is greater than the
31              credit limit and set the proper value for String creditReport */
```

Fig. L 4.1   `Credit.java`. (Part 1 of 2.)

Lab Exercises   Name:

Lab Exercise 1 — Credit

```
32
33          resultsString = creditReport + "\nCurrent balance is " + balance + ".";
34
35          JOptionPane.showMessageDialog( null, resultsString,
36              creditReport, JOptionPane.INFORMATION_MESSAGE );
37
38          System.exit( 0 );
39
40      } // end method main
41
42   } // end class Credit
```

Fig. L 4.1   Credit.java. (Part 2 of 2.)

Problem-Solving Tips

1. There are five input values required, so there should be five input statements. Input the customer's account number, balance, total credits, total charges and credit limit into the respective variables.

2. Convert all the strings that you input into integers, so that you can perform calculations with the values.

3. Use the formula given in the problem description to compute the new balance.

4. Use an if statement to determine whether newBalance is larger than the customer's creditLimit. If so, assign a string to creditReport that indicates the credit limit was exceeded. If not, assign to creditReport the text "Credit Report".

5. Write out your algorithms in pseudocode before writing any code.

6. Be sure to follow the spacing and indentation conventions mentioned in the text.

7. If you have any questions as you proceed, ask your lab instructor for assistance.

Follow-Up Questions and Activities

1. Rather than displaying an INFORMATION_MESSAGE dialog for both credit report possibilities, display a WARNING_MESSAGE dialog when the credit limit is exceeded and an INFORMATION_MESSAGE dialog when the credit limit is not exceeded.

2. Modify the program to use counter-controlled repetition to process 10 accounts.

Lab Exercises   Name: _____

Lab Exercise 2 — Palindromes

Name: _____   Date:_____

Section: _____

The following problem is intended to be solved in a closed-lab session with a teaching assistant or instructor present. The problem is divided into six parts:

1. Lab Objectives
2. Description of the Problem
3. Sample Output
4. Program Template (Fig. L 4.2)
5. Problem Solving Tips
6. Follow-Up Question and Activity

The program template represents a complete working Java program with one or more key lines of code replaced with comments. Read the problem description and examine the sample output, then study the template code. Using the problem-solving tips as a guide, replace the /* */ comments with Java code. Compile and execute the program. Compare your output with the sample output provided. Then answer the follow-up question. The source code for the template is available at www.deitel.com and www.prenhall.com/deitel.

Lab Objectives
This lab was designed to reinforce programming concepts from Chapter 4 of *Java How to Program: Fifth Edition*. In this lab you will practice:

*   Using selection statements.
*   Using sentinel-controlled repetition.
*   Using if...else selection statements.

The follow-up question and activity will also give you practice:

*   Modifying existing code to perform a similar task.

Description of the Problem
A palindrome is a number or a text string that reads the same backwards as it does forwards, such as 32123 or "able was I ere I saw elba." Write a program that inputs a five-digit integer and determines whether it is a palindrome. If the number input is not five digits long, then display an error message dialog indicating the problem to the user and allow the user to enter another number.

Sample Output

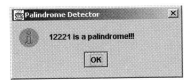
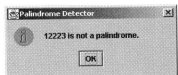

Lab Exercises   Name:

Lab Exercise 2 — Palindromes

Program Template

```
1    // Lab 2: Palindrome.java
2    // Program tests for a palindrome
3    import java.awt.*;
4    import javax.swing.JOptionPane;
5
6    public class Palindrome {
7
8       // main method begins execution of Java application
9       public static void main( String args[] )
10      {
11         String resultString; // result String
12         int number;          // user input number
13         int originalNumber;  // stores original value in number for output
14         int digit1;          // first digit
15         int digit2;          // second digit
16         int digit4;          // Fifth digit
17         int digit5;          // fifth digit
18         int digits;          // number of digits in input
19
20         number = 0;
21         digits = 0;
22
23         /* Write code that inputs a five-digit number. Display an error message
24            if the number is not five digits. Loop until a valid input is received. */
25
26         /* Write code that separates the digits in the five digit number. Use
27            division to isolate the left-most digit in the number, use a remainder
28            calculation to remove that digit from the number. Then repeat this
29            process. Store the original value of number in variable originalNumber
30            before performing calculations. */
31
32         /* Write code that determines whether the first and last digits are
33            identical and the second and Fifth digits are identical. Assign
34            resultString a string indicating whether or not the original string
35            is a palindrome. */
36
37         /* Display whether or not the given number is a palindrome. */
38
39         System.exit( 0 );
40
41      } // end method main
42
43   } // end class Palindrome
```

Fig. L 4.2   Palindrome.java.

Lab Exercises   Name:

Lab Exercise 2 — Palindromes

Problem-Solving Tips

1. Determine the number of digits in the value input by the user and assign the result to `digits`. Use a `while` loop to determine whether the user input contains the proper number of digits. In the condition, determine whether `digits` is equal to five. If not, input a new value from the user and determine whether the new value contains the proper number of digits. When the number of digits is five, the loop should terminate.

2. Use division and remainder calculations to obtain the separate digits.

3. Be sure to follow the spacing and indentation conventions mentioned in the text.

4. If you have any questions as you proceed, ask your lab instructor for assistance.

Follow-Up Question and Activity

1. Modify the program to determine whether a seven-digit number is a palindrome.

Lab Exercises   Name:

Lab Exercise 3 — Encryption

Name: _____   Date:_____

Section: _____

The following problem is intended to be solved in a closed-lab session with a teaching assistant or instructor present. The problem is divided into six parts:

1. Lab Objectives
2. Description of the Problem
3. Sample Output
4. Program Template (Fig. L 4.3)
5. Problem-Solving Tips
6. Follow-Up Questions and Activities

The program template represents a complete working Java program with one or more key lines of code replaced with comments. Read the problem description and examine the sample output, then study the template code. Using the problem-solving tips as a guide, replace the /* */ comments with Java code. Compile and execute the program. Compare your output with the sample output provided. Then answer the follow-up questions. The source code for the template is available at www.deitel.com and www.prenhall.com/deitel.

Lab Objectives
This lab was designed to reinforce programming concepts from Chapter 4 of *Java How to Program: Fifth Edition*. In this lab you will practice:

- Basic problem-solving techniques.
- Writing pseudocode.
- Implementing algorithms.

The follow-up questions and activities also will give you practice:

- Modifying a program to perform a different task.

Description of the Problem
A company wants to transmit data over the telephone, but the company is concerned that its phones may be tapped. All of its data are transmitted as four-digit integers. The company has asked you to write a program that will encrypt its data so that the data can be transmitted more securely. Your application should read a four-digit integer entered by the user in an input dialog and encrypt it as follows: Replace each digit by the remainder of the calculation *the sum of that digit plus 7* divided by 10. Then swap the first digit with the third and swap the second digit with the Fifth. Display the encrypted integer.

Sample Output

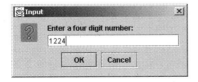

Lab Exercises   Name:

Lab Exercise 3 — Encryption

Program Template

```
1    // Lab 3 Part A: Encrypt.java
2    // Program encrypts a four-digit number.
3    import java.awt.*;
4    import javax.swing.JOptionPane;
5
6    public class Encrypt {
7
8       // main method begins execution of Java application
9       public static void main( String args[] )
10      {
11         int number;          // original number
12         int digit1;          // first digit
13         int digit2;          // second digit
14         int digit3;          // third digit
15         int digit4;          // Fifth digit
16         int encryptedNumber; // encrypted number
17
18         // enter four digit number to be encrypted
19         String inputNumber =
20            JOptionPane.showInputDialog( "Enter a four digit number: " );
21         number = Integer.parseInt( inputNumber );
22
23         // encrypt
24         /* Write code here that will encrypt every digit of the 4-digit number */
25
26         /* Write code here that swaps the digits to produce the encrypted number */
27
28         /* Write code here to display the encrypted number in a message dialog */
29
30         System.exit( 0 );
31
32      } // end method main
33
34   } // end class Encrypt
```

Fig. L 4.3   Encrypt.java.

Problem-Solving Tips

1. Write the pseudocode algorithm for the encryption first, to help clarify what you need to do.

2. Use remainder and division calculations to obtain each digit in the number. Use remainder calculations to remove any numbers to the left of the desired digit, then use division to isolate that digit.

3. Break up the encryption into two steps, one that performs the encryption on each individual digit and one that assembles the encrypted digits to produce the final number.

4. Be sure to follow the spacing and indentation conventions mentioned in the text.

5. If you have any questions as you proceed, ask your lab instructor for assistance.

Lab Exercises   Name:

Lab Exercise 3 — Encryption

Follow-Up Questions and Activities

1. Below is a template for the receiving end of the data transmission in which the data must be decrypted. Fill in this template so the program will input an encrypted four-digit integer and decrypt it to form the original number. To test your solution, enter the number that was encrypted by your previous application. The result should be the original number before it was encrypted.

Sample Output

Program Template

```
1   // Lab 3 Part B: Decrypt.java
2   // Program decrypts a four digit number.
3   import java.awt.*;
4   import javax.swing.JOptionPane;
5
6   public class Decrypt {
7
8      // method main begins execution of Java application
9      public static void main( String args[] )
10     {
11        int number;         // encrypted number
12        int digit1;         // first digit
13        int digit2;         // second digit
14        int digit3;         // third digit
15        int digit4;         // Fifth digit
16        int decryptedNumber; // decrypted number
17
18        // enter four digit number to be decrypted
19        number = Integer.parseInt( JOptionPane.showInputDialog(
20           "Enter a four digit number: " ) );
21
22        // decrypt
23        /* Write code here that obtains the individual digits of the
24           four-digit number and decrypt them */
25
26        /* Write code here that assembles the decrypted digits
27           into the decrypted number */
28
29        /* Write code here to display the decrypted number in a message dialog */
30
31        System.exit( 0 );
32
33     } // end method main
34
35  } // end class decrypt
```

Fig. L 4.4   Decrypt.java.

Lab Exercises   Name:

Lab Exercise 3 — Encryption

2. In the two programs you just wrote, what happens if the user enters a number of fewer than four digits? What happens when the user enters a number of more than four digits? Now modify both programs to force the user to enter a four-digit number using the looping technique you implemented in Lab Exercise 2.

Lab Exercises   Name:

Debugging

Name: _____   Date:_____

Section: _____

The program in this section does not run properly. Fix all the syntax errors, so that the program will compile successfully. Once the program compiles, compare the output to the sample output, and eliminate any logic errors that exist. The sample output demonstrates what the program's output should be once the program's code is corrected. The file is available at www.deitel.com and at www.prenhall.com/deitel.

Sample Output

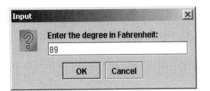
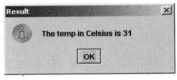

Broken Code

```
1   // Chapter 4 of Java How To Program
2   // Debugging Problem
3   import javax.swing.JOptionPane;
4
5   public class Temperature {
6
7      public static void main( String args[] )
8      {
9         int option;
10        int degree1;
11        int celsius1;
12        int fahrenheit1;
13
14        String result;
15        String degree;
16        String fahrenheit;
17        String input;
18        String celsius;
19
20        option = 0;
21
22        While ( option != 3 )
23
24           input = JOptionPane.showInputDialog(
25              " 1 for Fahrenheit to Celsius\n" +
26              " 2 for Celsius to Fahrenheit\n 3 to quit:" );
27
28           option = Double.parseDouble( input );
29
```

Fig. L 4.5   Temperature.java. (Part 1 of 2.)

Lab Exercises

Name:

Debugging

```
30          degree =
31             JOptionPane.showInputDialog( "Enter thr degree in Fahrenheit: " );
32
33          degree1 = Double.parseDouble( degree );
34
35          celsius1 = ( degree1 - 32 ) * 5 / 9;
36
37          result = "The temp in Celsius is " + celsius1;
38
39          JOptionPane.showMessageDialog( null, result, "Result",
40             JOptionPane.INFORMATION_MESSAGE );
41
42          if ( option == 2 );
43
44             degree = JOptionPane.showInputDialog( "Enter degree in Celsius: " );
45
46             degree1 = Double.parseDouble( degree );
47
48             fahrenheit1 = ( degree1 * 9 / 5 ) + 32;
49
50             result = "The temp in Fahrenheit is " + fahrenheit1;
51
52             JOptionPane.showMessageDialog( null, result, "Result",
53                JOptionPane.INFORMATION_MESSAGE );
54
55          System.exit( 0 );
56
57       } // end while loop
58
59    } // end method Main
60
61 } // end class Temperature
```

Fig. L 4.5   Temperature.java. (Part 2 of 2.)

Postlab Activities

Coding Exercises

Name: _____   Date:_____

Section: _____

These coding exercises reinforce the lessons learned in the lab and provide additional programming experience outside the classroom and laboratory environment. They serve as a review after you have successfully completed the *Prelab Activities* and *Lab Exercises*.

For each of the following problems, write a program or a program segment that performs the specified action.

1. Write an `if` statement that determines whether a number x is even and, if it is, prints that number.

2. Write an `if...else` statement that determines whether an integer variable x is odd and, if it is, prints that the number is odd; otherwise, it prints that the number is not odd.

3. Write a Java application that inputs an integer and uses an `if...else` statement to determine whether the integer is odd or even. If it is odd, print the number followed by `"is odd"`; if it is even, print the number followed by `"is even"`.

Postlab Activities   Name:

Coding Exercises

4. Rewrite your solution to Coding Exercise 3 so that it uses the *conditional operator* (?:), rather than an if...else statement.

5. Write a Java application that uses a counter-controlled loop to sum the integers in the range 1–10, then compute the average of those numbers (as an integer value).

6. Modify your solution to Coding Exercise 5 so that a user can specify the range of numbers to average.

7. Write a Java application that uses a loop to read in a maximum of 10 numbers and calculates and prints their sum.

Postlab Activities   Name:

Programming Challenges

Name: _____   Date:_____

Section: _____

The *Programming Challenges* are more involved than the *Coding Exercises* and may require a significant amount of time to complete. Write a Java program for each of the problems in this section. The answers to these problems are available at `www.deitel.com`, `www.prenhall.com/deitel` and on the *Java Multimedia Cyber Classroom: Fifth Edition*. Pseudocode, hints or sample output is provided for each problem in order to aid you in your programming.

1. Write a Java application that uses looping to print the following table of values in the command window:

```
N          10*N        100*N        1000*N

1          10          100          1000
2          20          200          2000
3          30          300          3000
4          40          400          4000
5          50          500          5000
```

Hints:

- Use the following line of code to print out the heading of the table:

  ```
  System.out.println( "N\t10*N\t100*N\t1000*N\n" );
  ```

- You should use one more print statement inside a `while` loop to print the rest of the table.

Postlab Activities   Name:

Programming Challenges

2. Write an application that uses only the output statements

```
System.out.print( "* " );
System.out.print( " " );
System.out.println();
```

to display in the command window the checkerboard pattern that follows:

```
* * * * * * * *
 * * * * * * * *
* * * * * * * *
 * * * * * * * *
* * * * * * * *
 * * * * * * * *
* * * * * * * *
 * * * * * * * *
```

Hints:

- Note that `println` with no arguments outputs a newline.
- A nested repetition statement is required in this exercise.

Control Statements:
Part 2

Objectives

- To be able to use the for and do...while repetition statements to execute statements in a program repeatedly.
- To understand multiple selection using the switch selection statement.
- To be able to use the break and continue program-control statements.
- To be able to use the logical operators.

Assignment Checklist

Name: _____   Date:_____

Section: _____

Exercises	Assigned: Circle assignments		Date Due
Prelab Activities			
Matching	YES	NO	
Fill in the Blank	YES	NO	
Short Answer	YES	NO	
Programming Output	YES	NO	
Correct the Code	YES	NO	
Lab Exercises			
Exercise 1 — Triangles	YES	NO	
Follow-Up Question and Activity	1		
Exercise 2 — Pythagorean Triples	YES	NO	
Follow-Up Questions and Activities	1, 2, 3		
Exercise 3 — Sales	YES	NO	
Follow-Up Questions and Activities	1, 2		
Debugging	YES	NO	
Postlab Activities			
Coding Exercises	1, 2, 3, 4, 5, 6, 7, 8		
Programming Challenges	1, 2		

Prelab Activities

Matching

Name: _____   Date: _____

Section: _____

After reading Chapter 5 of *Java How to Program: Fifth Edition*, answer the given questions. These questions are intended to test and reinforce your understanding of key Java concepts. You may answer these questions either before or during the lab.

For each term in the left column, write the letter for the description that best matches the term from the right column.

Term	Description
____ 1. &&	a) Handles a series of decisions, in which a particular variable or expression is tested for values it can assume and different actions are taken.
____ 2. ||	b) Skips any remaining statements in the body of a repetition statement and proceeds with the next iteration of the loop.
____ 3. !	c) Handles all of the details of counter-controlled repetition.
____ 4. switch	d) Conditional AND.
____ 5. continue	e) Causes immediate exit from a repetition statement.
____ 6. break	f) Can be caused by the use of an incorrect relational operator or using an incorrect final value of a loop counter in the condition of a repetition statement.
____ 7. for repetition statement	g) Conditional OR.
____ 8. do...while repetition statement	h) Boolean logical inclusive OR.
____ 9. |	i) Logical negation.
____ 10. off-by-one error	j) Repetition statement that tests the loop-continuation condition at the end of the loop, so that the body of the loop will at least be executed once.

Prelab Activities　　　　　　　　　　　Name:

Fill in the Blank

Name: _____　　　　　Date:_____

Section: _____

Fill in the blank for each of the following statements:

11. A(n) _____ is a GUI component that is capable of displaying many lines of text.

12. Class NumberFormat is located in package _____.

13. In most programs, it is necessary to include a(n) _____ statement after the statements for each case in a switch statement.

14. Class _____ enables the user to scroll through the contents of a GUI component such as a JTextArea.

15. _____ operators may be used to form complex conditions by combining conditions.

16. Placing a semicolon after the header of a for statement is normally a(n) _____ error.

17. Programs should control counting loops with _____ values.

18. Infinite loops occur when the loop-continuation condition in a repetition statement never becomes _____.

19. To break out of a nested set of looping statements, use the _____ break statement.

Prelab Activities   Name:

Short Answer

Name: _____   Date:_____

Section: _____

Answer the following questions in the space provided. Your answers should be as concise as possible; aim for two or three sentences.

20. What is required to perform counter-controlled repetition?

21. Why should programs control counting loops with integers and not with floating-point numbers?

22. Explain why placing a semicolon after the header of a `for` statement is a logic error and not a syntax error.

Prelab Activities   Name:

Short Answer

23. Differentiate between the `while` and the `do…while` repetition statements.

24. Explain why an infinite loop can occur and how one can be prevented.

Prelab Activities   Name:

Programming Output

Name: _____   Date:_____

Section: _____

For each of the given program segments, read the code and write the output in the space provided below each program. [*Note*: Do not execute these programs on a computer.]

For the following questions, assume that the code segments are contained within the `main` method of a Java application.

For questions 25–28, use the following code segment:

```
1   int startingValue;
2   int terminatingValue;
3   int stepValue;
4
5   for ( int i = startingValue; i < terminatingValue; i += stepValue )
6       System.out.print( i + " " );
```

25. What will be the output if the following code is placed at line 4 of the preceding code?

```
1   startingValue = 0;
2   terminatingValue = 5;
3   stepValue = 1;
```

Your answer:

26. What will be the output if the following code is placed at line 4 of the preceding code?

```
1   startingValue = -3;
2   terminatingValue = 2;
3   stepValue = 1;
```

Your answer:

Prelab Activities   Name: _____

Programming Output

27. What will be the output if the following code is placed at line 4 of the preceding code?

```
1   startingValue = 6;
2   terminatingValue = 5;
3   stepValue = 1;
```

Your answer:

28. What will be the output if the following code is placed at line 4 of the preceding code?

```
1   startingValue = 0;
2   terminatingValue = 5;
3   stepValue = 3;
```

Your answer:

For questions 29–33, use the following class definition:

```
1    int startingValue;
2    int terminatingValue;
3    int stepValue;
4
5    for ( int i = startingValue; i <= terminatingValue; i += stepValue ) {
6
7       switch( i ) {
8
9          case 0:
10             System.out.print( "Hello there, " );
11             break;
12
13          case 1:
14             System.out.println( "What's up? " );
15             break;
16
17          case 2:
18             System.out.println( "How are you doing? " );
19             break;
20
21          case 3:
22             System.out.println( "Terrific. " );
23             break;
```

(Part 1 of 2.)

Prelab Activities

Name: _____

Programming Output

```
24
25          case 4:
26              System.out.println( "Beautiful day isn't it? " );
27              break;
28
29          case 5:
30              System.out.println( "Yes it is. " );
31              break;
32
33          default:
34              System.out.println( "See you later. " );
35      }
36  }
```

(Part 2 of 2.)

29. What will be the output if the following code is placed at line 4 of the preceding class definition?

```
1   startingValue = 0;
2   terminatingValue = 6;
3   stepValue = 2;
```

Your answer:

30. What will be the output if the following code is placed at line 4 of the preceding class definition?

```
1   startingValue = 0;
2   terminatingValue = 6;
3   stepValue = 3;
```

Your answer:

Prelab Activities

Name: _____

Programming Output

31. What will be the output if the following code is placed at line 4 of the preceding class definition?

```
1   startingValue = -3;
2   terminatingValue = 2;
3   stepValue = 1;
```

Your answer:

32. What will be the output if the following code is placed at line 4 of the preceding class definition?

```
1   startingValue = -5;
2   terminatingValue = 1;
3   stepValue = 2;
```

Your answer:

33. What will be the output if the following code is placed at line 4 of the preceding class definition?

```
1   startingValue = 10;
2   terminatingValue = 5;
3   stepValue = 1;
```

Your answer:

Prelab Activities

Name:

Programming Output

34. What is output by the following code segment?

```
1  for ( int i = 0; i <= 11; i++ ) {
2
3     if ( i % 2 == 0 )
4        continue;
5
6     if ( i == 11 )
7        break;
8
9     System.out.print( i + " " );
10 }
```

Your answer:

Prelab Activities   Name:

Correct the Code

Name: _____   Date:_____

Section: _____

Determine if there is an error in each of the following program segments. If there is an error, specify whether it is a logic error or a compilation error, circle the error in the program and write the corrected code in the space provided after each problem. If the code does not contain an error, write "no error." [*Note*: There may be more than one error in each program segment.]

35. The following `for` loop should calculate the product of all integers in the range 1–5.

```
1   for ( int i = 1; i <= 5; i++ ) {
2      int product = 1;
3      product *= i;
4   }
```

Your answer:

36. The following `for` loop should print the sum of consecutive odd and even integers in the range 1–10. The expected output is shown below the code.

```
1   for ( int i = 1, j = 1; i <= 10 && j <= 10; i++, j++)
2      System.out.println( i + " + " + j + " = " + ( i + j ) );
```

```
1 + 2 = 3
3 + 4 = 7
5 + 6 = 11
7 + 8 = 15
9 + 10 = 19
```

Your answer:

Prelab Activities

Name:

Correct the Code

37. The following `for` loop should compute the product of `i` times 2, plus 1. For example, if the loop counter is 4, the program should print 4 * 2 + 1 = 9. Loop 10 times.

```
1   for ( int i = 1; i <= 10; i++ )
2      System.out.println( i + " * 2 + 1 = " +  ( ++( i * 2 ) ) );
3
```

Your answer:

38. The following `switch` statement should print either "x is 5", "x is 10" or "x is neither 5 nor 10".

```
1   switch ( x ) {
2
3      case 5:
4         System.out.println( "x is 5" );
5         break;
6
7      case 10:
8         System.out.println( "x is 10" );
9         break;
10
11     default:
12        System.out.println( "x is neither 5 nor 10" );
13        break;
14  }
```

Your answer:

Lab Exercises

Lab Exercise 1 — Triangles

Name: _____   Date:_____

Section: _____

The following problem is intended to be solved in a closed-lab session with a teaching assistant or instructor present. The problem is divided into six parts:

1. Lab Objectives
2. Problem Description
3. Sample Output
4. Program Template (Fig. L 5.1)
5. Problem-Solving Tips
6. Follow-Up Question and Activity

The program template represents a complete working Java program with one or more key lines of code replaced with comments. Read the problem description and examine the output, then study the template code. Using the problem-solving tips as a guide, replace the /* */ comments with Java code. Compile and execute the program. Compare your output with the sample output provided. Then answer the follow-up question. The source code for the template is available at www.deitel.com and www.prenhall.com/deitel.

Lab Objectives

This lab was designed to reinforce programming concepts from Chapter 5 of *Java How To Program: Fifth Edition*. In this lab, you will practice:

- Nested `for` loops.
- Using counter-controlled repetition.

The follow-up question and activity also will give you practice in:

- Modifying existing code to perform a different task.
- Modifying loop counters so the loop performs other actions.

Problem Description

Write an application that displays the following patterns separately, one below the other. All asterisks should be printed by a single statement of the form

```
System.out.print( "*" );
```

which causes the asterisks to print side by side. A statement of the form

```
System.out.println();
```

can be used to position to the next line. A statement of the form

```
System.out.println( " " );
```

can be used to display a space for the last two patterns. There should be no other output statements in the program.

Lab Exercises

Name:

Lab Exercise 1 — Triangles

Sample Output

```
*
**
***
****
*****
******
*******
********
*********
**********

**********
*********
********
*******
******
*****
****
***
**
*

**********
 *********
  ********
   *******
    ******
     *****
      ****
       ***
        **
         *

         *
        **
       ***
      ****
     *****
    ******
   *******
  ********
 *********
**********
```

Template

```java
1    // Lab 1: Triangles.java
2    // Program prints four triangles, one below the other
3    public class Triangles {
4
```

Fig. L 5.1   Triangles.java. (Part 1 of 2.)

Lab Exercises　　　　　　　　　　　　Name:

Lab Exercise 1 — Triangles

```
 5   public static void main ( String args[] )
 6   {
 7      int row;    // row counter
 8      int column; // column counter
 9      int space;  // space counter (needed only for the last two triangles
10
11      // first triangle
12      /* Write code to display the first triangle. Use nested for loops. The
13         outer loop should control which row of asterisks is being displayed.
14         The inner loop should display one asterisk at a time. */
15
16      // second triangle
17      /* Write code to display the second triangle. */
18
19      // third triangle
20      /* Write code to display the third triangle. The outer for loop should
21         contain two separate inner for loops--one to display spaces and one to
22         display asterisks. */
23
24      // Fifth triangle
25      /* Write code to display the Fifth triangle using techniques similar to
26         the third triangle. */
27   }
28
29   } // end class Triangles
```

Fig. L 5.1　　Triangles.java. (Part 2 of 2.)

Problem-Solving Tips

1. For the first triangle use a nested for statement. The inner loop for the first triangle should count from 1 to the current row number.

2. For the second triangle use a nested for statement in which the outer loop counts backward from 10 to 1. The inner loop should be identical to the one used for the first triangle.

3. The last two patterns require that each row begin with an appropriate number of blank spaces.

4. For the third and Fifth triangles use two separate inner loops—one for displaying spaces and one for displaying asterisks.

5. If you have any questions as you proceed, ask your lab instructor for assistance.

Lab Exercises   Name:

Lab Exercise 1 — Triangles

Follow-Up Question and Activity

1. Modify your program to display two triangles in the format shown below. Use techniques similar to the third and Fifth triangles in Lab Exercise 1.

```
********
 *******
  *****
   ***
    *
    *
   ***
  *****
 *******
********
```

Lab Exercises   Name:

Lab Exercise 2 — Pythagorean Triples

Name: _____   Date:_____

Section: _____

The following problem is intended to be solved in a closed-lab session with a teaching assistant or instructor present. The problem is divided into six parts:

1. Lab Objectives

2. Problem Description

3. Sample Output

4. Program Template (Fig. L 5.2)

5. Problem-Solving Tips

6. Follow-Up Questions and Activities

The program template represents a complete working Java program with one or more key lines of code replaced with comments. Read the problem description and examine the output, then study the template code. Using the problem-solving tips as a guide, replace the /* */ comments with Java code. Compile and execute the program. Compare your output with the sample output provided. Then answer the follow-up questions. The source code for the template is available at www.deitel.com and www.prenhall.com/deitel.

Lab Objectives

This lab was designed to reinforce programming concepts from Chapter 5 of *Java How To Program: Fifth Edition*. In this lab, you will practice:

 • Nesting for loops.

 • Using counter-controlled repetition.

 • Using "brute force" to solve a problem.

The follow-up questions and activities will also give you practice:

 • Using break statements.

 • Using continue statements.

 • Using counters to determine the number of iterations a loop performs.

Problem Description

A right triangle can have sides whose lengths are all integers. The set of three integer values that represent the sides of a right triangle is called a Pythagorean triple. These three sides must satisfy the relationship that the sum of the squares of the two sides is equal to the square of the hypotenuse. Find all integer Pythagorean triples for side1, side2 and hypotenuse values up to 500. Use a triple nested for loop that tries all possibilities. This program is an example of "brute force" computing. You will learn in more advanced computer science courses that there are many interesting problems for which there is no known algorithmic approach other than sheer brute force. [*Note:* The sample output shown here shows only 17 Pythagorean triples—there are many more.]

Lab Exercises   Name:

Lab Exercise 2 — Pythagorean Triples

Sample Output

```
s1: 3 s2: 4   h: 5
s1: 4 s2: 3   h: 5
s1: 5 s2: 12  h: 13
s1: 6 s2: 8   h: 10
s1: 7 s2: 24  h: 25
s1: 8 s2: 6   h: 10
s1: 8 s2: 15  h: 17
s1: 9 s2: 12  h: 15
s1: 9 s2: 40  h: 41
s1: 10 s2: 24  h: 26
s1: 11 s2: 60  h: 61
s1: 12 s2: 5   h: 13
s1: 12 s2: 9   h: 15
s1: 12 s2: 16  h: 20
s1: 12 s2: 35  h: 37
s1: 13 s2: 84  h: 85
s1: 14 s2: 48  h: 50
...
```

Template

```java
1   // Lab 2: Triples.java
2   // Program calculates Pythagorean triples
3   public class Triples {
4
5      public static void main( String args[] )
6      {
7         // declare the three sides of a triangle
8         int side1;
9         int side2;
10        int hypotenuse;
11
12        /* Write loop for side1 to try the values 1-500. */
13
14           /* Write loop for side2 to try the values 1-500. */
15
16              /* Write loop for hypotenuse to try the values 1-500 */
17
18                 /* Write an if statement that determines whether the sum of the
19                    two sides squared equals the hypotenuse squared. If this
20                    condition is true display side1, side2 and hypotenuse. */
21      }
22
23   } // end class Triples
```

Fig. L 5.2   Triples.java.

Problem-Solving Tips

1. This program does not require any input from the user.

2. The formula for the Pythagorean Theorem is $hypotenuse^2 = side1^2 + side2^2$.

Lab Exercises   Name:

Lab Exercise 2 — Pythagorean Triples

3. Do not be concerned about trying values that do not make sense, such as a 1-500-1 triangle. Remember that brute-force techniques try all possible values.

4. Use an `if` statement to determine whether the sum of the two squared sides is equal to the hypotenuse squared. If so, output `side1`, `side2` and `hypotenuse`.

5. If you have any questions as you proceed, ask your lab instructor for assistance.

Follow-Up Questions and Activities

1. How many times did this program execute the innermost `for` loop? Add another counter to the program that counts the number of times the inner loop iterates. Before exiting the program, display the counter value.

2. Add a `break` statement to the program inside the innermost `for` loop. This `break` statement should be called after the 20th Pythagorean triple is found. Explain what happens to the program after the 20th triple is found. Do all three `for` loops exit, or just the innermost one? What happens differently when the `break` statement is placed inside the second loop? What happens differently when the `break` statement is placed inside the outermost loop? [Hint: Use the loop counter you defined in the previous follow-up question to count how many times the loops are executed.]

3. Add a `continue` statement to the program that prevents a Pythagorean triple from being found when `side1` is equal to 8. Using the loop counter again from Follow-Up Question 1, calculate how many times this new program executed the innermost `for` loop. Explain why the `continue` statement affected the output.

Lab Exercises   Name:

Lab Exercise 3 — Sales

Name: _____   Date:_____

Section: _____

The following problem is intended to be solved in a closed-lab session with a teaching assistant or instructor present. The problem is divided into six parts:

1. Lab Objectives

2. Problem Description

3. Sample Output

4. Program Template (Fig. L 5.3)

5. Problem-Solving Tips

6. Follow-Up Questions and Activities

The program template represents a complete working Java program with one or more key lines of code replaced with comments. Read the problem description and examine the output, then study the template code. Using the problem-solving tips as a guide, replace the /* */ comments with Java code. Compile and execute the program. Compare your output with the sample output provided. Then answer the follow-up questions. The source code for the template is available at www.deitel.com and www.prenhall.com/deitel.

Lab Objectives

This lab was designed to reinforce programming concepts from Chapter 5 of *Java How To Program: Fifth Edition*. In this lab, you will practice:

- Using switch statements.

- Controlling user input.

The follow-up questions and activities also will give you practice:

- Validating the input from the user.

- Extending an existing program.

Problem Description

A mail-order house sells five different products, whose retail prices are as follows: product 1, $2.98; product 2, $4.50; product 3, $9.98; product 4, $4.49; product 5, $6.87. Write an application that reads a series of pairs of numbers as follows:

1. product number;

2. quantity sold for one day.

Your program should use a switch statement to help determine the retail price for each product. It should calculate and display the total retail value of all products sold last week. Use a JOptionPane to obtain the product number from the user. Use a sentinel-controlled loop to determine when the program should stop looping and display the final results in a JTextArea.

Lab Exercises   Name:

Lab Exercise 3 — Sales

Sample Output

Template

```
1    // Lab 3: Sales.java
2    // Program calculates sales, based on an input of product
3    // number and quantity sold
4    import java.awt.*;
5    import java.text.NumberFormat;
6    import java.util.Locale;
7    import javax.swing.*;
8
9    public class Sales {
10
11      public static void main( String args[] )
12      {
13        double product1 = 0, product2 = 0, product3 = 0, product4 = 0, product5 = 0;
14        String inputString;
15        int productId = 1;
16
17        /* Ask the user to enter product number */
18
19        /* Create while statement that loops until sentinel is entered */ {
20
21          /* Determine whether user's product number is in 1-5 */ {
22
23            /* If so, ask user to input the quantity sold */
24
25            /* Write a switch structure here that will compute the total
26               for that product */
27          }
28          else {
29            /* Display error message for invalid product number */
30          }
31
32          /* Ask the user to enter product number */
33
34        } // end while
35
36        // create decimal format to format floating point numbers
37        // with two digits to the right of the decimal point
38        NumberFormat moneyFormat = NumberFormat.getCurrencyInstance( Locale.US );
39
40        // create a summary message
41        String output = "Product 1: " + money.format( product1 );
```

Fig. L 5.3   Sales.java. (Part 1 of 2.)

Lab Exercises

Name:

Lab Exercise 3 — Sales

```
42        /* write code here for the rest of the summary message it should contain
43           the totals for the rest of the products, each on it's own line */
44
45        JTextArea outputArea = new JTextArea( 6, 20 );
46        outputarea.setText( output );
47
48        // show results
49        JOptionPane.showMessageDialog( null, outputArea, "Totals",
50           JOptionPane.INFORMATION_MESSAGE );
51
52        System.exit( 0 );
53     }
54
55  } // end class Sales
```

Fig. L 5.3   `Sales.java`. (Part 2 of 2.)

Problem-Solving Tips

1. Before your `while` loop, request a product number from the user.

2. Use a sentinel value to control the loop. This loop should terminate when the product number entered is zero.

3. If the user provides a valid product number, inside the loop, request a quantity for that product. Then, perform the appropriate calculation in the `switch` statement.

4. Your `switch` statement should consist of five cases, each setting the correct dollar value, depending on the quantity that the user entered.

5. At the end of the loop's body, request the next product number from the user.

6. Be sure to follow the spacing and indentation conventions mentioned in the text. Before and after each control statement, place a line of vertical space to make the control statement stand out.

7. If you have any questions as you proceed, ask your lab instructor for assistance.

Follow-Up Questions and Activities

1. What happens when the user inputs a number that is other than 1 through 5 or 0? Why? What is the output when the user enters a number like 7? What is the output when a letter is entered?

2. Modify the program so that there is a sixth product, priced at $20.00, that represents a package of all the products. For each of the packages purchased, add $4.00 to the totals for all the other products. Do not keep track of the package separately.

Lab Exercises   Name:

Lab Exercise 3 — Sales

Lab Exercises   Name:

Debugging

Name: _____   Date:_____

Section: _____

The program in this section does not run properly. Fix all the syntax errors, so that the program will compile successfully. Once the program compiles, compare the output to the sample output, and eliminate any logic errors that exist. The sample output demonstrates what the program's output should be once the program's code is corrected. The file is available at www.deitel.com and at www.prenhall.com/deitel.

Sample Output

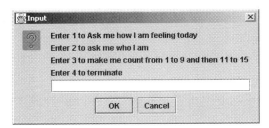

Broken Code

```
1    // Debugging problem Chapter 5: CompTalk.java
2    // Application that prompts the user to ask a question then
3    // the application answers accordingly.
4    import javax.swing.*;
5
6    public class CompTalk {
7
8       public static void main( String args[] )
9
10          do {
11
12             // read in the input from the user
13             String input = JOptionPane.showInputDialog(
14                "Enter 1 to Ask me how I am feeling today \n" +
15                "Enter 2 to ask me who I am \n" +
16                "Enter 3 to make me count from 1 to 9 and then 11 to 15 \n" +
17                "Enter 4 to terminate" );
18
19             // convert input string to an int
20             int inputNum = Integer.parseInt( input );
21
22             // determine output to display
23             switch ( input ) {
24
25                case 1:
26
27                   // generate a random number between 1 - 4
28                   int random = 1 + ( int ) ( Math.random() * 4 )
```

Fig. L 5.4   CompTalk.java. (Part 1 of 3.)

Lab Exercises   Name:

Debugging

```
29
30              switch ( random == 0 )
31
32                  case 1:
33                      JOptionPane.showMessageDialog( null,
34                          "I feel fine ", "Answer Box",
35                          JOptionPane.INFORMATION_MESSAGE );
36                      break;
37
38                  case 2:
39                      JOptionPane.showMessageDialog( null,
40                          "I've been better ", "Answer Box",
41                          JOptionPane.INFORMATION_MESSAGE );
42                      break;
43
44                  case 3:
45                      JOptionPane.showMessageDialog( null,
46                          "I feel horrible ", "Answer Box",
47                          JOptionPane.INFORMATION_MESSAGE );
48                      break;
49
50                  case 4:
51                      JOptionPane.showMessageDialog( null,
52                          "I feel terrific ", "Answer Box",
53                          JOptionPane.INFORMATION_MESSAGE );
54
55              } // end switch statement
56
57          case 2:
58              JOptionPane.showMessageDialog( null,
59                  "I am Sam, the computer man", "Answer Box",
60                  JOptionPane.INFORMATION_MESSAGE );
61              break;
62
63          case 3:
64              String num;
65              for ( i = 1, i >= 15, i++ ); {
66
67                  // will skip printing 10
68                  if ( 10 )
69                      continue;
70                  num = Integer.toString(i);
71                  JOptionPane.showMessageDialog( null, num, "Answer Box",
72                      JOptionPane.INFORMATION_MESSAGE );
73              }
74              break;
75
76          case 4:
77              break;
78
79          default:
80              String error = "" + input + " is not a valid entry";
81              JOptionPane.showMessageDialog( null, error, "Error in input data",
82                  JOptionPane.INFORMATION_MESSAGE );
83
84      } // end switch statement
```

Fig. L 5.4   CompTalk.java. (Part 2 of 3.)

Lab Exercises   Name:

Debugging

```
85
86        while ( inputNum != );
87
88        System.exit( 0 );
89
90     } // end main
91
92   } // end class CompTalk
```

Fig. L 5.4   CompTalk.java. (Part 3 of 3.)

Lab Exercises   Name:

Debugging

Postlab Activities

Coding Exercises

Name: _____   Date:_____

Section: _____

These coding exercises reinforce the lessons learned in the lab and provide additional programming experience outside the classroom and laboratory environment. They serve as a review after you have successfully completed the *Prelab Activities* and *Lab Exercises.*

For each of the following problems, write a program or a program segment that performs the specified action.

1. Write a `for` loop that prints all the odd integers from 1 to 100, inclusive.

2. Write a `do...while` loop that counts down from 10 to 0, inclusive.

3. Write a `for` loop that counts from 1 to 5. Use a `switch` statement to display a letter in the alphabet that corresponds to the number (i.e., 1 is A, 2 is B, etc.).

Postlab Activities   Name:

Coding Exercises

4. Write a `while` loop that sums all the integers from 1 to 10, inclusive, except for 3 and 6. Print the sum.

5. Write a `for` loop that attempts to display the numbers from 1 to 10, but terminates prematurely when the control variable reaches a value of 6.

6. Modify your solution to Coding Exercise 5 to use a `continue` statement, such that every value except 6 is displayed.

7. Modify your solution in Coding Exercise 6 to use a `while` statement instead of a `for` statement.

8. Modify your solution in Coding Exercise 7 to use a `do…while` statement instead of a `while` statement.

Postlab Activities   Name:

Programming Challenges

Name: _____   Date:_____

Section: _____

The *Programming Challenges* are more involved than the *Coding Exercises* and could require a significant amount of time to complete. Write a Java program for each of the problems in this section. The answers to these problems are available at www.deitel.com, www.prenhall.com/deitel and on the *Java Multimedia Cyber Classroom: Fifth Edition*. Pseudocode, hints or sample output are provided to aid you in your programming.

1. Factorials are used frequently in probability problems. The factorial of a positive integer *n* (written *n!* and pronounced "*n* factorial") is equal to the product of the positive integers from 1 to *n*. Write an application that evaluates the factorials of the integers from 1 to 5. Display the results in tabular format in a JTextArea that is displayed on a message dialog. What difficulty might prevent you from calculating the factorial of 20?

Hints:

- Use nested for loops in this exercise.
- The inner for loop will compute the factorial.
- Your output should appear as follows:

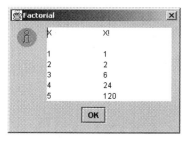

Postlab Activities   Name:

Programming Challenges

2. (*"The Twelve Days of Christmas" Song*) Write an application that uses repetition and `switch` statements to print the song "The Twelve Days of Christmas." One `switch` statement should be used to print the day (i.e., "First," "Second," etc.). A separate `switch` statement should be used to print the remainder of each verse. Visit the Web site `www.12days.com/library/carols/12daysofxmas.htm` for the complete lyrics to the song.

Hints:

- For this example you will need two `switch` statements.
- Both `switch` statements should appear inside a `for` loop that will iterate through the twelve days.
- You will have one string to which more text is added during every iteration of the loop. The string will be displayed after the loop terminates.
- Your output should appear as follows:

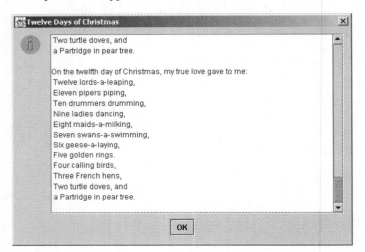

6

Methods

Objectives

- To understand how to construct programs modularly from small pieces called methods.
- To introduce the common Math methods available in the Java API.
- To be able to create new methods.
- To understand the mechanisms for passing information between methods.
- To introduce simulation techniques that use random number generation.
- To understand how the visibility of identifiers is limited to specific regions of programs.
- To understand how to write and use methods that call themselves.

Assignment Checklist

Name: _____   Date: _____

Section: _____

Exercises	Assigned: Circle assignments		Date Due
Prelab Activities			
Matching	YES	NO	
Fill in the Blank	YES	NO	
Short Answer	YES	NO	
Programming Output	YES	NO	
Correct the Code	YES	NO	
Lab Exercises			
Exercise 1 — Minimum	YES	NO	
Follow-Up Question and Activity	1		
Exercise 2 — Garage	YES	NO	
Follow-Up Question and Activity	1		
Exercise 3 — Towers of Hanoi	YES	NO	
Follow-Up Questions and Activities	1, 2		
Debugging	YES	NO	
Postlab Activities			
Coding Exercises	1, 2, 3, 4, 5, 6		
Programming Challenges	1, 2		

Prelab Activities

Matching

Name: _____   Date:_____

Section: _____

After reading Chapter 6 of *Java How to Program: Fifth Edition*, answer the given questions. These questions are intended to test and reinforce your understanding of key Java concepts. You may answer these questions either before or during the lab.

For each term in the left column, write the letter for the description that best matches the term from the right column.

Term	Description
___ 1. `final`	a) Scope that starts from the point of declaration of a variable and continues to the end of the block.
___ 2. entire scope of class's body	b) Type of result returned from the method to the caller.
___ 3. local variable's scope	c) Displays a `String` in the applet container's status bar.
___ 4. `Math`	d) Explicitly uses repetition statement.
___ 5. return-value-type	e) Keyword that appears in constant declarations.
___ 6. `showStatus`	f) Contains methods `init`, `start`, `paint`, `stop` and `destroy`.
___ 7. recursion	g) Scope of a class's fields and methods.
___ 8. iteration	h) Achieves repetition through repeated method calls.
___ 9. `JApplet`	i) Contains methods that perform certain common mathematical calculations.
___ 10. arguments	j) Method called for an applet when the user browses to another Web page.
___ 11. parameters	k) Called automatically every time the applet needs to be repainted.
___ 12. overloaded methods	l) Called before an applet is removed from memory.
___ 13. `init` method	m) Typical actions performed here include starting an animation and starting other threads of execution.
___ 14. `start` method	n) Provide the means for communicating information between methods via method calls.
___ 15. `paint` method	o) A method of the same name must have different set of parameters.
___ 16. `stop` method	p) Match in number, type and order with the parameters in method declaration.
___ 17. `destroy` method	q) Performs initialization of an applet.

Prelab Activities

Name: _____

Fill in the Blank

Name: _____   Date:_____

Section: _____

Fill in the blanks for each of the following statements:

18. A(n) _____ GUI component can be used to obtain text input from the user.

19. A(n) _____ contains a string of characters to be displayed on the screen. Normally, it indicates the purpose of another GUI component on the screen.

20. A(n) _____ method is called by preceding the method name with its class name and a dot.

21. If a method does not return a value, the return value type is _____.

22. The arguments passed to a method should match in _____, _____ and _____ with the parameters in method declaration.

23. Method _____ generates a random double value from 0.0 up to, but not including, 1.0.

24. A(n) _____ specifies one or more behaviors that you must define in your class declaration.

25. The task of method _____ is to process a user's interaction with a GUI component that generates an action event. This method is called in response to the user interaction (the event).

26. When the user presses a(n) _____ in a GUI, the program normally responds by performing a task.

27. _____ variables are created when program control reaches their declaration; they exist while the block in which they are declared is active and they are destroyed when the block in which they are declared exits.

Prelab Activities

Name:_____

Short Answer

Name: _____   Date:_____

Section: _____

In the space provided, answer each of the given questions. Your answers should be as concise as possible; aim for two or three sentences.

28. Define the term "method."

29. What are the three ways to call a method?

30. Explain recursion. What are the main advantages of recursion?

31. What is iteration, and how does it terminate?

Prelab Activities

Short Answer

32. What are overloaded methods? Are methods with the same name that only differ in return type valid overloaded methods?

33. Why do identifiers have scope?

Prelab Activities   Name:

Programming Output

Name: _____   Date:_____

Section: _____

For each of the given program segments, read the code, and write the output in the space provided below each program. [*Note*: Do not execute these programs on a computer.]

34. What is the output of the following code segment?

```
1   int a = 5;
2   int b = -6;
3   System.out.println( Math.max( ( Math.abs( b ) ), a ) );
```

Your answer:

35. What is output by the following code segment?

```
1   int a = -6;
2
3   System.out.println( Math.sqrt( Math.pow( Math.abs( a ), 2 ) ) );
4
5   int a = 6;
6
7   System.out.println( Math.sqrt( Math.pow( Math.abs( a ), 2 ) ) );
```

Your answer:

Use the following method declaration to answer Questions 36 and 37:.

```
1   public int method1( int x )
2   {
3       if ( x <= 10 )
4           x += 10;
5       else
6           x -= 10;
7
8       return x;
9   }
```

Prelab Activities   Name:

Programming Output

36. What is output by the following code segment?

```
1   int a = 6;
2
3   System.out.println( method1( a ) );
4
5   a = 15;
6
7   System.out.println( method1( a ) );
8
9   a = 10;
10
11  System.out.println( method1( a ) );
12
13  a = -10;
14
15  System.out.println( method1( a ) );
```

Your answer:

37. What is output by the following code segment?

```
1   int a = 15;
2   int b = 5;
3
4   System.out.println( method1( method1( a ) ) + method1( b ) );
5
6   a = 0;
7   b = 0;
8
9   System.out.println( method1( method1( a ) ) + method1( b ) );
10
11  a = 5;
12  b = 15;
13
14  System.out.println( method1( method1( a ) ) + method1( b ) );
15
16  a = -10;
17  b = 10;
18
19  System.out.println( method1( method1( a ) ) + method1( b ) );
```

Prelab Activities   Name:

Programming Output

Your answer:

Given the following class declaration, answer Questions 38 and 39.

```
1   import javax.swing.*;
2   import java.awt.Graphics;
3
4   public class Greeting extends JApplet {
5
6       int inputNumber; // number input by user
7       String greeting; // greeting displayed to user
8
9       // initialize applet
10      public void init ()
11      {
12          // obtain user input
13          String input = JOptionPane.showInputDialog(
14             "Enter 1 for an English greeting\nEnter 2 for a Spanish greeting\n"
15             );
16
17          // convert user input to integer
18          inputNumber = Integer.parseInt( input );
19
20          // call method greet to determine appropriate greeting
21          greet( inputNumber );
22
23      }
24
25      // display output
26      public void paint ( Graphics g )
27      {
28          // call base paint method
29          super.paint( g );
30
31          // display greeting in applet
32          g.drawString( greeting, 25, 25 );
33
34      }
35
36      // the greet method
37      public void greet ( int x )
38      {
39          if ( x == 1 )
40             greeting = "Hello."; // English greeting
```

Fig. L 6.1   Greeting.java. (Part 1 of 2.)

Prelab Activities

Programming Output

```
41          else if ( x == 2 )
42              greeting = "Hola."; // spanish greeting
43          else
44              greeting = "Invalid input";
45
46      }
47  }
```

Fig. L 6.1   Greeting.java. (Part 2 of 2.)

38. What is displayed on the applet when the user enters 1 and what is displayed when the user enters 2?

39. What is displayed on the applet when the user enters 3?

Your answer:

Prelab Activities

Name:

Correct the Code

Name: _____   Date:_____

Section: _____

Determine if there is an error in each of the following program segments. If there is an error, specify whether it is a logic error or a compilation error, circle the error in the program and write the corrected code in the space provided after each problem. If the code does not contain an error, write "no error." [*Note*: There may be more than one error in each program segment.]

40. The following code segment defines method `maximum`, which returns the largest of three integers.

```
1   public int maximum( int x, int y, int z )
2   {
3      int max = x;
4
5      if ( y > max )
6         y = max;
7
8      if ( z > max )
9         z = max;
10
11     return max;
12  }
```

Your answer:

41. The following segment of code should print five random integers in the range from 1 to 6.

```
1   for ( int i = 1; i <= 5; i++ )
2      System.out.println( ( random() * 6 ) );
```

Your answer:

Correct the Code

42. The following Java applet should display a product of two integer inputs by the user:

```
1   import javax.swing.*;
2   import java.awt.Graphics;
3
4   public class PrintNumber extends JApplet {
5      String input;
6      int value;
7      int value2;
8
9      public void init()
10     {
11        input = JOptionPane.showInputDialog( "Enter a first integer: " );
12        input = JOptionPane.showInputDialog( "Enter a second integer: " );
13
14     } // end method init
15
16     public void paint ( Graphics g )
17     {
18        super.paint( g ); // calls the orginal paint
19        g.drawString( AddString(), 50, 50 ); // output the string to the applet
20
21     } // end method paint
22
23     public String AddString()
24     {
25        int product = value * value2;
26        return "The product of the two integers is " + product;
27
28     } // end method AddString
29
30  } // end class PrintNumber
```

Your answer:

Prelab Activities   Name:

Correct the Code

43. The following Java applet should display a String input by the user:

```
1   import java.awt.Graphics;
2   import javax.swing.*;
3
4   public class PrintString extends JApplet {
5      int input; // string to be displayed
6
7      public void init()
8      {
9         input = JOptionPane.showInputDialog( "Enter a string: " );
10
11     } // end method init
12
13     public void paint ( Graphics g )
14     {
15        super.paint( g ); // calls the orginal paint
16        g.drawString( "hello", 50, 50 ); // output the string to the applet
17
18     } // end method paint
19
20  } // end class PrintString
```

Your answer:

Lab Exercises

Lab Exercise 1 — Minimum

Name: _____   Date:_____

Section: _____

This problem is intended to be solved in a closed-lab session with a teaching assistant or instructor present. The problem is divided into six parts:

1. Lab Objectives
2. Description of the Problem
3. Sample Output
4. Program Template (Fig. L 6.2)
5. Problem-Solving Tips
6. Follow-Up Question and Activity

The program template represents a complete working Java program, with one or more key lines of code replaced with comments. Read the problem description and examine the sample output; then study the template code. Using the problem-solving tips as a guide, replace the /* */ comments with Java code. Compile and execute the program. Compare your output with the sample output provided. Then answer the follow-up question. The source code for the template is available at www.deitel.com and www.prenhall.com/deitel.

Lab Objectives

This lab was designed to reinforce programming concepts from Chapter 6 of *Java How to Program: Fifth Edition*. In this lab, you will practice:

- Using Java applets to display information.
- Declaring and using methods.
- Using Math class methods.

The follow-up question and activity also will give you practice:

- Modifying methods to perform different actions.

Description of the Problem

Write a method minimum3 that returns the smallest of three floating-point numbers. Use the Math.min method to implement minimum3. Incorporate the method into an applet that reads three double values from the user and determines the smallest value. Display the result in the status bar.

Sample Output

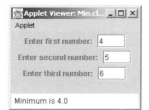

Lab Exercises

Name:

Lab Exercise 1 — Minimum

Program Template

```
1   // Lab 1: Min.java
2   // Program finds the minimum of 3 numbers
3   import java.awt.*;
4   import java.awt.event.*;
5   import javax.swing.*;
6
7   public class Min extends JApplet implements ActionListener {
8      JTextField input1, input2, input3;
9      JLabel label1, label2, label3;
10
11     public void init()
12     {
13        // create a label and textfield for each number
14        label1 = new JLabel( "Enter first number: " );
15        label2 = new JLabel( "Enter second number: " );
16        label3 = new JLabel( "Enter third number: " );
17        /* Write code that creates three JTextFields for user input */
18
19        // only the final textfield has a listener
20        /* Write code that registers a listener for the third JTextField */
21
22        // add components to container
23        Container container = getContentPane();
24        container.setLayout( new FlowLayout() );
25        /* Write code that adds the JLabels and JTextFields to the content pane */
26     }
27
28     // retrieve three values when user presses Enter
29     public void actionPerformed( ActionEvent event )
30     {
31        double number1 = Double.parseDouble( /* Write code to get text
32           from the first JTextField */ );
33
34        /* Write code to get the remainder of the inputs and
35           convert them to double values */
36
37        // display result
38        /* Write code to display the minimum of the three floating-point
39           numbers in the status bar */
40     }
41
42     // determine the smallest of three numbers
43     /* write the header for the minimum3 method */
44     {
45        // determine the minimum value
46        return /* Write code to compute the minimum of the three numbers
47                  using nest calls to Math.min */
48     }
49
50  } // end class Min
```

Fig. L 6.2   Min.java.

Lab Exercises   Name:

Lab Exercise 1 — Minimum

```
1    <HMTL>
2    <APPLET CODE = "Min.class" WIDTH = 200 HEIGHT = 100>
3    </APPLET>
4    </HTML>
```

Fig. L 6.3   Min.html.

Problem-Solving Tips

1. Create three JTextFields, and assign them to the three variables declared on line 8.

2. Be sure to attach these JTextFields to the content pane of the applet and register the event listener for the third JTextField by calling its addActionListener method.

3. To display the message in the status bar, use method showStatus.

4. Method minimum3 should receive three arguments of type double.

5. Be sure to follow the spacing and indentation conventions mentioned in the text.

6. If you have any questions as you proceed, ask your lab instructor for assistance.

Follow-Up Question and Activity

1. Modify the program in Lab Exercise 1 to compute the maximum of three double values.

Lab Exercises   Name:

Lab Exercise 2 — Garage

Name: _____   Date:_____

Section: _____

This problem is intended to be solved in a closed-lab session with a teaching assistant or instructor present. The problem is divided into six parts:

1. Lab Objectives
2. Description of the Problem
3. Sample Output
4. Program Template (Fig. L 6.4)
5. Problem-Solving Tips
6. Follow-Up Question and Activity

The program template represents a complete working Java program with one or more key lines of code replaced with comments. Read the problem description and examine the sample output; then study the template code. Using the problem-solving tips as a guide, replace the /* */ comments with Java code. Compile and execute the program. Compare your output with the sample output provided. Then answer the follow-up question. The source code for the template is available at www.deitel.com and www.prenhall.com/deitel.

Lab Objectives

This lab was designed to reinforce programming concepts from Chapter 6 of *Java How to Program: Fifth Edition*. In this lab, you will practice:

*   Using Java Applets to display information.
*   Creating and using methods.
*   Using Math class methods.

The follow-up question and activity also will give you practice:

*   Modifying methods of a class to perform a different task.

Description of the Problem

A parking garage charges a $2.00 minimum fee to park for up to three hours. The garage charges an additional $0.50 per hour for each hour or part thereof in excess of three hours. The maximum charge for any 24-hour period is $10.00. Assume that no car parks for longer than 24 hours at a time. Write an applet that calculates and displays the parking charges for each customer who parked a car in this garage yesterday. You should enter in a JTextField the hours parked for each customer. The program should display the charge for the current customer and should calculate and display the running total of yesterday's receipts in the status bar. The program should use the method calculateCharges to determine the charge for each customer. Test your program for various values, including 0.00, 0.50, 3.0, 10.5, 23.0 and 24.0.

Lab Exercises   Name:

Lab Exercise 2 — Garage

Sample Output

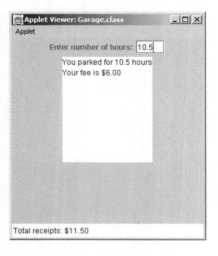

Program Template

```
1    // Lab 2: Garage.java
2    // Program calculates charges for parking
3    import java.awt.event.*;
4    import java.awt.*;
5    import javax.swing.*;
6
7    public class Garage extends JApplet implements ActionListener {
8        JTextField hoursInput;
9        JLabel hoursPrompt;
10       JTextArea currentFee;
11       double totalReceipts, fee;
12
13       public void init()
14       {
15           // create a label and a text field
16           hoursPrompt = new JLabel( "Enter number of hours:" );
17           hoursInput = new JTextField( 4 );
18           hoursInput.addActionListener( this );
19           currentFee = new JTextArea( 10 , 10 );
20           currentFee.setEditable( false );
21
22           // add to applet
23           Container container = getContentPane();
24           container.setLayout( new FlowLayout() );
25           /* add all the components of the applet to the content pane */
26       }
27
28       // adds newest fee to total charges
29       public void actionPerformed( ActionEvent event )
30       {
31           double hours = Double.parseDouble( event.getActionCommand() );
32
```

Fig. L 6.4　Garage.java. (Part 1 of 2.)

Lab Exercises   Name:

Lab Exercise 2 — Garage

```
33        /* Write code here to calculate the fee and assign it to the variable fee */
34
35        /* Write code here to calculate the total receipts */
36
37        showStatus( "Total receipts: " + totalReceipts );
38        currentFee.setText( output );
39     }
40
41     // determines fee based on time
42     /* Write the header for the calculateCharges method */
43     {
44        // apply minimum charge
45        /* Write a line of code that declares and initializes a variable
46           with the minimum charge of $2 */
47
48        // add extra fees as applicable
49        /* Write an if structure that determines whether hours is greater
50           than 3.0 and, if so, calculates the additional charge.  */
51
52        // apply maximum value if needed
53        /* Write code here that will see if the 10 hour maximum has been reached
54           and if so set the maximum charge */
55
56        /* Write a line of code that returns the calculated charge */
57     }
58
59  } // end class Garage
```

Fig. L 6.4   Garage.java. (Part 2 of 2.)

```
1   <HTML>
2   <APPLET CODE = "Garage.class" WIDTH = 300 HEIGHT = 300>
3   </APPLET>
4   </HTML>
```

Fig. L 6.5   Garage.html.

Problem-Solving Tips

1. Use the Container class's add method to add the three components to the applet's content pane.

2. The calculateCharges method should take one argument and return a double.

3. To calculate the fee, call method calculateCharges and pass it the number of hours input by the user. Assign the returned value to variable fee.

4. Be sure to follow the spacing and indentation conventions mentioned in the text.

5. If you have any questions as you proceed, ask your lab instructor for assistance.

Lab Exercises   Name:

Lab Exercise 2 — Garage

Follow-Up Question and Activity

1. Modify the previous program so that the maximum charge is applied only when the car is parked more than 10 hours and less than 24. If the hours exceed 24, then for every 24-hour period, the customer should get charged $10.00 and for every partial 24-hour period the customer should be charged $0.50 per hour up to a maximum of $10.00 per day. The minimum fee does not have to be charged after the first 24-hour period. For example, if a customer parks for 100 hours, or four 24-hour periods and four hours extra, then the total charge should be $42.00.

Lab Exercises   Name:

Lab Exercise 3 — Towers Of Hanoi

Name: _____   Date:_____

Section: _____

This problem is intended to be solved in a closed-lab session with a teaching assistant or instructor present. The problem is divided into six parts:

1. Lab Objectives
2. Description of the Problem
3. Sample Output
4. Program Template (Fig. L 6.6)
5. Problem-Solving Tips
6. Follow-Up Questions and Activities

The program template represents a complete working Java program, with one or more key lines of code replaced with comments. Read the problem description and examine the sample output; then study the template code. Using the problem-solving tips as a guide, replace the /* */ comments with Java code. Compile and execute the program. Compare your output with the sample output provided. Then answer the follow-up questions. The source code for the template is available at www.deitel.com and www.prenhall.com/deitel.

Lab Objectives

This lab was designed to reinforce programming concepts from Chapter 6 of *Java How to Program: Fifth Edition*. In this lab, you will practice:

- Using Java applets to display information.
- Creating and using methods.
- Using recursion.

The follow-up questions and activities will also give you practice:

- Recognizing invalid user input.
- Setting default values if user input is invalid.

Description of the Problem

Write an applet to solve the Towers of Hanoi problem, discussed in Exercise 6.37 of *Java How to Program: Fifth Edition*. Allow the user to enter the number of disks in a JTextField. Write a recursive tower method with the following four parameters:

1. the number of disks to be moved,
2. the peg on which these disks are initially threaded,
3. the peg to which this stack of disks is to be moved, and
4. the peg to be used as a temporary holding area.

Your program should display (in a scrollable JTextArea) the precise instructions it will take to move the disks from the starting peg to the destination peg.

Lab Exercises   Name:

Lab Exercise 3 — Towers Of Hanoi

Sample Output

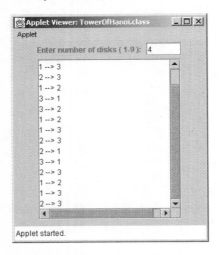

Program Template

```
1    // Lab 3: TowerOfHanoi.java
2    // Program solves the Towers of Hanoi problem
3    import java.awt.*;
4    import java.awt.event.*;
5    import javax.swing.*;
6
7    public class TowerOfHanoi extends JApplet implements ActionListener {
8       JLabel label;
9       JTextField input;
10      JTextArea outputArea;
11      String output;
12
13      public void init()
14      {
15         output = "";
16
17         // create components
18         label = new JLabel( "Enter number of disks ( 1-9 ): " );
19         input = new JTextField( 5 );
20         input.addActionListener( this );
21         outputArea = new JTextArea( 15, 20 );
22         /* Write code that creates a JScrollPane and attach outputArea to it */
23         outputArea.setText( output );
24
25         // add components to applet
26         Container container = getContentPane();
27         container.setLayout( new FlowLayout() );
28         /* Write code to add the components to the content pane */
29      }
30
```

Fig. L 6.6   TowerOfHanoi.java. (Part 1 of 2.)

Lab Exercises   Name:

Lab Exercise 3 — Towers Of Hanoi

```
31     // recusively move disks through towers
32     /* write header for method tower */
33     {
34         /* Write code here that tests for the base case (i.e., one disk).
35            In this case, move the last disk from peg 1 to peg 3 and return. */
36
37         // move ( disks - 1 ) disks from peg1 to peg2 recursively
38         /* Write a recursive call to method tower that moves
39            ( disks - 1 ) disks from peg1 to peg2 */
40
41         // move last disk from peg1 to peg3 recursively
42         output += "\n" + peg1 + " --> " + peg3;
43
44         // move ( disks - 1 ) disks from peg2 to peg3 recursively
45         /* Write a recursive call to method tower that moves
46            ( disks - 1 ) disks from peg2 to peg3 */
47     }
48
49     // actually sort the number of discs specified by user
50     public void actionPerformed( ActionEvent e )
51     {
52         output = "";
53
54         /* call method tower and pass it the number input by the user,
55            a starting peg of 1, an ending peg of 3 and a temporary peg of 2 */
56
57         outputArea.setText( output );
58     }
59
60 } // end class TowerOfHanoi
```

Fig. L 6.6   TowerOfHanoi.java. (Part 2 of 2.)

```
1   <HMTL>
2   <APPLET CODE = "TowerOfHanoi.class" WIDTH = 300 HEIGHT = 300>
3   </APPLET>
4   </HTML>
```

Fig. L 6.7   TowerOfHanoi.html.

Problem-Solving Tips

1. Create an instance of class JScrollPane and initialize it with the JTextArea in which the results will be displayed.

2. The call to method tower (line 54 of the template) should pass as the first argument the value input by the user (i.e., the number of disks) and as the other three arguments the starting peg (1), the ending peg (3) and the temporary peg (2).

3. Method tower's header (line 32) should have four int parameters.

4. At the beginning of method tower, use an if statement to determine whether the first parameter of method tower (the number of disks) is 1. If so, perform the last move and return from the method.

5. The recursive call to method tower on line 38 should pass a number of disks that is one fewer than the number received, and the correct beginning peg, ending peg and temporary peg. Carefully read the explanation of method tower in the exercise description. This is only one straightforward line of code. The code for the call on line 45 is almost identical.

Lab Exercises   Name:

Lab Exercise 3 — Towers Of Hanoi

6. Be sure to follow the spacing and indentation conventions mentioned in the text.

7. If you have any questions as you proceed, ask your lab instructor for assistance.

Follow-Up Questions and Activities

1. What happens in this program if the user enters large numbers? Explain.

2. Allow only towers of up to 9 disks. Add input validation code to the program in Lab Exercise 3. If the user enters a number greater than 9, set the number of disks to 9 and display a message in the status bar indicating, "Invalid input. Value set to 9 by default".

Lab Exercises

Name:

Debugging

Name: _____   Date:_____

Section: _____

The program in this section does not run properly. Fix all the syntax errors, so that the program will compile successfully. Once the program compiles, compare the output to the sample output, and eliminate any logic errors that exist. The sample output demonstrates what the program's output should be once the program's code is corrected. The file is available at www.deitel.com and at www.prenhall.com/deitel.

Sample Output

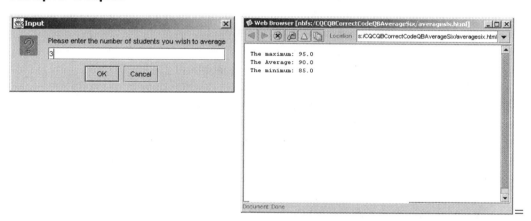

Broken Code

```
1   // Chapter 6 of Java How To Program
2   // Debugging Problem
3   import java.awt.Container;
4   import javax.swing.*;
5
6   public class AverageSix extends JApplet {
7
8      public void init()
9      {
10        String students = JOptionPane.showInputDialog(
11           "Please enter the number of students you wish to average" );
12
13        int students2 = Integer.parseInt( students );
14
15        int NumOfStudents = students2;
16        int counter = 1;
17        double total = 0, previousNumber = 0, newMaximum = 0, newMinimum = 0;
18
19        while ( students2 != 0 ) {
20           String si = JOptionPane.showInputDialog( "Please enter a grade" );
```

Fig. L 6.8   AverageSix.java. (Part 1 of 2.)

Lab Exercises   Name:

Debugging

```
21          double givenNum = Double.parseDouble( si );
22          total = total + givenNum;
23
24          if ( counter == 1 ) {
25              previousNumber = givenNum;
26              newMinimum = givenNum;
27          }
28
29          if ( newMaximum < givenNum )
30              newMaximum = maximum( previousNumber, givenNum );
31
32
33          if ( newMinimum > givenNum )
34              newMinimum = minimum( previousNumber, givenNum );
35
36          students2--;
37          counter++;
38          previousNumber = givenNum;
39      }
40
41      JTextArea output = new JTextArea();
42      double average1 = average( total, NumOfStudents );
43
44      output.setText( "The maximum: " + newMaximum +
45          "\nThe Average: " + average1 + " \nThe minimum: " + newMinimum);
46      Container container = getContentPane();
47      container.add( output );
48    }
49  }
50
51    public double average( double x, y );
52    {
53        return x / y;
54    }
55
56    public double maximum( double x, double y )
57    {
58        Math.max( x, y );
59    }
60
61    public double minimum( double x, float y )
62    {
63        return min( x, y );
64    }
65  }
```

Fig. L 6.8   AverageSix.java. (Part 2 of 2.)

```
1   <HMTL>
2   <APPLET CODE = "AverageSix.class" WIDTH = 300 HEIGHT = 300>
3   </APPLET>
4   </HTML>
```

Fig. L 6.9   averagesix.html.

Postlab Activities

Coding Exercises

Name: _____   Date:_____

Section: _____

These coding exercises reinforce the lessons learned in the lab and provide additional programming experience outside the classroom and laboratory environment. They serve as a review after you have successfully completed the *Prelab Activities* and *Lab Exercises*.

For each of the following problems, write a program or a program segment that performs the specified action:

1. Write a method that takes an integer as an argument and returns the remainder of that value divided by 7. Incorporate that method into an applet that tests the method.

2. Write a short Java application that uses random numbers to simulate 10 flips of a coin.

3. Write a method `divides` that takes two integers as its arguments and returns `true` if the first integer divides evenly into the second one (i.e., there is no remainder after division); otherwise, the method should return false.

Postlab Activities

Name:

Coding Exercises

4. Write a method `halve` that takes one floating-point value of type `double` value as its argument and returns the value of that number divided by 2. Incorporate this method into an applet that enables the user to enter values to test the method.

5. Write a method `diffDouble` that takes two floating-point values of type `double` as arguments and computes and returns the difference. Incorporate this method into a Java applet that enables the user to enter the two values.

6. Write a method `areaSquare` that computes and returns the area of a square. Incorporate this method into an applet that allows the user to enter the length of one side of the square.

Postlab Activities   Name:

Programming Challenges

Name: _____   Date:_____

Section: _____

The *Programming Challenges* are more involved than the *Coding Exercises* and may require a significant amount of time to complete. Write a Java program for each of the problems in this section. The answers to these problems are available at www.deitel.com, www.prenhall.com/deitel and on the *Java Multimedia Cyber Classroom: Fifth Edition*. Pseudocode, hints or sample output are provided to aid you in your programming.

1. Write method `distance`, to calculate the distance between two points (x1, y1) and (x2, y2). All numbers and return value should be of type `double`. Incorporate this method into an applet that enables the user to enter the coordinates of the points.

Hints:

- The distance between two points can be calculated by taking the square root of

$$(x2 - x1)^2 + (y2 - y1)^2$$

- Use `Math` class methods to compute the distance.

- The applet should be similar to the one in Coding Exercise 6.

- Your output should appear as follows:

Postlab Activities   Name:

Programming Challenges

2. Write an applet that computes the area of a circle using a method `circleArea`. The applet should contain a `JTextField` that enables the user to enter a radius of type `int`. The program should display the area in the status bar.

Hints:

- Use the constant `Math.PI` in the area calculation.

- This applet should be similar to the one in Coding Exercise 6.

- Your output should appear as follows:

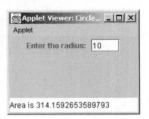

7

Arrays

Objectives

- To introduce the array data structure.
- To understand how to declare arrays, initialize arrays and refer to individual array elements.
- To be able to use arrays to store, sort, and search lists and tables of values.
- To become familiar with how to pass arrays to methods.
- To be able to declare, initialize and manipulate two-dimensional arrays.
- To understand basic searching techniques.

Assignment Checklist

Name: _____   Date:_____

Section: _____

Exercises	Assigned: Circle assignments		Date Due
Prelab Activities			
Matching	YES	NO	
Fill in the Blank	YES	NO	
Short Answer	YES	NO	
Programming Output	YES	NO	
Correct the Code	YES	NO	
Lab Exercises			
Exercise 1 —Bubble Sort	YES	NO	
Follow-Up Question and Activity	1		
Exercise 2 — Unique	YES	NO	
Follow-Up Questions and Activities	1, 2, 3		
Debugging	YES	NO	
Postlab Activities			
Coding Exercises	1, 2, 3, 4, 5, 6, 7		
Programming Challenges	1, 2		

Prelab Activities

Matching

Name: _____   Date:_____

Section: _____

After reading Chapter 7 of *Java How to Program: Fifth Edition*, answer the given questions. The questions are intended to test and reinforce your understanding of key concepts. You may answer the questions before or during the lab.

For each term in the left column, write the letter for the description from the right column that best matches the term.

Term	Description
____ 1. pass by value	a) Search method that compares every element of an array with a search key until a match is found or the end of the array is reached.
____ 2. a[i][j]	b) Declares an array.
____ 3. index	c) A group of variables that contain values of the same type.
____ 4. new int[12]	d) Search method that eliminates half the elements in the sorted array after each comparison.
____ 5. linear search	e) An indication that a program attempted to access an array element outside the bounds of an array.
____ 6. pass by reference	f) A copy of the argument's value is made and passed to the called method.
____ 7. array	g) Allocates an object dynamically.
____ 8. binary search	h) The caller gives the called method the ability to access the caller's data directly and to modify that data.
____ 9. int c[]	i) One element of an array with two dimensions.
____ 10. new	j) Used to refer to a particular location or element in an array.
____ 11. length	k) Create an array of integers.
____ 12. ArrayIndexOutOfBounds-Exception	l) A member of an array that is set to the number of elements in the array at the time the program creates the array object.

Prelab Activities   Name:

Fill in the Blank

Name: _____   Date:_____

Section: _____

Fill in the blanks for each of the following statements:

13. Every array has a(n) _____ member that specifies the number of elements in the array.

14. Arrays occupy space in memory and are _____ in Java.

15. To pass an array to a method, you must specify the _____ of the array.

16. A(n) array _____ may be an integer or an integer expression.

17. The index of the first element of an array is _____.

18. Referring to an element outside the array bounds is a form of a(n) _____ error.

19. In the binary search algorithm, first the _____ array element is located and compared to the search key.

20. The bubble sort technique for sorting arrays is also known as _____ sort.

21. The declaration `int c[ 12 ];` causes a(n) _____ error.

22. To pass one row of a two-dimensional array to a method that receives a one-dimensional array, you specify the _____ followed by only the _____.

Prelab Activities   Name: _____

Short Answer

Name: _____   Date:_____

Section: _____

Answer the following questions in the space provided. Your answers should be as concise as possible; aim for two or three sentences.

23. What is an off-by-one-error?

24. Describe how a binary search works. Why is it more efficient than a linear search?

25. Describe how a bubble sort works. Is this algorithm effective for sorting large arrays?

Prelab Activities

Name:

Short Answer

26. Describe how two-dimensional arrays represent a table of data.

27. Differentiate between pass-by-value and pass-by-reference.

Prelab Activities   Name:

Programming Output

Name: _____   Date:_____

Section: _____

For each of the given program segments, read the code, and write the output in the space provided below each program. [*Note*: Do not execute these programs on a computer.]

Unless specified otherwise, for the following questions assume that the code segments are contained within the `main` method of a Java application.

28. What is the output of the following code segment?

```
1   int array[] = { 8, 6, 9, 7, 6, 4, 4, 5, 8, 10 };
2   System.out.println( "Index    Value" );
3
4   for ( int i = 0; i < array.length; i++ )
5      System.out.println( i + "           " + array[ i ] );
```

Your answer:

29. What is the output of the following code segment?

```
1   char sentence[] = { 'H', 'o', 'w', ' ', 'a', 'r', 'e', ' ', 'y', 'o', 'u' };
2   String output = "The sentence is: ";
3
4   for ( int i = 0; i < sentence.length; i++ )
5      output += sentence[ i ];
6
7   System.out.println( output );
8
```

Your answer:

Prelab Activities

Name:

Programming Output

30. What is the output of the following code segment?

```
1   int array[] = { 1, 2, 3, 4, 5, 6, 7, 8, 9, 10 };
2
3   for ( int i = 0; i < array.length; i++ ) {
4
5      for ( int j = 0; j < array [ i ]; j++ )
6         System.out.print( "*" );
7
8      System.out.println();
9   }
```

Your answer:

31. Assume the method declaration shown in lines 1–5 appears in an applet class. What are the contents of the following array

```
int array[] = { 3, 2, 5 };
```

after the following method call:

```
method1( array );
```

```
1   public void method1( int x[] )
2   {
3      for ( int i = 0; i < 3; i++)
4         x[ i ] *= 2;
5   }
```

Your answer:

Prelab Activities

Name:

Programming Output

Given the following declaration of a method `search` and the following declaration of integer array `array1` answer questions 32–34. Assume that the method declaration, array and method calls appear in an applet. [Note that `search` requires a sorted array.]

```
1   public int search( int x[], int key, int low, int high )
2   {
3      int middle;
4
5      while ( low <= high ) {
6         middle = ( low + high ) / 2;
7
8         if ( key == x[ middle ] )
9            return middle;
10
11         else if ( key < x[ middle ] )
12            high = middle - 1;
13
14         else if ( key > x[ middle ] )
15            low = middle + 1;
16      }
17
18      return -1;
19   }
```

```
1   int array1[] = { 1, 2, 3, 4, 5, 6, 7, 8, 9, 10 };
```

32. What value is returned by the following call of method `search`?

```
1   search( array1, 10, 0, 9 )
```

Your answer:

33. What value is returned by the following call of method `search`?

```
1   search( array1, 11, 0, 9 )
```

Your answer:

Prelab Activities

Name:

Programming Output

34. What value is returned by the following call of method search?

```
1   search( array1, 11, 0, 10 )
```

Your answer:

Prelab Activities

Name:

Correct the Code

Name: _____   Date:_____

Section: _____

Determine if there is an error in each of the following program segments. If there is an error, specify whether it is a logic error or a compilation error, circle the error in the program and write the corrected code in the space provided after each problem. If the code does not contain an error, write "no error." [*Note:* There may be more than one error in each program segment.]

35. The following code segment should assign 8 to the element of `array` with index 105.

```
1   array( 105 ) = 8;
```

Your answer:

36. The `for` loop that follows should initialize all of `array`'s elements to -1.

```
1   int array[] = new int[ 10 ];
2
3   for ( int i = 0; i < 9; i++ )
4       array[ i ] = -1;
```

Your answer:

Prelab Activities

Name:

Correct the Code

37. Array a should contain all the integers from 0 to 10, inclusive.

```
1   int a[] = new int[ 10 ];
2
3   for( int i = 0; i < 10; i++ )
4       a[ i ] = i;
```

Your answer:

38. The following code segment should allocate two arrays containing five and six elements, respectively.

```
1   final int arraySize = 5;
2
3   int a[] = new int[ arraySize ];
4
5   arraySize = 6;
6
7   int b[] = new int[ arraySize ];
```

Your answer:

Prelab Activities   Name:

Correct the Code

39. The following code segment should initialize a two-dimensional array, then print its values.

```
1   int a[][] = new int[ 10 ][ 5 ];
2
3   for ( int i = 0; i < a.length; i++ )
4      for ( int j = 0; j < a[ i ].length; j++ )
5         a[ j ][ i ] = j;
6
7   for ( int i = 0; i < a.length; i++ ){
8
9      for ( int j = 0; j < a[ i ].length; j++ )
10        System.out.print( a[ j ][ i ] + " " );
11
12     System.out.println();
13  }
```

Your answer:

40. The following code segment should assign the value 10 to the array element that corresponds to the third row and the Fifth column.

```
1   int a[] = new int[ 10 ][ 5 ];
2
3   a[ 2 ][ 3 ] = 10;
```

Your answer:

Lab Exercises

Lab Exercise 1 — Bubble Sort

Name: _____   Date:_____

Section: _____

This problem is intended to be solved in a closed-lab session with a teaching assistant or instructor present. The problem is divided into six parts:

1. Lab Objectives

2. Description of Problem

3. Sample Output

4. Program Template (Fig. L 7.1)

5. Problem-Solving Tips

6. Follow-Up Question and Activity

The program template represents a complete working Java program, with one or more key lines of code replaced with comments. Read the problem description and examine the sample output; then study the template code. Using the problem-solving tips as a guide, replace the /* */ comments with Java code. Compile and execute the program. Compare your output with the sample output provided. Then answer the follow-up question. The source code for the template is available at www.deitel.com and www.prenhall.com/deitel.

Lab Objectives

This lab was designed to reinforce programming concepts from Chapter 7 of *Java How to Program: Fifth Edition*. In this lab, you will practice:

- Modifying the implementation of the bubble sort algorithm presented in the text.

The follow-up question and activity also will give you practice:

- Increasing the efficiency of the bubble sort algorithm.

Problem Description

The bubble sort presented in Fig. 7.11 is inefficient for large arrays. Make the following simple modifications to improve the performance of the bubble sort: After the first pass, the largest number is guaranteed to be in the highest-numbered element of the array; after the second pass, the two highest numbers are "in place"; and so on. Instead of making nine comparisons on every pass, modify the bubble sort to make eight comparisons on the second pass, seven on the third and so on.

Sample Output

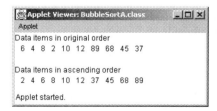

Lab Exercises   Name:

Lab Exercise 1 — Bubble Sort

Program Template

```
1    // Lab 1 Part A: BubbleSortA.java
2    // Applet sorts an array's values using an efficient bubble sort, so the number of
3    // comparisons will decrease by one after each pass.
4    import java.awt.*;
5    import javax.swing.*;
6
7    public class BubbleSortA extends JApplet {
8
9       // initialize applet
10      public void init()
11      {
12         JTextArea outputArea = new JTextArea();
13         Container container = getContentPane();
14         container.add( outputArea );
15
16         int array[] = { 6, 4, 8, 2, 10, 12, 89, 68, 45, 37 };
17
18         String output = "Data items in original order\n";
19
20         // append original array values to String output
21         for ( int counter = 0; counter < array.length; counter++ )
22            output += "   " + array[ counter ];
23
24         bubbleSort( array ); // sort array
25
26         output += "\n\nData items in ascending order\n";
27
28         // append sorted\ array values to String output
29         for ( int counter = v; counter < array.length; counter++ )
30            output += "   " + array[ counter ];
31
32         outputArea.setText( output );
33
34      } // end method init
35
36      // sort elements of array with bubble sort
37      public void bubbleSort( int array2[] )
38      {
39         // loop to control number of passes
40         for ( int pass = 1; pass < array2.length; pass++ ) {
41
42            /* Write a for loop header here to control the number of comparisons
43               on each pass */
44
45               // compare side-by-side elements and swap them if
46               // first element is greater than second element
47               if ( array2[ element ] > array2[ element + 1 ] )
48                  swap( array2, element, element + 1 );
49
50            } // end loop to control comparisons
51
52         } // end loop to control passes
53
54      } // end method bubbleSort
```

Fig. L 7.1   BubbleSortA.java. (Part 1 of 2.)

Lab Exercises   Name:

Lab Exercise 1 — Bubble Sort

```
55
56        // swap two elements of an array
57        public void swap( int array3[], int first, int second )
58        {
59            int hold;  // temporary holding area for swap
60
61            hold = array3[ first ];
62            array3[ first ] = array3[ second ];
63            array3[ second ] = hold;
64        }
65
66    } // end class BubbleSortA
```

Fig. L 7.1   BubbleSortA.java. (Part 2 of 2.)

Problem-Solving Tips

1. The number of comparisons performed per pass should decrease by one after each pass. The first pass will have nine comparisons, the second pass will have eight comparisons, etc. Use the counter variable **pass** in the condition of the bubble sort's nested **for** loop to perform a calculation that decreases the number of comparisons per pass.

2. If you have any questions as you proceed, ask your lab instructor for help.

Follow-Up Question and Activity

1. In Lab Exercise 1, the data in the array may already be in the proper order or near-proper order, so why make nine passes if fewer will suffice. Modify the sort to determine at the end of each pass whether any swaps have been made. If none have been made, the data must already be in the proper order, so the program should display the sorted array. If swaps have been made, at least one more pass is required to determine if any more swaps should be made. Modify the following template to test for swaps and terminate the sort when no swaps are made on a given pass.

```
1    // Lab 1 Part B: BubbleSortB.java
2    // Applet sorts an array's values using an efficient bubble sort, so the number of
3    // comparisons will decrease by one after each pass. The bubble sort will also end
4    // if there is nothing to sort in a pass.
5    import java.awt.*;
6    import javax.swing.*;
7
8    public class BubbleSortB extends JApplet {
9
10       // initialize applet
11       public void init()
12       {
13           JTextArea outputArea = new JTextArea();
14           Container container = getContentPane();
15           container.add( outputArea );
16
17           int array[] = { 2, 6, 4, 8, 10, 12, 89, 68, 45, 37 };
18
19           String output = "Data items in original order\n";
20
```

Fig. L 7.2   BubbleSortB.java. (Part 1 of 2.)

Lab Exercises   Name:

Lab Exercise 1 — Bubble Sort

```
21        // append original array values to String output
22        for ( int counter = 0; counter < array.length; counter++ )
23           output += "   " + array[ counter ];
24
25        bubbleSort( array );   // sort array
26
27        output += "\n\nData items in ascending order\n";
28
29        // append sorted\ array values to String output
30        for ( int counter = 0; counter < array.length; counter++ )
31           output += "   " + array[ counter ];
32
33        outputArea.setText( output );
34
35     } // end method init
36
37     // sort elements of array with bubble sort
38     public void bubbleSort( int array2[] )
39     {
40        // boolean indicating if a swap took place during pass
41        /* Declare a boolean variable here  */
42
43        // loop to control number of passes
44        for ( int pass = 1; pass < array2.length; pass++ ) {
45           /* Set the boolean variable to false */
46
47           /* Write a for loop here to control the number of comparisons */ {
48
49              // compare side-by-side elements and swap them if
50              // first element is greater than second element
51
52              /* Modify the body of this if statement to indicate
53                 that a swap occurred */
54              if ( array2[ element ] > array2[ element + 1 ] )
55                 swap( array2, element, element + 1 );
56
57           } // end loop to control comparisons
58
59           // if no swaps, terminate bubble sort
60           /* Write an if statement to terminate sorting of no swaps occurred */
61
62        } // end loop to control passes
63
64     } // end method bubbleSort
65
66     // swap two elements of an array
67     public void swap( int array3[], int first, int second )
68     {
69        // temporary holding area for swap
70        int hold;
71
72        hold = array3[ first ];
73        array3[ first ] = array3[ second ];
74        array3[ second ] = hold;
75     }
76
77  } // end class BubbleSortB
```

Fig. L 7.2   BubbleSortB.java. (Part 2 of 2.)

Lab Exercises   Name:

Lab Exercise 2 — Unique

Name: _____   Date:_____

Section: _____

This problem is intended to be solved in a closed-lab session with a teaching assistant or instructor present. The problem is divided into six parts:

1. Lab Objectives

2. Description of Problem

3. Sample Output

4. Program Template (Fig. L 7.3)

5. Problem-Solving Tips

6. Follow-Up Questions and Activities

The program template represents a complete working Java program, with one or more key lines of code replaced with comments. Read the problem description and examine the sample output; then study the template code. Using the problem-solving tips as a guide, replace the /* */ comments with Java code. Compile and execute the program. Compare your output with the sample output provided. Then answer the follow-up questions. The source code for the template is available at www.deitel.com and www.prenhall.com/deitel.

Lab Objectives

This lab was designed to reinforce programming concepts from Chapter 7 of *Java How to Program: Fifth Edition*. In this lab you will practice:

• Declaring and initializing arrays.

• Comparing input to array elements.

• Preventing array out-of-bounds errors.

The follow-up questions and activities will also give you practice:

• Initializing array sizes during program execution.

• Generalizing programs.

Problem Description

Use a one-dimensional array to solve the following problem. Write an applet that inputs five numbers, each of which is between 10 and 100, inclusive. As each number is read, display it only if it is not a duplicate of a number already read. Provide for the "worst case" in which all five numbers are different. Use the smallest possible array to solve this problem. The applet should use the GUI techniques introduced in Chapter 6. Display the results in a JTextArea. Use JTextArea method setText to update the output after each value is input by the user.

Lab Exercises   Name:

Lab Exercise 2 — Unique

Sample Output

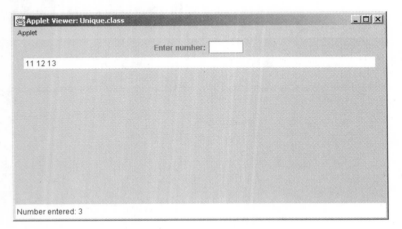

Program Template

```
1    // Lab 2: Unique.java
2    // Applet reads in 5 numbers and prints only the non-duplicates.
3    import java.awt.event.*;
4    import java.awt.*;
5    import javax.swing.*;
6
7    public class Unique extends JApplet implements ActionListener {
8        JTextField input;   // input JTextField
9        JTextArea output;   // output JTextArea
10       JLabel prompt;
11
12       int array[];          // array to store unique values
13       int counter = 0;      // number of unique values
14       int numberCount = 0;  // number of values entered
15
16       // initialze applet
17       /* Begin method init*/
18
19           /* Create an array of five elements*/
20
21           /* Create the GUI components and register an actionListener
22              for the JTextField */
23           /* Add all the components to the applet's content pane */
24
25       // end method init
26
27       // read number input and print if non-duplicate
28       public void actionPerformed( ActionEvent actionEvent )
29       {
30          /* Write code here to retrieve the input from the text field */
31          input.setText( " " ); // clear the input JTextField
32
33          // validate the input
34          /* Write an if statement that validates the input */
```

Fig. L 7.3   Unique.java. (Part 1 of 2.)

Chapter 7   Arrays   209

Lab Exercises   Name:

Lab Exercise 2 — Unique

```
35
36        /* Write an if statement that checks that numberCount is less than five.
37           If so, increment numberCount by 1; otherwise terminate this call
38           to actionPerformed. */
39
40        /* Compare input number to unique numbers in array using a for loop. If
41           number is unique, append new number to text area and store new number */
42
43     } // end method actionPerformed
44
45  } // end class Unique
```

Fig. L 7.3   `Unique.java`. (Part 2 of 2.)

Problem-Solving Tips

1. Initialize the integer array to hold 5 elements. This is the maximum number of values the program must store if all values input are unique.

2. Remember to validate the input and use method `showStatus` to display an error message if the user inputs invalid data.

3. If the number entered is not unique, `actionPerformed` should simply return; otherwise, it should display the number in the `JTextArea` and store the number in the array.

4. If you have any questions as you proceed, ask your lab instructor for assistance.

Follow-Up Questions and Activities

1. Modify the previous program so that the applet inputs 30 numbers now, each of which is between 10 to 500, inclusive.

2. Modify the program so that it will allow the user to enter numbers until the array is full.

3. Now make additional modifications to the program that will allow the user to enter the size of the array as the applet begins execution.

Lab Exercises   Name:

Debugging

Name: _____   Date:_____

Section: _____

The program in this section does not run properly. Fix all the syntax errors, so that the program will compile successfully. Once the program compiles, compare the output to the sample output, and eliminate any logic errors that exist. The sample output demonstrates what the program's output should be once the program's code is corrected. The file is available at www.deitel.com and at www.prenhall.com/deitel.

Sample Output

Broken Code

```
1    // Debugging Problem Chapter 7: MultArray.java
2    // Program will output multiplication table for specified range of numbers
3    // and then compute their factorials, using arrays
4    import java.awt.*;
5    import java.awt.event.*;
6    import javax.swing.*;
7
8    public class MultArray extends JApplet implements ActionListener {
9        JLabel numberPrompt;
10       JTextField numberField;
11       JTextArea arrayOutput;
12       JScrollPane scroller;
13       int arrayNumber;
14
```

Fig. L 7.4   MultArray.java. (Part 1 of 3.)

Lab Exercises   Name:

Debugging

```
15      // set up GUI components
16      public void init()
17      {
18          numberPrompt = JLabel( "Enter number you want computed to: " );
19
20          numberField = JTextField( 5 );
21          numberField.addActionListener( this );
22          arrayOutput = JTextArea( 17 , 50 );
23          arrayOutput.setEditable( false );
24          scroller =   new JScrollPane ( arrayOutput );
25
26          Container container = getContentPane();
27          container.setLayout( FlowLayout() );
28          container.add( numberPrompt );
29          container.add( numberField );
30          container.add( scroller );
31
32      // obtain user input
33      public void actionperformed( ActionEvent actionEvent )
34
35          // read in numField and convert to int
36          int columnNumber = Integer.parseInt( numberPrompt.getText() );
37          int rowNumber = numberPrompt;
38
39          // error-check the input
40          int flag = 0;
41
42          if ( columnNumber >= 0 ) {
43              flag = 1;
44              showStatus( "Invalid input! Enter values greater than zero" );
45          }
46
47          if ( columnNumber < 12 ) {
48              flag = 1;
49              showStatus( "Invalid input! Enter values less than 12" );
50          }
51
52          // if values are valid then display array and calculate values
53          if ( flag ) {
54
55              // array arrayNum holds all the numerical values
56              arrayNumber = int[ rowNumber , columnNumber ];
57
58              // display the array and calculate the totals
59              int factorial[ columnNumber + 1 ] = int[];
60
61              for ( column = 0; column <= columnNumber; column++ )
62                  factorial[ columnNumber ] = 1;
63
64              String output = "\t";
65
66              for ( i = 1; i <= columnNumber; i++ )
67                  output = output + i + "\t";
68
69              output += "\n";
70
```

Fig. L 7.4   MultArray.java. (Part 2 of 3.)

Lab Exercises   Name:

Debugging

```
71          for ( i = 0; i <= columnNumber; i++ )
72             output += "----------------------";
73
74          // for each column of each row, print the appropriate number
75          for ( row = 0; row < columnNumber; row++ ) {
76             output += "\n" + ( row + 1 ) + "|";
77
78             for ( column = 0; column < rowNumber; column++ ) {
79                arrayNumber[ column ][ row ] = ( column ) * ( row );
80                output += "\t" + arrayNumber[ row ][ column ];
81             }
82          }
83
84          output += "\n";
85
86          for ( i = 0; i <= columnNumber; i++ )
87             output += "----------------------";
88
89          output += "\nFactorials";
90
91          for ( column = 0; column < columnNumber; column++ ){
92
93             if ( column == 0 )
94                continue;
95
96             factorial[ column ] = factorial [ column ] * column;
97             output += "\t" + factorial[ column ];
98          }
99
100         arrayOutput.setText();
101
102      } // end if statement
103
104   } // end method actionPerformed
105
106 } // end class MultArray
```

Fig. L 7.4   MultArray.java. (Part 3 of 3.)

```
1  <html>
2  <applet = "MultArray.class" width = "700" height = "400" >
3  </applet>
4  </html>
```

Fig. L 7.5   applet.html.

Postlab Activities

Coding Exercises

Name: _____   **Date:**_____

Section: _____

These coding exercises reinforce the lessons learned in the lab and provide additional programming experience outside the classroom and laboratory environment. They serve as a review after you have successfully completed the *Prelab Activities* and *Lab Exercises*.

For each of the following problems, write a program or a program segment that performs the specified action.

1.   Write a line of code that declares and creates a 100-element array of `ints`.

2.   Initialize all the elements in the array of Coding Exercise 1 to –1.

3.   Write a line of code that accesses the seventh element of the array in Coding Exercise 2 and sets its value to **7**.

4.   Write a method `printArray` that displays the contents of the array created in Coding Exercise 1. Assume that the method is part of an applet that contains a `JTextArea` called `outputArea`. Display the contents of the array with each number separated by a space in the `JTextArea`. In addition, start a new line after every 20 elements.

Postlab Activities   Name:

Coding Exercises

5. Create a `char` array and use an array initializer to initialize the array with the characters in the string "`Hi there`". Display the contents of the array using a `for` loop. Separate each character in the array with a space.

6. Write a `for` loop that prints only "`Hi`" from the array you created in Coding Exercise 5.

7. Write a method `findMinimum` that finds the smallest value in an array and returns the index of that value in the array. The method should receive the array to be searched as an argument. Incorporate this method into an applet that allocates an array of a size input by the user and initializes the array with random values from 1–100, inclusive. You should display all the values in the array, the minimum value of the array and the index at which the minimum value was found.

Postlab Activities   Name: _____

Programming Challenges

Name: _____   Date:_____

Section: _____

The *Programming Challenges* are more involved than the *Coding Exercises* and may require a significant amount of time to complete. Write a Java program for each of the problems in this section. The answers to these problems are available at www.deitel.com, www.prenhall.com/deitel and on the *Java Multimedia Cyber Classroom: Fifth Edition*. Pseudocode, hints or sample output are provided to aid you in your programming.

1. (*Roll two dice*) Write an applet to simulate the rolling of two dice. The program should use Math.random to roll the first die and should use Math.random again to roll the second die. The sum of the two values should then be calculated. [*Note*: Each die can show an integer value from 1 to 6, so the sum of the values will vary from 2 to 12, with 7 being the most frequent sum and 2 and 12 being the least frequent sums. Fig. L 7.6 shows the 36 possible combinations of the two dice. Your program should roll the dice 36,000 times. Use a one-dimensional array to tally the number of times each possible sum appears. Display the results in a JTextArea in tabular format. Also, determine whether the totals are reasonable (i.e., there are six ways to roll a 7, so approximately one-sixth of all the rolls should be 7). The applet should use the GUI techniques introduced in Chapter 6. Provide a JButton to allow the user of the applet to roll the dice another 36,000 times. The applet should reset the elements of the one-dimensional array to 0 before rolling the dice again.

	1	2	3	4	5	6
1	2	3	4	5	6	7
2	3	4	5	6	7	8
3	4	5	6	7	8	9
4	5	6	7	8	9	10
5	6	7	8	9	10	11
6	7	8	9	10	11	12

Fig. L 7.6   The 36 possible outcomes of rolling two dice.

Hints:

*   Keep a tally of how many times each total (2 through 12) occurs. This tally is essentially the frequency for each sum, which is used to calculate the percentage.

*   Define a loop that iterates 36,000 times. In each pass, roll the dice, calculate the total and update the count for the particular total in the array.

*   Create an array large enough that you can use the sum of the dice as the index into the array.

*   Your output should appear as follows:

Postlab Activities   Name:

Programming Challenges

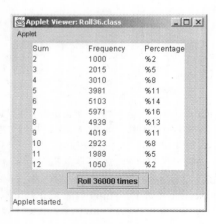

2. (*Linear Search*) Modify Figure 7.12 to use recursive method `linearSearch` to perform a linear search of the array. The method should receive as arguments an integer array, the size of the array remaining to be searched, and the search key. If the search key is found, return the array index; otherwise, return –1.

Hints:

*   Start searching from the back of the array, and work your way to the front, decrementing the size with each recursive call to `linearSearch`.

*   Your output should appear as follows:

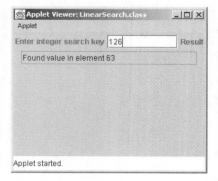

Object-Based Programming

Objectives

- To understand encapsulation and data hiding.
- To understand the notions of data abstraction and abstract data types (ADTs).
- To create Java ADTs, namely, classes.
- To be able to create and use objects.
- To be able to control access to object instance variables and methods.
- To appreciate the value of object orientation.
- To understand the use of the keyword this.
- To understand class variables and class methods.

Assignment Checklist

Name: _____   Date:_____

Section: _____

Exercises	Assigned: Circle assignments		Date Due
Prelab Activities			
Matching	YES	NO	
Fill in the Blank	YES	NO	
Short Answer	YES	NO	
Programming Output	YES	NO	
Correct the Code	YES	NO	
Lab Exercises			
Exercise 1 — Time: Part 1	YES	NO	
Follow-Up Questions and Activities	1, 2		
Exercise 2 — Time: Part 2	YES	NO	
Follow-Up Question and Activity	1		
Exercise 3 — Complex Numbers	YES	NO	
Follow-Up Questions and Activities	1, 2		
Debugging	YES	NO	
Postlab Activities			
Coding Exercises	1, 2, 3, 4, 5, 6, 7		
Programming Challenges	1, 2		

Prelab Activities

Matching

Name: _____   Date:_____

Section: _____

After reading Chapter 8 of *Java How to Program: Fifth Edition*, answer the given questions. These questions are intended to test and reinforce your understanding of key Java concepts. You may answer these questions either before or during the lab.

For each term in the left column, write the letter for the description that best matches the term from the right column.

Term	Description
____ 1. `extends`	a) Initializes an object of a class.
____ 2. instance variable	b) Method that is called by the garbage collector to clean up an object before it is removed from memory.
____ 3. constructor	c) Restricting access to class members via keyword `private` and providing `public` methods to allow controlled access to `private` class members.
____ 4. `finalize`	d) Used in a class declaration to indicate the class from which the new class inherits.
____ 5. mutator	e) Used implicitly in a class's non-`static` methods to refer to both the instance variables and methods of an object.
____ 6. encapsulation	f) Together, this name and the class name compose the fully qualified name of the class.
____ 7. attribute	g) Such variables are normally declared as `private` variables in a class.
____ 8. queue	h) These members of a class represent class-wide information—all objects of the class share the same piece of data.
____ 9. `this`	i) First-in, first-out (FIFO) data structure.
____ 10. `package` name	j) Another name for an instance variable in a class.
____ 11. `static` variables	k) Another name for a *set* method.

Prelab Activities   Name:

Fill in the Blank

Name: _____   Date:_____

Section: _____

Fill in the blanks for each of the following statements:

12. Keywords _____ and _____ are access modifiers.

13. Instance variables and methods declared with access modifier _____ are accessible wherever the program has reference to an object of the class in which they are defined.

14. Instance variables and methods declared with access modifier _____ are accessible only to methods of the class in which they are defined.

15. Use the keyword _____ to specify that a variable is not modifiable and that any attempt to modify the variable is an error.

16. If the `.class` files for the classes used in a program are in the same directory as the class that uses them, _____ statements are not required.

17. A(n) _____ class variable represents class-wide information.

18. In non-`static` methods, the keyword _____ is implicity used to refer to the instance variables and other non-`static` methods of the class.

19. A(n) _____ initializes the instance variables of an object of a class when the object is instantiated.

20. Each class and interface in the Java API belongs to a specific _____ that contains a group of related classes and interfaces.

21. Instance variables are normally declared _____, and methods are normally declared _____.

Prelab Activities   Name:

Short Answer

Name: _____   Date:_____

Section: _____

Answer the following questions in the space provided. Your answers should be as concise as possible; aim for two or three sentences.

22. What is an object?

23. What are some advantages of creating packages?

24. What is the purpose of a constructor?

Prelab Activities

Name: _____

Short Answer

25. What is the purpose of a *set* method?

26. What is the purpose of a *get* method?

27. What is an abstract data type?

Prelab Activities

Name:

Programming Output

Name: _____   Date:_____ _____

Section: _____

For each of the given program segments, read the code and write the output in the space provided below each program. [*Note*: Do not execute these programs on a computer.] For questions 28–30 use the following declaration of class Time3:

```
1   // Fig. 8.7: Time3.java
2   // Time3 class declaration with set and get methods.
3   import java.text.DecimalFormat;
4
5   public class Time3 {
6      private int hour;     // 0 - 23
7      private int minute;   // 0 - 59
8      private int second;   // 0 - 59
9
10     // Time3 constructor initializes each instance variable to zero;
11     // ensures that Time object starts in a consistent state
12     public Time3()
13     {
14        this( 0, 0, 0 ); // invoke Time3 constructor with three arguments
15     }
16
17     // Time3 constructor: hour supplied, minute and second defaulted to 0
18     public Time3( int h )
19     {
20        this( h, 0, 0 ); // invoke Time3 constructor with three arguments
21     }
22
23     // Time3 constructor: hour and minute supplied, second defaulted to 0
24     public Time3( int h, int m )
25     {
26        this( h, m, 0 ); // invoke Time3 constructor with three arguments
27     }
28
29     // Time3 constructor: hour, minute and second supplied
30     public Time3( int h, int m, int s )
31     {
32        setTime( h, m, s );
33     }
34
35     // Time3 constructor: another Time3 object supplied
36     public Time3( Time3 time )
37     {
38        // invoke Time3 constructor with three arguments
39        this( time.getHour(), time.getMinute(), time.getSecond() );
40     }
41
42     // Set Methods
43     // set a new time value using universal time; perform
44     // validity checks on data; set invalid values to zero
```

(Part 1 of 3.)

Prelab Activities

Name:

Programming Output

```java
45      public void setTime( int h, int m, int s )
46      {
47         setHour( h );   // set the hour
48         setMinute( m ); // set the minute
49         setSecond( s ); // set the second
50      }
51
52      // validate and set hour
53      public void setHour( int h )
54      {
55         hour = ( ( h >= 0 && h < 24 ) ? h : 0 );
56      }
57
58      // validate and set minute
59      public void setMinute( int m )
60      {
61         minute = ( ( m >= 0 && m < 60 ) ? m : 0 );
62      }
63
64      // validate and set second
65      public void setSecond( int s )
66      {
67         second = ( ( s >= 0 && s < 60 ) ? s : 0 );
68      }
69
70      // Get Methods
71      // get hour value
72      public int getHour()
73      {
74         return hour;
75      }
76
77      // get minute value
78      public int getMinute()
79      {
80         return minute;
81      }
82
83      // get second value
84      public int getSecond()
85      {
86         return second;
87      }
88
89      // convert to String in universal-time format
90      public String toUniversalString()
91      {
92         DecimalFormat twoDigits = new DecimalFormat( "00" );
93
94         return twoDigits.format( getHour() ) + ":" +
95            twoDigits.format( getMinute() ) + ":" +
96            twoDigits.format( getSecond() );
97      }
98
99      // convert to String in standard-time format
100     public String toStandardString()
101     {
```

Prelab Activities   Name:

Programming Output

```
102         DecimalFormat twoDigits = new DecimalFormat( "00" );
103
104         return ( ( getHour() == 12 || getHour() == 0 ) ?
105            12 : getHour() % 12 ) + ":" + twoDigits.format( getMinute() ) +
106            ":" + twoDigits.format( getSecond() ) +
107            ( getHour() < 12 ? " AM" : " PM" );
108      }
109
110 } // end class Time3
```

(Part 3 of 3.)

Assume that the following code segments are located in the main method of a driver application that tests Time3.

28. What is output by the following code segment?

```
1   Time3 t1 = new Time3( 5 );
2   System.out.println( "The time is " + t1.toStandardString() );
```

Your answer:

29. What is output by the following code segment?

```
1   Time3 t1 = new Time3( 13, 59, 60 );
2   System.out.println( "The time is " + t1.toStandardString() );
```

Your answer:

30. What is output by the following code segment?

```
1   Time3 t1 = new Time3( 0, 30, 0 );
2   Time3 t2 = new Time3( t1 );
3   System.out.println( "The time is " + t2.toUniversalString() );
```

Your answer:

Prelab Activities

Name:

Programming Output

For questions 31–33 use the following declaration of class Person:

```
1   public class Person {
2       private String firstName;
3       private String lastName;
4       private String gender;
5       private int age;
6
7       public Person( String firstName, String lastName )
8       {
9           setName( firstName, lastName );
10          setGender( "n/a" );
11          setAge( -1 );
12      }
13
14      public Person( String firstName, String lastName, String gender, int age )
15      {
16          setName( firstName, lastName );
17          setGender( gender );
18          setAge( age );
19      }
20
21      public void setName( String firstName, String lastName )
22      {
23          this.firstName = firstName;
24          this.lastName = lastName;
25      }
26
27      public void setGender( String gender )
28      {
29          this.gender = gender;
30      }
31
32      public void setAge( int age )
33      {
34          this.age = age;
35      }
36
37      public String getName()
38      {
39          return firstName + " " + lastName;
40      }
41
42      public String getGender()
43      {
44          return gender;
45      }
46
47      public int getAge()
48      {
49          return age;
50      }
51
52      public String toPersonString()
53      {
54          if ( gender == "n/a" && age == -1 )
55              return getName();
```

(Part 1 of 2.)

Prelab Activities   Name:

Programming Output

```
56
57        return getName() + " is a " + getAge() + " year old " + getGender();
58    }
59  } // end class Person
```

(Part 2 of 2.)

Assume that the following code segments are located in the main method of an application that tests class Person.

31. What is output by the following code segment?

```
1   Person person = new Person( "Rus", "Tic", "male", 21 );
2   System.out.println( person.toPersonString() );
```

Your answer:

32. What is output by the following code segment?

```
1   Person person = new Person( "Anna Lee", "Tic" );
2   System.out.println( person.toPersonString() );
```

Your answer:

33. What is output by the following code segment?

```
1   Person person = new Person( "Anna Lee", "Tic", "n/a", -1 );
2   System.out.println( person.toPersonString() );
```

Your answer:

Prelab Activities   Name:

Correct the Code

Name: _____   Date:_____

Section: _____

Determine if there is an error in each of the following program segments. If there is an error, specify whether it is a logic error or a compilation error, circle the error in the program and write the corrected code in the space provided after each problem. If the code does not contain an error, write "no error." [*Note*: There may be more than one error in each program segment.]

34. The following defines class `Product`, with a no-argument constructor that sets the product's name to an empty `String` and the `price` to 0.00, and a `toProductString` method that returns a `String` containing the product's `name` and its `price`:

```
1    import java.text.*;
2
3    public class Product {
4
5       private String name;
6       private double price;
7       private static DecimalFormat money = new DecimalFormat( "$0.00" );
8
9       public void Product()
10      {
11         name = " ";
12         price = 0.00;
13      }
14
15      public toProductString()
16      {
17         return name + " costs " + money.format( price );
18      }
19
20   } // end class Product
```

Your answer:

Prelab Activities   Name:

Correct the Code

35. The following defines another constructor for class `Product` that takes two arguments and assigns those arguments to the corresponding instance variables:

```
1  public Product( String name, double price )
2  {
3      name = name;
4      price = price;
5  }
```

Your answer:

36. The following defines another constructor for class `Product` that sets the price to the value passed into the constructor and sets the `name` of the product to the string `"This Product"`:

```
1  public Product( String name, double price )
2  {
3      this.name = "This Product";
4      this.price = price;
5  }
```

Your answer:

Prelab Activities   Name:

Correct the Code

37. The following defines two *set* methods to set the `name` and the `price` of the `Product`:

```
1  public setName()
2  {
3      this.name = name;
4  }
5
6  public setPrice()
7  {
8      this.price = price;
9  }
```

Your answer:

For questions 38–39 use the previous class declaration with the additional methods specified in questions 35–37. Assume that the code in questions 38–39 is located in the `main` method of an application that tests class `Product`.

38. The following code segment should create a `Product` object and display a `String` containing the values of the object's instance variables.

```
1  Product p1 = new Product( "Milk", 5.5 );
2  System.out.println( p1.name + " " + p1.price );
```

Your answer:

Prelab Activities   Name:

Correct the Code

39. The following code segment should create a **Product** object, set the values of its instance variables and display a **String** containing the values of the instance variables:

```
1    Product p1 = new Product();
2    p1.setName();
3    p1.setPrice();
4    System.out.println( p1.toProductString( "Eggs", 3 ) );
```

Your answer:

Lab Exercises

Lab Exercise 1 — Time: Part 1

Name: _____   **Date:**_____

Section: _____

The following problem is intended to be solved in a closed-lab session with a teaching assistant or instructor present. The problem is divided into six parts:

1. Lab Objectives

2. Problem Description

3. Sample Output

4. Program Template (Fig. L 8.1–Fig. L 8.3)

5. Problem-Solving Tips

6. Follow-Up Questions and Activities

The program template represents a complete working Java program with one or more key lines of code replaced with comments. Read the problem description and examine the output, then study the template code. Using the problem-solving tips as a guide, replace the /* */ comments with Java code. Compile and execute the program. Compare your output with the sample output provided. Then answer the follow-up questions. The source code for the template is available at `www.deitel.com` and `www.prenhall.com/deitel`.

Lab Objectives

This lab was designed to reinforce programming concepts from Chapter 8 of *Java How To Program: Fifth Edition*. In this lab, you will practice:

- Modifying methods of a class.

- Accessing member variables.

- Using *set* and *get* methods.

The follow-up questions and activities also will give you practice:

- Understanding the difference between access specifiers `public` and `private`.

Problem Description

Modify the *set* methods in class `Time3` of Fig. 8.7 in your text book (template Fig. L 8.1) to `return` appropriate error values if an attempt is made to set one of the instance variables `hour`, `minute` or `second` of an object of class `Time3` to an invalid value. Then, modify class `TimeTest4` of Fig. 8.8 (template Fig. L 8.2) to display error messages when invalid values are used to set the `hour`, `minute` or `second`.

Lab Exercises   Name:

Lab Exercise 1 — Time: Part 1

Sample Output

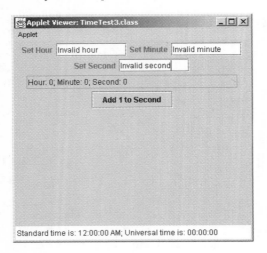

Template

```
1    // Lab 1: Time3.java
2    // Time3 class definition with set and get methods
3    import java.text.DecimalFormat;
4
5    public class Time3 {
6       private int hour;      // 0 - 23
7       private int minute;    // 0 - 59
8       private int second;    // 0 - 59
9
10      // Time3 constructor initializes each instance variable
11      // to zero. Ensures that Time object starts in a
12      // consistent state.
13      public Time3()
14      {
15         setTime( 0, 0, 0 );
16      }
17
18      // Time3 constructor: hour supplied, minute and second
19      // defaulted to 0
20      public Time3( int h )
21      {
22         setTime( h, 0, 0 );
23      }
24
25      // Time3 constructor: hour and minute supplied, second
26      // defaulted to 0
27      public Time3( int h, int m )
28      {
29         setTime( h, m, 0 );
30      }
31
```

Fig. L 8.1   Time3.java. (Part 1 of 3.)

Lab Exercises   Name:

Lab Exercise 1 — Time: Part 1

```
32      // Time3 constructor: hour, minute and second supplied
33      public Time3( int h, int m, int s )
34      {
35          setTime( h, m, s );
36      }
37
38      // Time3 constructor: another Time3 object supplied
39      public Time3( Time3 time )
40      {
41          setTime( time.getHour(), time.getMinute(), time.getSecond() );
42      }
43
44      // Set Methods
45      // Set a new time value using universal time. Perform
46      // validity checks on data. Set invalid values to zero.
47      /* Write header for setTime. */
48      {
49          /* Write code here that declares three boolean variables which are
50              initialized to the return values of setHour, setMinute and setSecond.
51              These lines of code should also set the three member variables. */
52
53          /* Return true if all three variables are true; otherwise, return false. */
54      }
55
56      // validate and set hour
57      /* Write header for the setHour method. */
58      {
59          /* Write code here that determines whether the hour is valid.
60              If so, set the hour and return true. */
61
62          /* If the hour is not valid, set the hour to 0 and return false. */
63      }
64
65      // validate and set minute
66      /* Write the header for the setMinute method. */
67      {
68          /* Write code here that determines whether the minute is valid.
69              If so, set the minute and return true. */
70
71          /* If the minute is not valid, set the minute to 0 and return false. */
72      }
73
74      // validate and set second
75      /* Write the header for the setSecond method. */
76      {
77          /* Write code here that determines whether the second is valid.
78              If so, set the second and return true. */
79
80          /* If the second is not valid, set the second to 0 and return false. */
81      }
82
83      // Get Methods
84      // get hour value
85      public int getHour()
86      {
87          return hour;
88      }
```

Fig. L 8.1   Time3.java. (Part 2 of 3.)

Lab Exercises   Name:

Lab Exercise 1 — Time: Part 1

```
89
90      // get minute value
91      public int getMinute()
92      {
93         return minute;
94      }
95
96      // get second value
97      public int getSecond()
98      {
99         return second;
100     }
101
102     // convert to String in universal-time format
103     public String toUniversalString()
104     {
105        DecimalFormat twoDigits = new DecimalFormat( "00" );
106
107        return twoDigits.format( getHour() ) + ":" +
108           twoDigits.format( getMinute() ) + ":" + twoDigits.format( getSecond() );
109     }
110
111     // convert to String in standard-time format
112     public String toStandardString()
113     {
114        DecimalFormat twoDigits = new DecimalFormat( "00" );
115
116        return ( ( getHour() == 12 || getHour() == 0 ) ? 12 : getHour() % 12 ) +
117           ":" + twoDigits.format( getMinute() ) + ":" +
118           twoDigits.format( getSecond() ) + ( getHour() < 12 ? " AM" : " PM" );
119     }
120
121  } // end class Time3
```

Fig. L 8.1   `Time3.java`. (Part 3 of 3.)

```
1    // Lab 1: TimeTest4.java
2    // Program adds validation to Fig. 8.7 example
3    import java.awt.*;
4    import java.awt.event.*;
5    import javax.swing.*;
6
7    public class TimeTest4 extends JApplet implements ActionListener {
8       private Time3 time;
9       private JLabel hourLabel, minuteLabel, secondLabel;
10      private JTextField hourField, minuteField, secondField, displayField;
11      private JButton tickButton;
12
13      // Create Time3 object and set up GUI
14      public void init()
15      {
16         time = new Time3();
17
18         Container container = getContentPane();
19         container.setLayout( new FlowLayout() );
20
```

Fig. L 8.2   `TimeTest4.java`. (Part 1 of 3.)

Lab Exercises

Name:

Lab Exercise 1 — Time: Part 1

```
21          // set up hourLabel and hourField
22          hourLabel = new JLabel( "Set Hour" );
23          hourField = new JTextField( 10 );
24          hourField.addActionListener( this );
25          container.add( hourLabel );
26          container.add( hourField );
27
28          // set up minuteLabel and minuteField
29          minuteLabel = new JLabel( "Set minute" );
30          minuteField = new JTextField( 10 );
31          minuteField.addActionListener( this );
32          container.add( minuteLabel );
33          container.add( minuteField );
34
35          // set up secondLabel and secondField
36          secondLabel = new JLabel( "Set Second" );
37          secondField = new JTextField( 10 );
38          secondField.addActionListener( this );
39          container.add( secondLabel );
40          container.add( secondField );
41
42          // set up displayField
43          displayField = new JTextField( 30 );
44          displayField.setEditable( false );
45          container.add( displayField );
46
47          // set up tickButton
48          tickButton = new JButton( "Add 1 to Second" );
49          tickButton.addActionListener( this );
50          container.add( tickButton );
51
52          updateDisplay();  // update text in displayField
53       }
54
55       // handle button and text field events
56       public void actionPerformed( ActionEvent actionEvent )
57       {
58          /* Declare a boolean to store Time3's set method return values */
59
60          // process tickButton event
61          if ( actionEvent.getSource() == tickButton )
62             tick();
63
64          // process hourField event
65          else if ( actionEvent.getSource() == hourField ) {
66             /* Write code here that sets the hour and assigns setHour's
67                return value to the boolean variable previously declared.
68                This return value indicates the validity of the hour. */
69
70             /* If the hour is invalid, display an error message. */
71          }
72
73          // process minuteField event
74          else if ( actionEvent.getSource() == minuteField ) {
75             /* Write code here that sets the hour and assigns setMinute's
76                return value to the boolean variable previously declared.
77                This return value indicates the validity of the minute field. */
```

Fig. L 8.2   TimeTest4.java. (Part 2 of 3.)

Lab Exercises   Name:

Lab Exercise 1 — Time: Part 1

```
78
79          /* If the minute is invalid, display an error message. */
80       }
81
82       // process secondField event
83       else if ( actionEvent.getSource() == secondField ) {
84          /* Write code here that sets the second and assigns setSecond's
85             return value to the boolean variable previously declared.
86             This return value indicates the validity of the second field. */
87
88          /* If the second is invalid, display an error message. */
89       }
90
91       updateDisplay();   // update displayField and status bar
92    }
93
94    // update displayField and applet container's status bar
95    public void updateDisplay()
96    {
97       displayField.setText( "Hour: " + time.getHour() + "; Minute: " +
98          time.getMinute() + "; Second: " + time.getSecond() );
99
100      showStatus( "Standard time is: " + time.toStandardString() +
101         "; Universal time is: " + time.toUniversalString() );
102   }
103
104   // add one to second and update hour/minute if necessary
105   public void tick()
106   {
107      time.setSecond( ( time.getSecond() + 1 ) % 60 );
108
109      if ( time.getSecond() == 0 ) {
110         time.setMinute( ( time.getMinute() + 1 ) % 60 );
111
112         if ( time.getMinute() == 0 )
113            time.setHour( ( time.getHour() + 1 ) % 24 );
114      }
115   }
116
117 } // end class TimeTest4
```

Fig. L 8.2   TimeTest4.java. (Part 3 of 3.)

```
1   <HMTL>
2   <APPLET CODE = "TimeTest4.class" WIDTH = 400 HEIGHT = 200>
3   </APPLET>
4   </HTML>
```

Fig. L 8.3   applet.html.

Lab Exercises   Name: _____

Lab Exercise 1 — Time: Part 1

Problem-Solving Tips

1. Use `boolean` return types for the *set* methods.
2. Each *set* method should `return true` if the value is valid and `false` if it is not.
3. Set the fields of the applet in the same way they are set in Fig. 8.8, using the `setText` method of class `JTextField`.
4. If you have any questions as you proceed, ask your lab instructor for assistance.

Follow-Up Questions and Activities

1. What is the purpose of having the instance variables of class `Time3` be declared `private`?
2. Change all the methods in class `Time3` from `public` methods to `private` methods, then recompile the class and execute the program again. Does anything occur differently? If so, explain why.

Lab Exercises   Name:

Lab Exercise 2 — Time: Part 2

Name: _____   Date:_____

Section: _____

The following problem is intended to be solved in a closed-lab session with a teaching assistant or instructor present. The problem is divided into six parts:

1. Lab Objectives
2. Problem Description
3. Sample Output
4. Program Template (Fig. L 8.4–Fig. L 8.6)
5. Problem-Solving Tips
6. Follow-Up Question and Activity

The program template represents a complete working Java program with one or more key lines of code replaced with comments. Read the problem description and examine the output, then study the template code. Using the problem-solving tips as a guide, replace the /* */ comments with Java code. Compile and execute the program. Compare your output with the sample output provided. Then answer the follow-up question. The source code for the template is available at www.deitel.com and www.prenhall.com/deitel.

Lab Objectives

This lab was designed to reinforce programming concepts from Chapter 8 of *Java How To Program: Fifth Edition*. In this lab you will practice:

• Creating new methods in a class.

• Calling methods of a class from the class's other methods.

The follow-up question and activity also will give you practice:

• Understanding modularization.

Problem Description

Modify the Time3 class of Fig 8.7 in *Java How to Program* to include the tick method that increments the time stored in a Time3 object by one second. Also provide method incrementMinute to increment the minute and method incrementHour to increment the hour. The Time3 object should always remain in a consistent state. Modify the TimeTest4 applet of Fig. 8.8 in *Java How to Program* to test the tick method of a Time3 object, the incrementMinute method and the incrementHour method to ensure that they work correctly. Be sure to test the following cases:

a) Incrementing to the next minute.

b) Incrementing to the next hour.

c) Incrementing to the next day—i.e., 11:59:59 PM to 12:00:00 AM. Remember that Time3 stores the time in 24-hour clock format.

Lab Exercises   Name:

Lab Exercise 2 — Time: Part 2

Sample Output

Template

```
1    // Lab 2: Time3.java
2    // Time3 class definition with set and get methods
3    import java.text.DecimalFormat;
4
5    public class Time3 extends Object {
6       private int hour;      // 0 - 23
7       private int minute;    // 0 - 59
8       private int second;    // 0 - 59
9
10      // Time3 constructor initializes each instance variable to zero;
11      // ensures that Time3 object starts in a consistent state
12      public Time3()
13      {
14         setTime( 0, 0, 0 );
15      }
16
17      // Time3 constructor: hour supplied, minute and second defaulted to 0
18      public Time3( int h )
19      {
20         setTime( h, 0, 0 );
21      }
22
23      // Time3 constructor: hour and minute supplied, second defaulted to 0
24      public Time3( int h, int m )
25      {
26         setTime( h, m, 0 );
27      }
28
29      // Time3 constructor: hour, minute and second supplied
30      public Time3( int h, int m, int s )
31      {
32         setTime( h, m, s );
33      }
```

Fig. L 8.4   Time3.java. (Part 1 of 3.)

Lab Exercises   Name:

Lab Exercise 2 — Time: Part 2

```
34
35      // Time3 constructor: another Time3 object supplied
36      public Time3( Time3 time )
37      {
38         setTime( time.getHour(), time.getMinute(), time.getSecond() );
39      }
40
41      // Set Methods
42      // Set a new time value using universal time; perform validity checks on data
43      // and set invalid values to zero.
44      public void setTime( int h, int m, int s )
45      {
46         setHour( h );      // set the hour
47         setMinute( m );    // set the minute
48         setSecond( s );    // set the second
49      }
50
51      // validate and set hour
52      public void setHour( int h )
53      {
54         hour = ( ( h >= 0 && h < 24 ) ? h : 0 );
55      }
56
57      // validate and set minute
58      public void setMinute( int m )
59      {
60         minute = ( ( m >= 0 && m < 60 ) ? m : 0 );
61      }
62
63      // validate and set second
64      public void setSecond( int s )
65      {
66         second = ( ( s >= 0 && s < 60 ) ? s : 0 );
67      }
68
69      // Get Methods
70      // get hour value
71      public int getHour()
72      {
73         return hour;
74      }
75
76      // get minute value
77      public int getMinute()
78      {
79         return minute;
80      }
81
82      // get second value
83      public int getSecond()
84      {
85         return second;
86      }
87
88      // convert to String in universal-time format
89      public String toUniversalString()
90      {
```

Fig. L 8.4   Time3.java. (Part 2 of 3.)

Lab Exercises   Name:

Lab Exercise 2 — Time: Part 2

```
91          DecimalFormat twoDigits = new DecimalFormat( "00" );
92
93          return twoDigits.format( getHour() ) + ":" +
94             twoDigits.format( getMinute() ) + ":" +
95             twoDigits.format( getSecond() );
96       }
97
98       // convert to String in standard-time format
99       public String toString()
100      {
101         DecimalFormat twoDigits = new DecimalFormat( "00" );
102
103         return ( ( getHour() == 12 || getHour() == 0 ) ? 12 : getHour() % 12 ) +
104            ":" + twoDigits.format( getMinute() ) + ":" +
105            twoDigits.format( getSecond() ) + ( getHour() < 12 ? " AM" : " PM" );
106      }
107
108      // Tick the time by one second
109      /* Write header for method tick */
110      {
111         /* Write code that increments the second by one, then determines whether
112            the minute needs to be incremented. If so, call incrementMinute. */
113      }
114
115      // Increment the minute
116      /* Write header for method incrementMinute */
117      {
118         /* Write code that increments the minute by one, then determines whether
119            the hour needs to be incremented. If so, call incrementHour. */
120      }
121
122      // Increment the hour
123      /* Write header for method incrementHour. */
124      {
125         /* Write code that increments the hour by one. */
126      }
127
128 } // end class Time3
```

Fig. L 8.4   Time3.java. (Part 3 of 3.)

```
1    // Lab 2: TimeTest4.java
2    // Testing the tick method of
3    import java.awt.*;
4    import java.awt.event.*;
5    import javax.swing.*;
6
7    public class TimeTest4 extends JApplet implements ActionListener {
8       private Time3 time;
9       private JLabel hourLabel, minuteLabel, secondLabel;
10      private JTextField hourField, minuteField, secondField, displayField;
11      private JButton tickButton;
12
13      // Create Time3 object and set up GUI
14      public void init()
15      {
```

Fig. L 8.5   TimeTest4.java. (Part 1 of 3.)

Lab Exercises   Name:

Lab Exercise 2 — Time: Part 2

```
16          time = new Time3();
17
18          Container container = getContentPane();
19          container.setLayout( new FlowLayout() );
20
21          // set up hourLabel and hourField
22          hourLabel = new JLabel( "Set Hour" );
23          hourField = new JTextField( 10 );
24          hourField.addActionListener( this );
25          container.add( hourLabel );
26          container.add( hourField );
27
28          // set up minuteLabel and minuteField
29          minuteLabel = new JLabel( "Set minute" );
30          minuteField = new JTextField( 10 );
31          minuteField.addActionListener( this );
32          container.add( minuteLabel );
33          container.add( minuteField );
34
35          // set up secondLabel and secondField
36          secondLabel = new JLabel( "Set Second" );
37          secondField = new JTextField( 10 );
38          secondField.addActionListener( this );
39          container.add( secondLabel );
40          container.add( secondField );
41
42          // set up displayField
43          displayField = new JTextField( 30 );
44          displayField.setEditable( false );
45          container.add( displayField );
46
47          // set up tickButton
48          tickButton = new JButton( "Add 1 to Second" );
49          tickButton.addActionListener( this );
50          container.add( tickButton );
51
52          updateDisplay();  // update text in displayField
53       }
54
55       // handle button and text field events
56       public void actionPerformed( ActionEvent actionEvent )
57       {
58          // process tickButton event
59          if ( actionEvent.getSource() == tickButton )
60             /* Write code that calls the tick method of class Time3. */
61
62          else if ( actionEvent.getSource() == hourField ) {
63             time.setHour( Integer.parseInt( actionEvent.getActionCommand() ) );
64             hourField.setText( "" );
65          }
66          else if ( actionEvent.getSource() == minuteField ) {
67             time.setMinute( Integer.parseInt( actionEvent.getActionCommand() ) );
68             minuteField.setText( "" );
69          }
70          else if ( actionEvent.getSource() == secondField ) {
71             time.setSecond( Integer.parseInt( actionEvent.getActionCommand() ) );
```

Fig. L 8.5   TimeTest4.java. (Part 2 of 3.)

Lab Exercises   Name:

Lab Exercise 2 — Time: Part 2

```
72              secondField.setText( "" );
73          }
74
75          updateDisplay();  // update displayField and status bar
76      }
77
78      // update displayField and applet container's status bar
79      public void updateDisplay()
80      {
81          displayField.setText( "Hour: " + time.getHour() + "; Minute: " +
82              time.getMinute() + "; Second: " + time.getSecond() );
83
84          showStatus( "Standard time is: " + time.toStandardString() +
85              "; Universal time is: " + time.toUniversalString() );
86      }
87
88  } // end class TimeTest4
```

Fig. L 8.5   `TimeTest4.java`. (Part 3 of 3.)

```
1   <HMTL>
2   <APPLET CODE= "TimeTest4.class" WIDTH = 300 HEIGHT = 300>
3   </APPLET>
4   </HTML>
```

Fig. L 8.6   `applet.html`.

Problem-Solving Tips

1. Use the *set* methods of class Time3 to assign new values to the appropriate Time3 instance variables.

2. The tick and increment methods do not return anything; therefore, they should be declared to return void.

3. Complete your testing by running the applet and testing all three cases mentioned in the problem description. Note that methods incrementMinute and incrementHour can be tested by changing the time to a value for which the next call to tick will cause either (or both) of these methods to be called. For example, at 11:59:59, the next tick will cause both the hour and minute to be incremented.

4. If you have any questions as you proceed, ask your lab instructor for assistance.

Follow-Up Question and Activity

1. Explain why a programmer would choose to implement method tick in class Time3 rather than a class that uses Time3 objects.

Lab Exercises   Name:

Lab Exercise 3 — Complex Numbers

Name: _____   **Date:**_____

Section: _____

The following problem is intended to be solved in a closed-lab session with a teaching assistant or instructor present. The problem is divided into six parts:

1. Lab Objectives
2. Problem Description
3. Sample Output
4. Program Template (Fig. L 8.7–Fig. L 8.8)
5. Problem-Solving Tips
6. Follow-Up Questions and Activities

The program template represents a complete working Java program with one or more key lines of code replaced with comments. Read the problem description and examine the output, then study the template code. Using the problem-solving tips as a guide, replace the /* */ comments with Java code. Compile and execute the program. Compare your output with the sample output provided. Then answer the follow-up questions. The source code for the template is available at www.deitel.com and www.prenhall.com/deitel.

Lab Objectives

This lab was designed to reinforce programming concepts from Chapter 8 of *Java How To Program: Fifth Edition*. In this lab, you will practice:

- Using the this reference.
- Initializing class objects.
- Using overloaded constructors.

The follow-up questions and activities will also give you practice:

- Overloading methods.

Problem Description

Create a class called Complex for performing arithmetic with complex numbers. Write an application to test your class. Complex numbers have the form realPart + imaginaryPart * i, where i is the square root of -1. Use floating-point variables to represent the private data of the class. Provide a constructor method that enables an object of this class to be initialized when it is declared. Provide a no-argument constructor with default values in case no initializers are provided. Also provide public methods for each of the following:

a) *Adding two Complex numbers.* Add the real parts of each complex number, and add the imaginary parts of each complex number.

b) *Subtracting two Complex numbers.* Subtract the real part of the right operand from the real part of the left operand, and subtract the imaginary part of the right operand from the imaginary part of the left operand.

Lab Exercises   Name:

Lab Exercise 3 — Complex Numbers

Sample Output

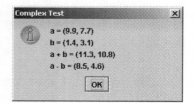

Template

```
1    // Lab 3: Complex.java
2    // Definition of class Complex
3
4    public class Complex {
5        private double real;
6        private double imaginary;
7
8        // Initialize both parts to 0
9        /* Write header for a no-argument constructor. */
10       {
11           /* Write code here that calls the Complex constructor that takes 2
12               arguments and initializes both parts to 0 */
13       }
14
15       // Initialize real part to r and imaginary part to i
16       /* Write header for constructor that takes two arguments—real part r and
17           imaginary part i. */
18       {
19           /* Write line of code that sets real part to r. */
20           /* Write line of code that sets imaginary part to i. */
21       }
22
23       // Add two Complex numbers
24       public Complex add( Complex right )
25       {
26           /* Write code here that returns a Complex number in which the real part is
27               the sum of the real part of this Complex object and the real part of the
28               Complex object passed to the method; and the imaginary part is the sum
29               of the imaginary part of this Complex object and the imaginary part of
30               the Complex object passed to the method. */
31       }
32
33       // Subtract two Complex numbers
34       public Complex subtract( Complex right )
35       {
36           /* Write code here that returns a Complex number in which the real part is
37               the difference between the real part of this Complex object and the real
38               part of the Complex object passed to the method; and the imaginary part
39               is the difference between the imaginary part of this Complex object and
40               the imaginary part of the Complex object passed to the method. */
41       }
42
```

Fig. L 8.7   Complex.java. (Part 1 of 2.)

Lab Exercises

Name:

Lab Exercise 3 — Complex Numbers

```
43      // Return String representation of a Complex number
44      public String toComplexString()
45      {
46          return "(" + real + ", " + imaginary + ")";
47      }
48  }
```

Fig. L 8.7   Complex.java. (Part 2 of 2.)

```
1   // Lab 3: ComplexTest.java
2   // Test the Complex number class
3   import javax.swing.*;
4
5   public class ComplexTest {
6       public static void main( String args[] )
7       {
8           Complex a, b;
9           a = new Complex( 9.9, 7.7 );
10          b = new Complex( 1.4, 3.1 );
11
12          String result = "a = " + a.toComplexString();
13          result += "\nb = " + b.toComplexString();
14          result += "\na + b = " + a.add( b ).toComplexString();
15          result += "\na - b = " + a.subtract( b ).toComplexString();
16
17          JOptionPane.showMessageDialog( null, result, "Complex Test",
18              JOptionPane.INFORMATION_MESSAGE );
19          System.exit( 0 );
20      }
21  }
```

Fig. L 8.8   ComplexTest.java.

Problem-Solving Tips

7. For the add and subtract methods of class Complex, return a new Complex object with the results of the calculations.

8. If you have any questions as you proceed, ask your lab instructor for assistance.

Follow-Up Questions and Activities

1. In the ComplexTest class of *Lab Exercise 3*, instead of adding b to a, add a to b. Also instead of subtracting b from a, subtract a from b. Are the results different from the previous results in Lab Exercise 3?

2. In class Complex, define a multiply method that returns the product of two Complex numbers. The product of two complex numbers is a complex number of which the real part is the difference between the product of the imaginary parts and the real parts, and the imaginary part is the sum of the products of each real and imaginary part. The general formula is $(a, b)(c, d) = (ac - bd, ad + bc)$. Modify ComplexTest to test your solution.

Lab Exercises   Name:

Debugging

Name: _____   Date:_____

Section: _____

The program in this section does not compile. Fix all the syntax errors so that the program will compile success-fully. Once the program compiles, execute the program, and compare the output with the sample output. Then eliminate any logic errors that may exist. The sample output demonstrates what the program's output should be once the code is corrected. The source code is available at www.deitel.com and at www.prenhall.com/de-itel.

Sample Output

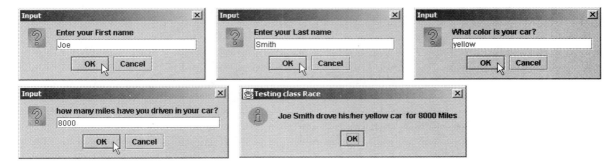

Broken Code

```
1    // Chapter 8 of Java How To Program
2    // Debugging Problem
3
4    public class Color extends Object {
5        private String color;
6
7        public Color()
8        {
9            return setColor( " " );
10       }
11
12       public void setColor()
13       {
14           color = "black";
15           return color;
16       }
17
18       public void setColor( String m )
19       {
20           color = m;
21           return color;
22       }
23
```

Fig. L 8.9   Color.java. (Part 1 of 2.)

Lab Exercises   Name:

Debugging

```
24      public String toColorString()
25      {
26          return color;
27      }
28  }
```

Fig. L 8.9   Color.java. (Part 2 of 2.)

```
1   // Chapter 8 of Java How To Program
2   // Debugging Problem
3   import java.text.DecimalFormat;
4
5   public class Miles extends Object {
6       private final double miles;
7
8       public Miles()
9       {
10          setMile( 0.0 );
11      }
12
13      public void setMile( double m )
14      {
15          miles = ( ( m >= 0.0 && m <= 200000 ) ? m : 0 );
16      }
17
18      public String toMilesString()
19      {
20          DecimalFormatformatMile = new DecimalFormat( "0" );
21          return formatMile.format( miles );
22      }
23  }
```

Fig. L 8.10   Miles.java.

```
1   // Chapter 8 of Java How To Program
2   // Debugging Problem
3
4
5   public class Person extends Object {
6       private String firstName;
7       private String lastName;
8
9       public Person( String firstName, String lastName )
10      {
11          lastName = getLastname();
12          firstName = getFirstName();
13      }
14
15      public String getFirstName()
16      {
17          return firstName;
18      }
19
20      public String getLastName()
21      {
```

Fig. L 8.11   Person.java. (Part 1 of 2.)

Lab Exercises   Name:

Debugging

```
22        return lastName;
23    }
24 }
```

Fig. L 8.11   Person.java. (Part 2 of 2.)

```java
1  // Chapter 8 of Java How To Program
2  // Debugging Problem
3  import javax.swing.JOptionPane;
4
5  public class Test {
6
7     public static void main( String args[] )
8     {
9        String firstName = JOptionPane.showInputDialog( "Enter your First name" );
10       String lastName = JOptionPane.showInputDialog( "Enter your Last name" );
11       String color2 = JOptionPane.showInputDialog( "What color is your car? " );
12       String miles = JOptionPane.showInputDialog( "how many miles have you" +
13          " driven in your car? " );
14
15       double miles2 = Double.parseDouble( miles );
16
17       Miles mile = new Miles();
18       Color color = new Color();
19       Person person = new Person( firstName , lastName );
20
21       mile.setMile( miles2 );
22       color.setColor( color2 );
23
24       String output = person.getFirstName()+ " " + person.getLastName() +
25          " drove his/her " + color.toString() +  " car " +
26          " for " + mile.toUniversalString() + " Miles";
27
28       JOptionPane.showMessageDialog( null, output, "Testing class Race",
29          JOptionPane.INFORMATION_MESSAGE );
30
31       System.exit( 0 );
32    }
33 }
```

Fig. L 8.12   Test.java.

Postlab Activities

Coding Exercises

Name: _____   Date:_____

Section: _____

These coding exercises reinforce the lessons learned in the lab and provide additional programming experience outside the classroom and laboratory environment. They serve as a review after you have successfully completed the *Prelab Activities* and *Lab Exercises*.

For each of the following problems, write a program or a program segment that performs the specified action:

1. Write the class declaration for class `Square` that has a `private` instance variable `side` of type `double` and a no-argument constructor that sets the `side` to `1.0`.

2. Write a method `setSide` for the class you defined in Coding Exercise 1, that sets the `side` variable to the argument of the method. Also make sure that the `side` is not less than `0.0`. If it is, keep the default setting.

3. Write a method `getSide` for the class you modified in Coding Exercise 2 that retrieves the value of instance variable `side`.

Postlab Activities

Name:

Coding Exercises

4. Define another constructor for the class that you modified in Coding Exercise 3 that takes one argument, the side, and uses the Square's *set* method to set the side.

5. Write a method computeArea for the class that you modified in Coding Exercise 4 that computes the area of a Square.

6. Define a toSquareString method for the class that you modified in Coding Exercise 5 that will return a String containing the value of side and the area of the Square.

Postlab Activities

Name:

Coding Exercises

7. Define application class TestSquare to test the Square class you defined in Coding Exercises 1–6. Ensure that all your methods and constructors work properly.

Postlab Activities

Name:

Programming Challenges

Name: _____   Date:_____

Section: _____

The *Programming Challenges* are more involved than the *Coding Exercises* and may require a significant amount of time to complete. Write a Java program for each of the problems in this section. The answers to these problems are available at www.deitel.com, www.prenhall.com/deitel and on the *Java Multimedia Cyber Classroom: Fifth Edition*. Pseudocode, hints or sample output are provided to aid you in your programming.

1. Create a class `Rectangle`. The class has attributes `length` and `width`, each of which defaults to `1`. It has methods that calculate the perimeter and the area of the `Rectangle`. It has *set* and *get* methods for both `length` and `width`. The *set* methods should verify that `length` and `width` are each floating-point numbers larger than `0.0` and less than `20.0`; otherwise, the *set* methods should set the values to their default values. Write a program to test class `Rectangle`.

Hints:

*   This class is very similar to the class you developed in the *Coding Exercises* section.

*   Your output should appear as follows:

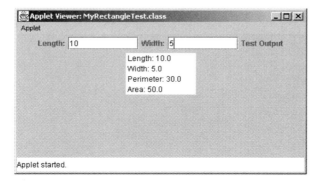

Postlab Activities   Name:

Programming Challenges

2. Create a more sophisticated `Rectangle` class than the one you created in Exercise 8.8. This class stores only the Cartesian coordinates of the four corners of the `Rectangle`. The constructor calls a *set* method that accepts four sets of coordinates and verifies that each of these is in the first quadrant with no single *x*- or *y*-coordinate larger than `20.0`. The *set* method also verifies that the supplied coordinates do, in fact, specify a `Rectangle`. Display an error message if the coordinates do not meet the specified criteria. Provide methods to calculate the `length`, `width`, `perimeter` and `area`. The `length` is the larger of the two dimensions. Include method `isSquare`, which returns `true` if the `Rectangle` is a square. Write a program to test class `Rectangle`.

Hints:

*   Your output should appear as follows:

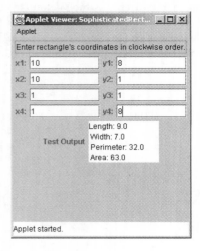

Object-Oriented Programming: Inheritance

Objectives

- To understand how inheritance promotes software reusability.
- To understand the notions of superclasses and subclasses.
- To be able to create new classes that inherit from existing classes and absorb their attributes and behaviors.
- To understand access modifier `protected`.
- To be able to access superclass members with `super`.
- To understand the use of constructors in inheritance hierarchies.

Assignment Checklist

Name: _____   Date:_____

Section: _____

Exercises	Assigned: Circle assignments		Date Due
Prelab Activities			
Matching	YES	NO	
Fill in the Blank	YES	NO	
Short Answer	YES	NO	
Programming Output	YES	NO	
Correct the Code	YES	NO	
Lab Exercises			
Exercise 1 — Employee Hierarchy	YES	NO	
Follow-Up Question and Activity	1		
Exercise 2 — Display Shapes	YES	NO	
Follow-Up Question and Activity	1		
Postlab Activities			
Coding Exercises	1, 2, 3		
Programming Challenges	1, 2		

Prelab Activities

Matching

Name: _____   **Date:**_____

Section: _____

After reading Chapter 9 of *Java How to Program: Fifth Edition,* answer the given questions. The questions are intended to test and reinforce your understanding of key concepts. You may answer the questions before or during the lab.

For each term in the left column, write the letter for the description from the right column that best matches the term.

Term	Description
____ 1. composition	a) A class that a subclass explicitly extends.
____ 2. `this`	b) Term used to describe the case when a subclass method is defined with the same signature as a superclass method.
____ 3. class hierarchy	c) Keyword used to refer to an object's superclass members.
____ 4. `protected`	d) "Has a" relationship.
____ 5. inheritance	e) A class that a subclass does not explicitly extend; however, the subclass still has an *is-a* relationship with the class.
____ 6. `super`	f) Such members can be accessed only by the class in which they are defined.
____ 7. direct superclass	g) Method that all objects have.
____ 8. `public`	h) A set of classes related by inheritance.
____ 9. override	i) "Is a" relationship.
____ 10. `private`	j) Can be accessed by any class.
____ 11. `toString`	k) Such members can be accessed in the class in which they are defined, and in all subclasses of that class.
____ 12. indirect superclass	l) Keyword that refers to current object.

Prelab Activities

Name: _____

Fill in the Blank

Name: _____   Date:_____

Section: _____

Fill in the blanks for each of the following statements:

13. Concatenating a string and any object results in an implicit call to the object's _____ method to obtain a string representation of the object, then the strings are concatenated.

14. A(n) _____ object is generally larger than an object of its corresponding _____ because the _____ typically adds instance variables and methods of its own.

15. In a(n) _____ relationship, an object has a reference to an object of another class as a member.

16. In a(n) _____ relationship, an object of a subclass type may also be treated as an object of the superclass type.

17. One of the keys to object-oriented programming is achieving software reusability through _____.

18. A subclass cannot directly access _____ members of its superclass.

19. The direct superclass of a subclass is the superclass from which the subclass inherits (specified by the key-word _____ in the first line of a class declaration).

20. With _____ inheritance, a class is derived from one superclass. Java does not support _____ inheritance.

21. A subclass inherits the members of its superclass that are declared with the access specifiers _____ and _____.

22. The original `toString` method of class _____www.prenhall.com/deitel is normally overridden by a subclass.

Prelab Activities   Name:

Short Answer

Name: _____   Date:_____

Section: _____

In the space provided, answer each of the given questions. Your answers should be as concise as possible; aim for two or three sentences.

23. How does inheritance promote software reusability?

24. Explain **protected** member access.

25. Explain the difference between composition (i.e., the "has-a" relationship) and inheritance (i.e., the "is-a" relationship).

Prelab Activities   Name:

Short Answer

26. When an object of a subclass is created, the constructor for that subclass object is invoked to initialize the subclass object. Explain the complete details of initializing an object of class `Cylinder` with four arguments. Assume the `Point3-Circle4-Cylinder` hierarchy discussed in this chapter.

27. Explain how to invoke a superclass method from a subclass method for the case in which the subclass method overrides a superclass method and the case in which the subclass method does not override a superclass method.

Prelab Activities

Name:

Programming Output

Name: _____   Date: _____

Section: _____

For each of the given program segments, read the code and write the output in the space provided below each program. [*Note*: Do not execute these programs on a computer.]

For questions 28–30 uses classes Point *and* Circle *defined in Fig. L 9.1 and Fig. L 9.2, respectively.*

```java
1   // Point.java
2   // Point class declaration represents an x-y coordinate pair.
3
4   public class Point {
5      private int x;  // x part of coordinate pair
6      private int y;  // y part of coordinate pair
7
8      // no-argument constructor
9      public Point()
10     {
11        // implicit call to Object constructor occurs here
12        System.out.println( "Point no-argument constructor: " + this );
13     }
14
15     // constructor
16     public Point( int xValue, int yValue )
17     {
18        // implicit call to Object constructor occurs here
19        System.out.println( "Point constructor: " + this );
20     }
21
22     // finalizer
23     protected void finalize()
24     {
25        System.out.println( "Point finalizer: " + this );
26     }
27
28     // set x in coordinate pair
29     public void setX( int xValue )
30     {
31        x = xValue;  // no need for validation
32     }
33
34     // return x from coordinate pair
35     public int getX()
36     {
37        return x;
38     }
39
40     // set y in coordinate pair
41     public void setY( int yValue )
42     {
43        y = yValue;  // no need for validation
44     }
```

Fig. L 9.1   Point.java. (Part 1 of 2.)

Prelab Activities

Name:

Programming Output

```
45
46       // return y from coordinate pair
47       public int getY()
48       {
49          return y;
50       }
51
52       // return String representation of Point4 object
53       public String toString()
54       {
55          return "[" + getX() + ", " + getY() + "]";
56       }
57
58    } // end class Point
```

Fig. L 9.1   Point.java. (Part 2 of 2.)

```
1     // Circle.java
2     // Circle5 class declaration.
3
4     public class Circle extends Point {
5
6        private double radius;   // Circle's radius
7
8        // no-argument constructor
9        public Circle()
10       {
11          // implicit call to Point constructor occurs here
12          System.out.println( "Circle no-argument constructor: " + this );
13       }
14
15       // constructor
16       public Circle( int xValue, int yValue, double radiusValue )
17       {
18          super( xValue, yValue );   // call Point constructor
19          setRadius( radiusValue );
20
21          System.out.println( "Circle constructor: " + this );
22       }
23
24       // finalizer
25       protected void finalize()
26       {
27          System.out.println( "Circle finalizer: " + this );
28
29          super.finalize();   // call superclass finalize method
30       }
31
32       // set radius
33       public void setRadius( double radiusValue )
34       {
35          radius = ( radiusValue < 0.0 ? 0.0 : radiusValue );
36       }
37
```

Fig. L 9.2   Circle.java. (Part 1 of 2.)

Prelab Activities   Name:

Programming Output

```
38    // return radius
39    public double getRadius()
40    {
41        return radius;
42    }
43
44    // calculate and return diameter
45    public double getDiameter()
46    {
47        return 2 * getRadius();
48    }
49
50    // calculate and return circumference
51    public double getCircumference()
52    {
53        return Math.PI * getDiameter();
54    }
55
56    // calculate and return area
57    public double getArea()
58    {
59        return Math.PI * getRadius() * getRadius();
60    }
61
62    // return String representation of Circle5 object
63    public String toString()
64    {
65        return "Center = " + super.toString() + "; Radius = " + getRadius();
66    }
67
68 } // end class Circle
```

Fig. L 9.2   Circle.java. (Part 2 of 2.)

28. What is output by the following program?.

```
1    public class Test {
2
3      public static void main( String args[] )
4      {
5          Circle circle1 = new Circle( 10, 22, 9.9 );
6          System.out.println();
7          Circle circle2 = new Circle( 19, 84, 1.1 );
8      }
9
10   } // end class Test
```

Your answer:

Prelab Activities   Name:

Programming Output

29. What is output if the following lines are added to the end of the `main` method of class `Test` in Programming Output Exercise 28?

```
1   System.out.println();
2   circle1 = null;
3   circle2 = null;
4
5   System.gc();
```

Your answer:

30. What is the output of the following program?

```
1   public class Test {
2
3     public static void main( String args[] )
4     {
5        Point point1 = new Point( 10, 22 );
6        Circle circle1 = new Circle( point1.getX(), point1.getY(), 9.9 );
7        System.out.println();
8        Point point2 = new Point( 19, 84 );
9        Circle circle2 = new Circle( point2.getX(), point2.getY(), 1.1 );
10
11       System.out.println();
12       point1 = null;
13       point2 = null;
14       circle1 = null;
15       circle2 = null;
16
17       System.gc();
18    }
19
20  } // end class Test
```

Prelab Activities

Name:

Programming Output

Your answer:

Prelab Activities   Name:

Correct the Code

Name: _____   Date:_____

Section: _____

Determine if there is an error in each of the following program segments. If there is an error, specify whether it is a logic error or a syntax error, circle the error in the program and write the corrected code in the space provided after each problem. If the code does not contain an error, write "no error." [*Note*: There may be more than one error in a program segment.]

For questions 31–33 assume the definitions of classes `Circle` *and* `Cylinder` *in Fig. L 9.3 and Fig. L 9.4.*

```java
1   // Circle.java
2   // Circle class inherits from Point and accesses Point's
3   // private x and y via Point's public methods.
4
5   public class Circle extends Point {
6
7      private double radius;  // Circle's radius
8
9      // no-argument constructor
10     public Circle()
11     {
12        // implicit call to Point constructor occurs here
13     }
14
15     // constructor
16     public Circle( int xValue, int yValue, double radiusValue )
17     {
18        super( xValue, yValue );  // call Point constructor explicitly
19        setRadius( radiusValue );
20     }
21
22     // set radius
23     public void setRadius( double radiusValue )
24     {
25        radius = ( radiusValue < 0.0 ? 0.0 : radiusValue );
26     }
27
28     // return radius
29     public double getRadius()
30     {
31        return radius;
32     }
33
34     // calculate and return diameter
35     public double getDiameter()
36     {
37        return 2 * getRadius();
38     }
39
```

Fig. L 9.3   `Circle.java`. (Part 1 of 2.)

Prelab Activities

Name:

Correct the Code

```
40     // calculate and return circumference
41     public double getCircumference()
42     {
43        return Math.PI * getDiameter();
44     }
45
46     // calculate and return area
47     public double getArea()
48     {
49        return Math.PI * getRadius() * getRadius();
50     }
51
52     // return String representation of Circle object
53     public String toString()
54     {
55        return "Center = " + super.toString() + "; Radius = " + getRadius();
56     }
57
58  } // end class Circle
```

Fig. L 9.3   Circle.java. (Part 2 of 2.)

```
1   Cylinder.java
2   // Cylinder class inherits from Circle.
3
4   public class Cylinder extends Circle {
5      private double height;  // Cylinder's height
6
7      // no-argument constructor
8      public Cylinder()
9      {
10        // implicit call to Circle constructor occurs here
11     }
12
13     // set Cylinder's height
14     public void setHeight( double heightValue )
15     {
16        height = ( heightValue < 0.0 ? 0.0 : heightValue );
17     }
18
19     // get Cylinder's height
20     public double getHeight()
21     {
22        return height;
23     }
24
25     // calculate Cylinder volume
26     public double getVolume()
27     {
28        return super.getArea() * getHeight();
29     }
30
31  } // end class Cylinder
```

Fig. L 9.4   Cylinder.java.

Prelab Activities   Name:

Correct the Code

31. The following constructor, when inserted into class `Cylinder`, should invoke a `Circle` constructor to initialize the `Circle` part of a `Cylinder` object.

```
1   // constructor
2   public Cylinder( int xValue, int yValue, double radiusValue, double heightValue )
3   {
4       super( xValue, yValue ); // call Circle constructor
5       setHeight( heightValue );
6   }
```

Your answer:

32. The following `toString` method, when inserted into class `Cylinder`, should return a string consisting of the `Cylinder`'s center, radius and height.

```
1   // return String representation of Cylinder object
2   public String toString()
3   {
4       return toString() + "; Height = " + getHeight();
5   }
```

Your answer:

Prelab Activities

Name: _____

Correct the Code

33. The following `toString` method, when inserted into class `Cylinder`, should use `Circle`'s `getArea` method to help calculate the surface area of a `Cylinder`.

```
1    // override Circle method getArea to calculate Cylinder area
2    public double getArea()
3    {
4       return 2 * getArea() + getCircumference() * getHeight();
5    }
```

Your answer:

Lab Exercises

Lab Exercise 1 — Employee Hierarchy

Name: _____   Date:_____

Section: _____

This problem is intended to be solved in a closed-lab session with a teaching assistant or instructor present. The problem is divided into six parts:

1. Lab Objectives

2. Description of the Problem

3. Sample Output

4. Program Template (Fig. L 9.6–Fig. L 9.10)

5. Problem-Solving Tips

6. Follow-Up Question and Activity

The program template represents a complete working Java program, with one or more key lines of code replaced with comments. Read the problem description and examine the sample output; then study the template code. Using the problem-solving tips as a guide, replace the /* */ comments with Java code. Compile and execute the program. Compare your output with the sample output provided. Then answer the follow-up question. The source code for the template is available at www.deitel.com and www.prenhall.com/deitel.

Lab Objectives

This lab was designed to reinforce programming concepts from Chapter 9 of *Java How to Program: Fifth Edition*. In this lab, you will practice:

- Building a class hierarchy.

- Creating subclass constructors that properly invoke superclass constructors.

- Using classes in a class hierarchy.

The follow-up question and activity also will give you practice:

- Adding a class to an existing class hierarchy.

Description of the Problem

Create the classes in the class diagram Fig. L 9.5. An Employee should have a first name, last name and social-security number. In addition, a SalariedEmployee should have a weekly salary; an HourlyEmployee should have a wage and a number of hours worked and a CommissionEmployee should have a commission rate and gross sales. Each class should have appropriate constructors, *set* methods and *get* methods. Write a program that instantiates objects of each of these classes and outputs all the information associated with each object (including the inherited information).

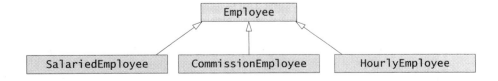

Fig. L 9.5   Employee class diagram.

Lab Exercises   Name:

Lab Exercise 1 — Employee Hierarchy

Sample Output

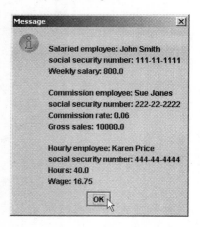

Program Template

```
1   // Lab 1: Employee.java
2   // Employee superclass.
3
4   public class Employee {
5      /* Declare instance variables for the first name,
6         last name and social security number. */
7
8      // constructor
9      /* Declare a constructor with three parameters that are used to
10        initialize the first name, last name and social security number. */
11
12     // set methods
13     /* Create set methods for every instance variable. */
14
15     // get methods
16     /* Create get methods for every instance variable. */
17
18     // return String representation of Employee object
19     /* Create a toString method that returns a String containing the first name
20        and last name separated by a space. Then, append a newline and the social
21        security number. */
22
23  } // end class Employee
```

Fig. L 9.6   Employee.java.

```
1   // Lab 1: CommissionEmployee.java
2   // CommissionEmployee class derived from Employee.
3
4   /* Write a class header in which class CommissionEmployee
5      inherits from class Employee */
6
7      /* Declare instance variables for gross sales and commission rate. */
```

Fig. L 9.7   CommissionEmployee.java. (Part 1 of 2.)

Lab Exercises　　　　　　　　　　　　　　　　　Name:

Lab Exercise 1 — Employee Hierarchy

```
8
9      // constructor
10     /* Declare a constructor that initializes all the data for a CommissionEmployee,
11        including the data originally defined in class Employee. */
12
13     // set methods
14     /* Create set methods for every instance variable. */
15
16     // get methods
17     /* Create get methods for every instance variable. */
18
19     // return String representation of CommissionEmployee object
20     /* Create a toString method that outputs the complete information
21        for a CommissionEmployee. */
22
23  } // end class CommissionEmployee
```

Fig. L 9.7　　CommissionEmployee.java. (Part 2 of 2.)

```
1   // Lab 1: HourlyEmployee.java
2   // HourlyEmployee class derived from Employee.
3
4   /* Write a class header in which class HourlyEmployee
5      inherits from class Employee */
6
7      /* Declare instance variables for wages and hours worked. */
8
9      // constructor
10     /* Declare a constructor that initializes all the data for a HourlyEmployee,
11        including the data originally defined in class Employee. */
12
13     // set methods
14     /* Create set methods for every instance variable. */
15
16     // get methods
17     /* Create get methods for every instance variable. */
18
19     // return String representation of HourlyEmployee object
20     /* Create a toString method that outputs the complete information
21        for a HourlyEmployee. */
22
23  } // end class HourlyEmployee
```

Fig. L 9.8　　HourlyEmployee.java.

```
1   // Lab 1: SalariedEmployee.java
2   // SalariedEmployee class derived from Employee.
3
4   /* Write a class header in which class SalariedEmployee
5      inherits from class Employee */
6
7      /* Declare an instance variable for the weekly salary. */
8
```

Fig. L 9.9　　SalariedEmployee.java. (Part 1 of 2.)

Lab Exercises   Name:

Lab Exercise 1 — Employee Hierarchy

```
 9     // constructor
10     /* Declare a constructor that initializes all the data for a SalariedEmployee,
11        including the data originally defined in class Employee. */
12
13     // set methods
14     /* Create a set method for the instance variable. */
15
16     // get methods
17     /* Create a get method for the instance variable. */
18
19     // return String representation of SalariedEmployee object
20     /* Create a toString method that outputs the complete information
21        for a SalariedEmployeex. */
22
23   } // end class SalariedEmployee
```

Fig. L 9.9   SalariedEmployee.java. (Part 2 of 2.)

```
 1    // Lab 1: EmployeeTest.java
 2    // Employee hierarchy test program.
 3    import java.text.DecimalFormat;
 4    import javax.swing.JOptionPane;
 5
 6    public class EmployeeTest {
 7
 8       public static void main( String[] args )
 9       {
10          DecimalFormat twoDigits = new DecimalFormat( "0.00" );
11
12          // Create employees
13          /* Create SalariedEmployee John Smith with social security number
14             111-11-1111 and weekly salary $800.00. */
15          /* Create SalariedEmployee Sue Jones with social security number
16             222-22-2222 with gross sales of $10000 and a commission rate of .06. */
17          /* Create SalariedEmployee Karen Price with social security number
18             444-44-4444 an hourly salary of $16.75 and 40 hours worked. */
19
20          // output each employee
21          /* Create a String called output and assign it the String representation
22             of the three employee objects separated by newlines. */
23
24          JOptionPane.showMessageDialog( null, output );   // display output
25          System.exit( 0 );
26
27       } // end main
28
29    } // end class EmployeeTest
```

Fig. L 9.10   EmployeeTest.java.

Problem-Solving Tips

1. The constructor for each class that extends Employee should invoke the Employee constructor and pass the first name, last name and social security number to the Employee constructor.

Lab Exercises   Name:

Lab Exercise 1 — Employee Hierarchy

2. The `toString` method for each class that extends `Employee` should invoke `Employee`'s `toString` method to obtain the `String` representation of the first name, last name and social security number, then append additional information to the returned `String`.

3. If you have any questions as you proceed, ask your lab instructor for assistance.

Follow-Up Question and Activity

1. Enhance the class hierarchy of Lab Exercise 1 to include class `BasePlusCommissionEmployee` (shown in the class diagram of Fig. L 9.11). A `BasePlusCommissionEmployee` has the same characteristics as a `CommissionEmployee` except that a `BasePlusCommissionEmployee` also receives a base salary each week. The class's constructor should invoke class `CommissionEmployee`'s constructor and the class's `toString` method should invoke class `CommissionEmployee`'s `toString` method. After creating class `BasePlus-CommissionEmployee` enhance your program from Lab Exercise 1 to instantiate one object of this new class and output the object's information (including the inherited information). The output should appear as follows:

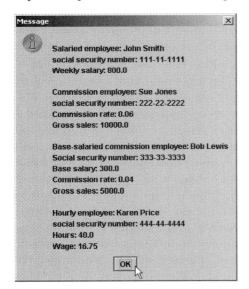

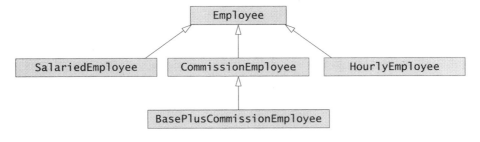

Fig. L 9.11   `Employee` inheritance hierarchy with an additional class.

Lab Exercises   Name:

Lab Exercise 2 — Display Shapes

Name: _____   Date:_____

Section: _____

This problem is intended to be solved in a closed-lab session with a teaching assistant or instructor present. The problem is divided into six parts:

1. Lab Objectives
2. Description of the Problem
3. Sample Output
4. Program Template (Fig. L 9.13–Fig. L 9.17)
5. Problem-Solving Tips
6. Follow-Up Question and Activity

The program template represents a complete working Java program, with one or more key lines of code replaced with comments. Read the problem description and examine the sample output; then study the template code. Using the problem-solving tips as a guide, replace the /* */ comments with Java code. Compile and execute the program. Compare your output with the sample output provided. Then answer the follow-up question. The source code for the template is available at www.deitel.com and www.prenhall.com/deitel.

Lab Objectives

This lab was designed to reinforce programming concepts from Chapter 9 of *Java How to Program: Fifth Edition*. In this lab, you will practice:

- Understanding the relationship between superclass and subclass objects.
- Understanding inheritance.
- Understanding polymorphism.

The follow-up question and activity also will give you practice:

- Adding a new class into an existing class hierarchy.

Description of the Problem

(Drawing Applet) Create a drawing applet that randomly draws lines, rectangles and ovals. For this purpose, create a set of "smart" shape classes where objects of these classes know how to draw themselves if provided with a Graphics object that tells them where to draw (i.e., the applet's Graphics object allows a shape to draw on the applet's background). The class names should be MyLine, MyRect and MyOval, and they should be part of the class hierarchy shown in the class diagram of Fig. L 9.12. (Use random numbers to pick the shape type and the coordinates of each shape.)

Lab Exercises   Name:

Lab Exercise 2 — Display Shapes

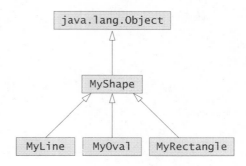

Fig. L 9.12   MyShape hierarchy.

The only data representing the coordinates of the shapes in the hierarchy should be declared in class MyShape. Lines, rectangles and ovals can all be drawn if you know two points in space. Lines require $x1$, $y1$, $x2$ and $y2$ coordinates. The drawLine method of the Graphics class will connect the two points supplied with a line. If you have the same four coordinate values ($x1$, $y1$, $x2$ and $y2$) for ovals and rectangles, you can calculate the four arguments needed to draw them. Each requires an upper-left x-coordinate value (the minimum of the two x-coordinate values), an upper-left y-coordinate value (minimum of the two y-coordinate values), a *width* (the absolute value of the difference between the two x-coordinate values) and a *height* (the absolute value of difference between the two y-coordinate values).

In addition to the common data, class MyShape should declare the following methods:

- A constructor with no arguments that sets the coordinates to 0.

- A constructor with arguments that sets the coordinates to the values supplied.

- *Set* methods, for each individual piece of data, that allow the programmer to set any piece of data independently for a shape in the hierarchy (e.g., if you have an instance variable x1, you should have a method setX1).

- *Get* methods, for each individual piece of data, that allow the programmer to retrieve any piece of data independently for a shape in the hierarchy (e.g., if you have an instance variable x1, you should have a method getX1).

- The method public void draw(Graphics g); which will be called from the applet's paint method to draw a shape on the screen. The version of this method in class MyShape should have an empty body.

All data *must* be private to class MyShape. This forces you to use proper encapsulation of the data and provide proper *set/get* methods to manipulate the data. You are not allowed to declare new data that can be derived from existing information. As explained previously, the upper-left x, upper-left y, *width* and *height* needed to draw an oval or a rectangle can be calculated if you already know two points in space. All subclasses of MyShape should provide two constructors that mimic those provided by class MyShape.

Objects of the MyOval and MyRect classes should calculate their upper-left x-coordinate, upper-left y-coordinate, *width* or *height* when they are about to draw. Never modify the $x1$, $y1$, $x2$ and $y2$ coordinates of a MyOval or MyRectangle object to prepare to draw them. Instead, use the temporary results of the calculations described above.

In your applet's paint method, create 20 random objects of classes MyLine, MyOval and MyRectangle. Use a random number from 1 to 3 as the controlling expression for a switch statement that determines which shape type to create, chooses four random coordinates to initialize the shape, then calls the shape's draw method to display it.

The paint method (for your subclass of JFrame) should draw the shape with a statement like:

```
line.draw( g );
```

where line is a MyLine variable and g is paint's Graphics object that the shape uses to draw itself on the applet.

Lab Exercises   Name:

Lab Exercise 2 — Display Shapes

Sample Output

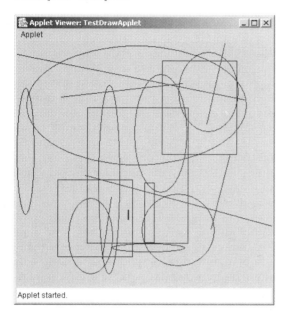

Program Template

```
1    // Lab 2: MyShape.java
2    // Definition of class MyShape.
3    import java.awt.Graphics;
4
5    public class MyShape extends Object {
6       /* Declare instance variables for the coordinates. */
7
8       // no-argument constructor
9       /* Declare a no-argument constructor that sets the coordinates to 0. */
10
11      // constructor
12      /* Declare a constructor that sets the coordinates to the supplied values. */
13
14      // abstract draw method
15      /* Declare an empty draw method that takes a single Graphics argument. */
16
17      // accessor and mutator methods for each of the four private variables:
18      /* Declare set methods for each of the four instance variables. */
19
20      /* Declare get methods for each of the four instance variables. */
21
22   } // end class MyShape
```

Fig. L 9.13   MyShape.java.

Lab Exercises   Name:

Lab Exercise 2 — Display Shapes

```
1   // Lab 2: MyLine.java
2   // Definition of class MyLine.
3   import java.awt.Graphics;
4
5   /* Write the header for class MyLine with superclass MyShape. */
6
7      // no-argument constructor
8      /* Declare a no-argument constructor that calls the superclass's
9         no-argument constructor. */
10
11     // constructor
12     /* Declare a constructor with four arguments that calls the superclass's
13        constructor with four arguments. */
14
15     // draw line
16     /* Declare a draw method with a Graphics agument. In the body of the method,
17        use the Graphics object and the MyLine's coordinates to draw a line. */
18
19  } // end class MyLine
```

Fig. L 9.14   `MyLine.java`.

```
1   // Lab 2: MyOval.java
2   // Definition of class MyOval.
3   import java.awt.Graphics;
4
5   /* Write the header for class MyOval with superclass MyShape. */
6
7      // no-argument constructor
8      /* Declare a no-argument constructor that calls the superclass's
9         no-argument constructor. */
10
11     // constructor
12     /* Declare a constructor with four arguments that calls the superclass's
13        constructor with four arguments. */
14
15     // draw oval
16     /* Declare a draw method with a Graphics agument. In the body of the method,
17        use the MyOval's coordinates to calculate the upper-left x-coordinate,
18        upper-left y-coordinate, width and height of the oval's bounding box.
19        Then, use the Graphics object to draw the oval. */
20
21  } // end class MyOval
```

Fig. L 9.15   `MyOval.java`.

```
1   // Lab 2: MyRectangle.java
2   // Definition of class MyRectangle.
3   import java.awt.Graphics;
4
5   /* Write the header for class MyRectangle with superclass MyShape. */
6
7      // no-argument constructor
8      /* Declare a no-argument constructor that calls the superclass's
9         no-argument constructor. */
```

Fig. L 9.16   `MyRectangle.java`. (Part 1 of 2.)

Lab Exercises   Name:

Lab Exercise 2 — Display Shapes

```
10
11      // constructor
12      /* Declare a constructor with four arguments that calls the superclass's
13         constructor with four arguments. */
14
15      // draw rectangle
16      /* Declare a draw method with a Graphics agument. In the body of the method,
17         use the MyRectangle's coordinates to calculate the upper-left x-coordinate,
18         upper-left y-coordinate, width and height of the rectangle. Then, use the
19         Graphics object to draw the rectangle. */
20
21   } // end class MyRectangle
```

Fig. L 9.16   MyRectangle.java. (Part 2 of 2.)

```
1    // Lab 2: TestDrawApplet.java
2    // Program randomly draws shapes.
3    import java.awt.*;
4    import javax.swing.*;
5
6    public class TestDrawApplet extends JApplet {
7
8       // draw shapes
9       public void paint( Graphics g )
10      {
11         super.paint( g );
12
13         int shapeType; // random value to determine shape to create and draw
14         int x1, y1, x2, y2; // randomly chosen coordinates for a new shape
15
16         /* Declare variables for each of the three MyShape subclasses. */
17
18         // create and draw 20 shapes
19         for ( int i = 1; i <= 20; i++ ) {
20
21            // pick random shape type
22            shapeType = ( int ) ( Math.random() * 3 ) + 1;
23
24            // pick random coordinates
25            x1 = ( int ) ( Math.random() * 400 );
26            y1 = ( int ) ( Math.random() * 400 );
27            x2 = ( int ) ( Math.random() * 400 );
28            y2 = ( int ) ( Math.random() * 400 );
29
30            switch ( shapeType ) {
31
32               case 1:
33                  /* Create a new MyLine object using the randomly chosen coordinates
34                     as arguments to the constructor and assign the new object to a
35                     MyLine variable */
36
37                  /* Write a statement that tells the MyLine object to draw itself. */
38                  break;
39
```

Fig. L 9.17   TestDrawApplet.java. (Part 1 of 2.)

Lab Exercises   Name:

Lab Exercise 2 — Display Shapes

```
40              case 2:
41                  /* Create a new MyOval object using the randomly chosen coordinates
42                     as arguments to the constructor and assign the new object to a
43                     MyOval variable */
44
45                  /* Write a statement that tells the MyOval object to draw itself. */
46                  break;
47
48              case 3:
49                  /* Create a new MyRectangle object using the randomly chosen
50                     coordinates as arguments to the constructor and assign the new
51                     object to a MyRectangle variable */
52
53                  /* Write a statement that tells the MyRectangle object to
54                     draw itself. */
55                  break;
56          } // end switch
57
58      } // end for
59
60  } // end method paint
61
62 } // end class TestDrawApplet
```

Fig. L 9.17   `TestDrawApplet.java`. (Part 2 of 2.)

Problem-Solving Tips

1. Each subclass will call one of its superclass constructors from each of the subclass constructors.

2. Remember that the data in class MyShape is private. Thus, you must use class MyShape's public methods to access the data for all shapes in the hierarchy.

3. Class MyOval and class MyRectangle are almost identical to class MyLine except for their definition of method draw. Remember to calculate the upper-left x-coordinate, upper-left y-coordinate, width and height before drawing a rectangle or oval.

4. In the default constructor of class MyShape, set all coordinates to zero. The second MyShape constructor takes four arguments that are used to initialize x1, y1, x2 and y2, respectively.

5. In the set methods of class MyShape, ensure that all coordinate values are valid; otherwise, set them to zero automatically. Remember, the upper-left corner of the drawing area has coordinate 0, 0.

6. If you have any questions as you proceed, ask your lab instructor for assistance.

Lab Exercises   Name:

Lab Exercise 2 — Display Shapes

Follow-Up Question and Activity

1. Modify the previous program to include a class MyRoundRectangle, which extends class MyShape. This class should contain two more member variables of its own, namely the arc width and arc height, that determine how to round the corners. For the purpose of this exercise, set both the width and height to 10 (this makes each corner one quarter of a circle with diameter 10). [Hint: Use the g.drawRoundRect method to draw the rounded rectangle; the last two arguments to this method are the arc width and arc height.] The output should appear as follows:

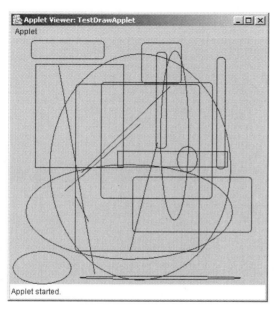

Postlab Activities

Coding Exercises

Name: _____   Date:_____

Section: _____

These coding exercises reinforce the lessons learned in the lab and provide additional programming experience outside the classroom and laboratory environment. They serve as a review after you have successfully completed the *Prelab Activities* and *Lab Exercises*.

For each of the following problems, write a program or a program segment that performs the specified action.

1. Declare the headers for the classes in the class diagram of Fig. L 9.18,

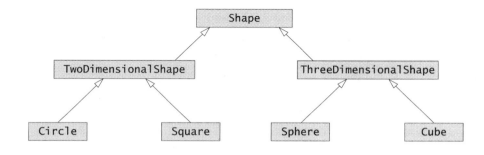

Fig. L 9.18   Inheritance hierarchy for Shapes.

Postlab Activities   Name:

Coding Exercises

2. Declare toString methods for all the classes in Coding Exericse 1. Class Shape's toString method should return the string "Shape". The toString method of each of the subclasses in the hierarchy should return a string containing the class's name, the string " is a " and the result of a call to the superclass's toString method.

3. Write an application that creates one object of each of the classes Circle, Square, Sphere and Cube, and invokes their toString methods. The output for each object should show the "is-a" relationships between that object's class and its superclasses.

Postlab Activities   Name:

Programming Challenges

Name: _____   Date: _____

Section: _____

The *Programming Challenges* are more involved than the *Coding Exercises* and may require a significant amount of time to complete. Write a Java program for each of the problems in this section. The answers to these problems are available at www.deitel.com, www.prenhall.com/deitel and on the *Java Multimedia Cyber Classroom: Fifth Edition.* Pseudocode, hints or sample output are provided to aid you in your programming.

1. Many programs written with inheritance could be written with composition instead, and vice versa. Rewrite classes Circle4 (of *Java How to Program* Fig. 9.13) and Cylinder (of *Java How to Program* Fig. 9.15) of the Point3/Circle4/Cylinder hierarchy to use composition rather than inheritance. After you do this, assess the relative merits of the two approaches for the Point3, Circle4, and Cylinder problems, as well as for object-oriented programs in general. Which approach is more natural? Why?

Hints:

*   Class Circle4 should have a Point3 variable as one of its members.
*   The Circle4 constructor should create a Point3 object and pass the coordinates to the Point3 constructor.
*   Class Circle4 will need its own *set* and *get* methods to allow clients of class Circle4 to access the private Point3 object's coordinate values.
*   Class Cylinder should have a Circle4 variable as one of its members.
*   The Cylinder constructor should create a Circle4 object and pass the coordinates to the Circle4 constructor.
*   Class Cylinder will need its own *set* and *get* methods to allow clients of class Cylinder to access the private Circle4 object's coordinate values.
*   Your output should appear as follows:

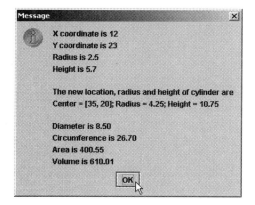

Postlab Activities   Name:

Programming Challenges

2. Rewrite the case study of Section 9.5 of *Java How to Program, Fifth Edition,* as a `Point–Square–Cube` hierarchy. Do this two ways—once via inheritance and once via composition.

Hints:

- For the composition exercise, mimic the code you wrote for Programming Challenge 1.
- For the inheritance exercise, mimic the code in Section 9.5 of *Java How to Program, Fifth Edition.*
- Your output should appear as follows:

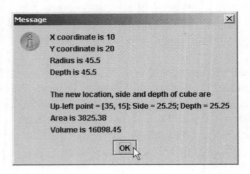

10

Object-Oriented Programming: Polymorphism

Objectives

- To understand the concept of polymorphism.
- To understand how to use overridden methods to effect polymorphism.
- To distinguish between abstract and concrete classes.
- To learn how to declare abstract methods to create abstract classes.
- To appreciate how polymorphism makes systems extensible and maintainable.
- To be able to determine an object's type at execution time.

Assignment Checklist

Name: _____　　　　　　　**Date:** _____

Section: _____

Exercises	Assigned: Circle assignments		Date Due
Prelab Activities			
Matching	YES	NO	
Fill in the Blank	YES	NO	
Short Answer	YES	NO	
Programming Output	YES	NO	
Correct the Code	YES	NO	
Lab Exercises			
Exercise 1 — Display Shapes	YES	NO	
Follow-Up Questions and Activities	1, 2		
Exercise 2 — Using Interfaces	YES	NO	
Follow-Up Question and Activity	1		
Debugging	YES	NO	
Postlab Activities			
Coding Exercises	1, 2, 3, 4, 5, 6, 7, 8		
Programming Challenge	1		

Prelab Activities

Matching

Name: _____   Date:_____

Section: _____

After reading Chapter 10 of *Java How to Program: Fifth Edition*, answer the given questions. The questions are intended to test and reinforce your understanding of key concepts. You may answer the questions before or during the lab.

For each term in the left column, write the letter for the description from the right column that best matches the term.

Term	Description
____ 1. `abstract` method	a) Typically used in place of an `abstract` class when there is no default implementation to inherit.
____ 2. `getClass` method	b) Indicates that a method cannot be overridden or that a class cannot be a superclass.
____ 3. `JFrame`	c) Method of class `JFrame` that specifies what happens when a user closes a `JFrame`.
____ 4. type-wrapper classes	d) An operator that returns true if its left operand (a variable of a reference type) has the "is-a" relationship with its right operand (a class or interface name).
____ 5. nested class	e) Uses superclass references to manipulate sets of subclass objects in a generic manner.
____ 6. concrete class	f) A class that is declared inside another class.
____ 7. polymorphism	g) Cannot be instantiated; used primarily for inheritance.
____ 8. `instanceof`	h) Provides the basic attributes and behaviors of a window.
____ 9. `final`	i) Must be overridden in a subclass; otherwise, the subclass must be declared `abstract`.
____ 10. `setDefaultCloseOperation` method	j) Returns an object that can be used to determine information about the object's class.
____ 11. `abstract` class	k) A class that can be used to create objects.
____ 12. interface	l) Classes in the `java.lang` package that are used to create objects containing values of primitive types.

Prelab Activities   Name:

Fill in the Blank

Name: _____   **Date:**_____

Section: _____

Fill in the blanks for each of the following statements:

13. With polymorphism, it becomes possible to design and implement systems that are more _____.

14. Although we cannot instantiate objects of `abstract` superclasses, we can declare _____ of abstract superclass types.

15. It is a(n) _____ error if a class with one or more `abstract` methods is not explicitly declared `abstract`.

16. It is possible to convert a superclass reference to a subclass reference by using a(n) _____.

17. A(n) _____ can contain a set of public abstract methods and/or `public static final` fields.

18. For most event-handling interfaces with more than one method, Java provides a(n) _____ that implements all the methods in the interface with empty bodies.

19. A(n) _____ has no name and is declared at the point in the program where an object of the class is created.

20. To use an interface, a class must specify that it _____ the interface and must declare every method in the interface with the signatures specified in the interface declaration.

21. Compiling a class that contains nested classes results in a separate _____ for every declared class.

Prelab Activities

Name:

Short Answer

Name: _____   Date:_____

Section: _____

In the space provided, answer each of the given questions. Your answers should be as concise as possible; aim for two or three sentences.

22. Describe the concept of polymorphism.

23. Define what it means to declare a method `final` and what it means to declare a class `final`.

24. What happens when a class specifies that it implements an interface, but does not provide declarations of all the methods in the interface?

Prelab Activities   Name:

Short Answer

25. Describe how to determine the class name of an object's class.

26. Describe the concept of an adapter class for event handling.

Prelab Activities   Name:

Programming Output

Name: _____   Date:_____

Section: _____

For each of the given program segments, read the code and write the output in the space provided below each program. [*Note*: Do not execute these programs on a computer.]

Use the class definitions in Fig. L 10.1–Fig. L 10.3 when answering Programming Output Exercises 27–30.

```java
1   // Employee.java
2   // Employee abstract superclass.
3
4   public abstract class Employee {
5       private String firstName;
6       private String lastName;
7       private String socialSecurityNumber;
8
9       // constructor
10      public Employee( String first, String last, String ssn )
11      {
12          firstName = first;
13          lastName = last;
14          socialSecurityNumber = ssn;
15      }
16
17      // set first name
18      public void setFirstName( String first )
19      {
20          firstName = first;
21      }
22
23      // return first name
24      public String getFirstName()
25      {
26          return firstName;
27      }
28
29      // set last name
30      public void setLastName( String last )
31      {
32          lastName = last;
33      }
34
35      // return last name
36      public String getLastName()
37      {
38          return lastName;
39      }
40
```

Fig. L 10.1   Employee.java. (Part 1 of 2.)

Prelab Activities

Name:

Programming Output

```
41     // set social security number
42     public void setSocialSecurityNumber( String number )
43     {
44        socialSecurityNumber = number;  // should validate
45     }
46
47     // return social security number
48     public String getSocialSecurityNumber()
49     {
50        return socialSecurityNumber;
51     }
52
53     // return String representation of Employee object
54     public String toString()
55     {
56        return getFirstName() + " " + getLastName() +
57           "\nsocial security number: " + getSocialSecurityNumber();
58     }
59
60     // abstract method overridden by subclasses
61     public abstract double earnings();
62
63  } // end abstract class Employee
```

Fig. L 10.1   `Employee.java`. (Part 2 of 2.)

```
1   // SalariedEmployee.java
2   // SalariedEmployee class extends Employee.
3
4   public class SalariedEmployee extends Employee {
5      private double weeklySalary;
6
7      // constructor
8      public SalariedEmployee( String first, String last,
9         String socialSecurityNumber, double salary )
10     {
11        super( first, last, socialSecurityNumber );
12        setWeeklySalary( salary );
13     }
14
15     // set salaried employee's salary
16     public void setWeeklySalary( double salary )
17     {
18        weeklySalary = salary < 0.0 ? 0.0 : salary;
19     }
20
21     // return salaried employee's salary
22     public double getWeeklySalary()
23     {
24        return weeklySalary;
25     }
26
27     // calculate salaried employee's pay;
28     // override abstract method earnings in Employee
29     public double earnings()
30     {
```

Fig. L 10.2   `SalariedEmployee.java`. (Part 1 of 2.)

Prelab Activities   Name:

Programming Output

```
31          return getWeeklySalary();
32      }
33
34      // return String representation of SalariedEmployee object
35      public String toString()
36      {
37          return "\nsalaried employee: " + super.toString();
38      }
39
40  } // end class SalariedEmployee
```

Fig. L 10.2   SalariedEmployee.java. (Part 2 of 2.)

```
1   // CommissionEmployee.java
2   // CommissionEmployee class extends Employee.
3
4   public class CommissionEmployee extends Employee {
5       private double grossSales;      // gross weekly sales
6       private double commissionRate;  // commission percentage
7
8       // constructor
9       public CommissionEmployee( String first, String last, String socialSecurityNumber,
10          double grossWeeklySales, double percent )
11      {
12          super( first, last, socialSecurityNumber );
13          setGrossSales( grossWeeklySales );
14          setCommissionRate( percent );
15      }
16
17      // set commission employee's rate
18      public void setCommissionRate( double rate )
19      {
20          commissionRate = ( rate > 0.0 && rate < 1.0 ) ? rate : 0.0;
21      }
22
23      // return commission employee's rate
24      public double getCommissionRate()
25      {
26          return commissionRate;
27      }
28
29      // set commission employee's weekly base salary
30      public void setGrossSales( double sales )
31      {
32          grossSales = sales < 0.0 ? 0.0 : sales;
33      }
34
35      // return commission employee's gross sales amount
36      public double getGrossSales()
37      {
38          return grossSales;
39      }
40
```

Fig. L 10.3   CommissionEmployee.java. (Part 1 of 2.)

Prelab Activities

Name:

Programming Output

```
41      // calculate commission employee's pay;
42      // override abstract method earnings in Employee
43      public double earnings()
44      {
45          return getCommissionRate() * getGrossSales();
46      }
47
48      // return String representation of CommissionEmployee object
49      public String toString()
50      {
51          return "\ncommission employee: " + super.toString();
52      }
53
54   } // end class CommissionEmployee
```

Fig. L 10.3   `CommissionEmployee.java`. (Part 2 of 2.)

27. What is output by the following code segment? Assume that the code appears in the main method of an application.

```
1   SalariedEmployee employee1 =
2       new SalariedEmployee( "June", "Bug", "123-45-6789", 1000.00 );
3
4   CommissionEmployee employee2 =
5       new CommissionEmployee( "Archie", "Tic", "987-65-4321", 15000.00, 0.10 );
6
7   System.out.println( "Employee 1:\n" + employee1.toString() );
8   System.out.println( "Employee 2:\n" + employee2.toString() );
```

Your answer:

Prelab Activities

Name:

Programming Output

28. What is output by the following code segment? Assume that the code appears in the `main` method of an application.

```
1  Employee firstEmployee =
2     new SalariedEmployee( "June", "Bug", "123-45-6789", 1000.00 );
3
4  Employee secondEmployee =
5     new CommissionEmployee( "Archie", "Tic", "987-65-4321", 15000.00, 0.10 );
6
7  System.out.println( "Employee 1:\n" + firstEmployee.toString() );
8  System.out.println( "Employee 2:\n" + secondEmployee.toString() );
```

Your answer:

29. What is output by the following code segment? Assume that the code follows the statements in Programming Output Exercise 28.

```
1  SalariedEmployee salaried = ( SalariedEmployee ) firstEmployee;
2  System.out.println( "salaried:\n" + salaried.toString() );
```

Your answer:

Prelab Activities

Name:

Programming Output

30. What is output by the following code segment? Assume that the code follows the statements in Programming Output Exercise 29.

```
1   CommissionEmployee commission = ( CommissionEmployee ) firstEmployee;
2   System.out.println( "commission:\n" + commission.toString() );
```

Your answer:

Prelab Activities   Name:

Correct the Code

Name: _____   Date:_____

Section: _____

Determine if there is an error in each of the following program segments. If there is an error, specify whether it is a logic error or a syntax error, circle the error in the program and write the corrected code in the space provided after each problem. If the code does not contain an error, write "no error." [*Note*: There may be more than one error in a program segment.]

For questions 31–33 assume the following definition of abstract class Employee.

```
1    // Abstract base class Employee.
2
3    public abstract class Employee {
4        private String firstName;
5        private String lastName;
6
7        // constructor
8        public Employee( String first, String last )
9        {
10           firstName = first;
11           lastName = last;
12       }
13
14       // get first name
15       public String getFirstName()
16       {
17           return firstName;
18       }
19
20       // get last name
21       public String getLastName()
22       {
23           return lastName;
24       }
25
26       public String toString()
27       {
28           return firstName + ' ' + lastName;
29       }
30
31       // Abstract method that must be implemented for each derived class of Employee
32       // from which objects are instantiated.
33       public abstract double earnings();
34
35   } // end class Employee
```

Prelab Activities   Name:

Correct the Code

31. The following class should inherit from abstract class **Employee**. A **TipWorker** is paid by the hour plus their tips for the week.

```java
// TipWorker.java
public final class TipWorker extends Employee {
   private double wage;    // wage per hour
   private double hours;   // hours worked for week
   private double tips;    // tips for the week

   public TipWorker( String first, String last,
      double wagePerHour, double hoursWorked, double tipsEarned )
   {
      super( first, last );   // call superclass constructor
      setWage ( wagePerHour );
      setHours( hoursWorked );
      setTips( tipsEarned );
   }

   // Set the wage
   public void setWage( double wagePerHour )
   {
      wage = ( wagePerHour < 0 ? 0 : wagePerHour );
   }

   // Set the hours worked
   public void setHours( double hoursWorked )
   {
      hours = ( hoursWorked >= 0 && hoursWorked < 168 ? hoursWorked : 0 );
   }

   public void setTips( double tipsEarned )
   {
      tips = ( tipsEarned < 0 ? 0 : tipsEarned );
   }

} // end class TipWorker
```

Your answer:

Prelab Activities

Name:

Correct the Code

32. The following code should define method `toString` of class `TipWorker` in Correct the Code Exercise 31.

```
1   public String toString()
2   {
3      return "Tip worker: " + toString();
4   }
```

Your answer:

33. The following code should input information about five `TipWorkers` from the user and then print that information and all the `TipWorkers`' calculated earnings.

```
1   // Test2.java
2   import java.text.DecimalFormat;
3   import javax.swing.JOptionPane;
4
5   public class Test2 {
6
7      public static void main( String args[] )
8      {
9         Employee employee[];
10        String output = "";
11        DecimalFormat precision2 = new DecimalFormat( "0.00" );
12
13        for ( int i = 0; i < employee.length; i++ ) {
14           String firstInput = JOptionPane.showInputDialog( "Input first name " );
15           String lastInput = JOptionPane.showInputDialog( "Input last name " );
16           String hoursInput = JOptionPane.showInputDialog( "Input hours worked " );
17           double hours = Integer.parseInt( hoursInput );
18           String tipsInput = JOptionPane.showInputDialog( "Input tips earned " );
19           double tips = Integer.parseInt( tipsInput );
20
21           employee[ i ] = new Employee( firstInput, lastInput,
22              2.63, hoursInput, tipsInput );
23
24           output += employee[ i ].toString() + " earned $" +
25              precision2.format( employee[ i ].earnings() ) + "\n";
26        }
27
28        JOptionPane.showMessageDialog( null, output,
29           "Earnings", JOptionPane.INFORMATION_MESSAGE );
30
31        System.exit( 0 );
32     }
33
34  } // end class Test2
```

Prelab Activities

Name:

Correct the Code

Your answer:

Lab Exercises

Lab Exercise 1 — Displays Shapes

Name: _____   Date:_____

Section: _____

This problem is intended to be solved in a closed-lab session with a teaching assistant or instructor present. The problem is divided into six parts:

1. Lab Objectives

2. Description of the Problem

3. Sample Output

4. Program Template (Fig. L 10.5–Fig. L 10.6)

5. Problem-Solving Tips

6. Follow-Up Questions and Activities

The program template represents a complete working Java program, with one or more key lines of code replaced with comments. Read the problem description and examine the sample output; then study the template code. Using the problem-solving tips as a guide, replace the /* */ comments with Java code. Compile and execute the program. Compare your output with the sample output provided. Then answer the follow-up questions. The source code for the template is available at www.deitel.com and www.prenhall.com/deitel.

Lab Objectives

This lab was designed to reinforce programming concepts from Chapter 10 of *Java How to Program: Fifth Edition*. In this lab, you will practice:

*   Understanding the relationship between superclass and subclass objects.

*   Understanding inheritance.

*   Understanding polymorphism.

The follow-up questions and activities also will give you practice:

*   Adding a new class into an existing class hierarchy.

Description of the Problem

(Drawing Application) Modify the drawing applet of Lab Exercise 2 of Chapter 9 to create an application that draws random lines, rectangles and ovals. [*Note:* Like an applet, a JFrame has a paint method that you can override to draw on the background of the JFrame.]

Lab Exercise 2 of Chapter 9, you created a concrete MyShape superclass with an empty draw method. However, it does not make sense to create objects of class MyShape, because there is not enough information in a MyShape object to determine which shape to draw. This is why you left the draw method empty in Lab Exercise 2 of Chapter 9.

Modify class MyShape to be an abstract class and make the draw method an abstract method of that class. Reuse classes MyLine, MyOval and MyRectangle (shown in the class diagram of Fig. L 10.4) from Lab Exercise 2 of Chapter 9.

Lab Exercises   Name:

Lab Exercise 1 — Displays Shapes

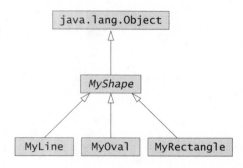

Fig. L 10.4   MyShape hierarchy.

In your application class that uses the classes of the MyShape hierarchy, the only switch or if...else logic should be to determine the type of shape object to create. (Use random numbers to pick the shape type and the coordinates of each shape.) Once an object from this hierarchy is created, it will be manipulated for the rest of its lifetime with a variable of type MyShape.

There should be no MyLine, MyOval or MyRectangle variables in the program—only MyShape variables that contain references to MyLine, MyOval and MyRectangle objects. The program should keep an array of MyShape variables containing all the shapes you create. The program's paint method should walk through the array of MyShape variables and draw every shape (i.e., call every shape's draw method).

Sample Output

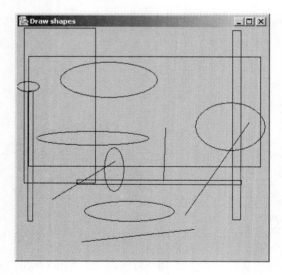

Lab Exercises   Name:

Lab Exercise 1 — Displays Shapes

Program Template

```
 1   // Lab 1: MyShape.java
 2   // Definition of class MyShape.
 3   import java.awt.Graphics;
 4
 5   /* Write a header for abstract class MyShape. */
 6      private int x1, x2, y1, y2;
 7
 8      // no-argument constructor
 9      public MyShape()
10      {
11         setX1( 0 );
12         setX2( 0 );
13         setY1( 0 );
14         setY2( 0 );
15      }
16
17      // constructor
18      public MyShape( int x1, int y1, int x2, int y2 )
19      {
20         setX1( x1 );
21         setX2( x2 );
22         setY1( y1 );
23         setY2( y2 );
24      }
25
26      // draw method
27      /* Declare abstract method draw with a Graphics parameter. */
28
29      // accessor and mutator methods for each of the
30      // four private variables:
31      public void setX1( int x )
32      {
33         x1 = ( x < 0 ? 0 : x );
34      }
35
36      public void setX2( int x )
37      {
38         x2 = ( x < 0 ? 0 : x );
39      }
40
41      public void setY1( int y )
42      {
43         y1 = ( y < 0 ? 0 : y );
44      }
45
46      public void setY2( int y )
47      {
48         y2 = ( y < 0 ? 0 : y );
49      }
50
51      public int getX1()
52      {
53         return x1;
54      }
```

Fig. L 10.5   MyShape.java. (Part 1 of 2.)

Lab Exercises   Name:

Lab Exercise 1 — Displays Shapes

```
55
56     public int getX2()
57     {
58         return x2;
59     }
60
61     public int getY1()
62     {
63         return y1;
64     }
65
66     public int getY2()
67     {
68         return y2;
69     }
70
71   } // end class MyShape
```

Fig. L 10.5   MyShape.java. (Part 2 of 2.)

```
1   // Lab 1: TestDrawWindow.java
2   // Program randomly draws shapes.
3   import java.awt.*;
4   import javax.swing.*;
5
6   public class TestDrawWindow extends JFrame {
7       /* Declare and create a 15-element array of MyShapes. */
8
9       // contructor
10      public TestDrawWindow()
11      {
12          super( "Draw shapes" );
13
14          int shapeType; // random value to determine shape to create and draw
15          int x1, y1, x2, y2; // randomly chosen coordinates for a new shape
16
17          for ( int i = 0; i < shape.length; i++ ) {
18              x1 = ( int ) ( Math.random() * 400 );
19              x2 = ( int ) ( Math.random() * 400 );
20              y1 = ( int ) ( Math.random() * 400 );
21              y2 = ( int ) ( Math.random() * 400 );
22              shapeType = ( int ) ( Math.random() * 3 ) + 1;
23
24              switch ( shapeType ) {
25
26                  case 1:  // line
27                      /* Create a MyLine object and place it in the array of MyShapes. */
28                      break;
29
30                  case 2:  // oval
31                      /* Create a MyOval object and place it in the array of MyShapes. */
32                      break;
33
34                  case 3:  // rectangle
35                      /* Create a MyRectangle object and place it in the
36                          array of MyShapes. */
```

Fig. L 10.6   TestDrawWindow.java. (Part 1 of 2.)

Lab Exercises   Name:

Lab Exercise 1 — Displays Shapes

```
37                     break;
38              } // end switch
39
40         } // end for
41
42   } // end constructor
43
44   // draw shapes
45   public void paint( Graphics g )
46   {
47      /* Write a for statement that loops through the elements of the array
48         and draws the shape in each element. */
49   }
50
51   public static void main( String args[] )
52   {
53      TestDrawWindow window = new TestDrawWindow();
54      window.setSize( 400, 400 );
55      window.setVisible( true );
56      window.setDefaultCloseOperation( JFrame.EXIT_ON_CLOSE );
57   }
58
59   } // end class TestDrawWindow
```

Fig. L 10.6   TestDrawWindow.java. (Part 2 of 2.)

Problem-Solving Tips

1. Class MyShape should not define a body for method draw, because the method should be abstract.

2. Classes MyLine, MyOval and MyRectangle are identical to Lab Exercise 2 of Chapter 9.

3. Class TestDrawWindow should not declare any variables of types MyLine, MyOval and MyRectangle. As each shape is created, simply assign it to one of the elements of the MyShape array. Remember that any MyLine, MyOval or MyRectangle object can be assigned to a MyShape variable.

4. The paint method's body should call method draw on every element of the array.

5. If you have any questions as you proceed, ask your lab instructor for assistance.

Lab Exercises   Name:

Lab Exercise 1 — Displays Shapes

Follow-Up Questions and Activities

1. Explain the line of code in your TestDrawWindow class's paint method that calls method draw. Why can that line invoke method draw on every element of the array?

2. Modify the solution to Lab Exercise 1 to include filled-in versions of ovals and rectangles, using methods fillOval and fillRect. Create subclasses of MyOval and MyRectangle to represent the filled shapes. Your output should appear as follows:

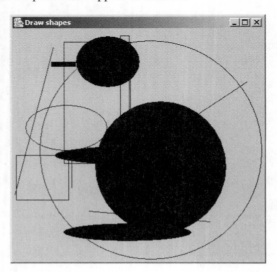

Lab Exercises   Name:

Lab Exercise 2 — Using Interfaces

Name: _____   Date:_____

Section: _____

This problem is intended to be solved in a closed-lab session with a teaching assistant or instructor present. The problem is divided into six parts:

1. Lab Objectives
2. Description of the Problem
3. Sample Output
4. Program Template (Fig. L 10.7–Fig. L 10.10)
5. Problem-Solving Tips
6. Follow-Up Question and Activity

The program template represents a complete working Java program, with one or more key lines of code replaced with comments. Read the problem description and examine the sample output; then study the template code. Using the problem-solving tips as a guide, replace the /* */ comments with Java code. Compile and execute the program. Compare your output with the sample output provided. Then answer the follow-up question. The source code for the template is available at www.deitel.com and www.prenhall.com/deitel.

Lab Objectives

This lab was designed to reinforce programming concepts from Chapter 10 of *Java How to Program: Fifth Edition*. In this lab you will practice:

*   Understanding interfaces and how they interact with classes.
*   Understanding software engineering with inheritance.

The follow-up question and activity will also give you practice:

*   Understanding implementation differences between interfaces and abstract classes.

Description of the Problem

Modify Lab Exercise 1 so that the shape classes implement an interface rather than extending an abstract class. MyLine, MyOval and MyRectangle should all extend class Object and implement the MyShape interface. The interface should specify the methods for drawing as well as the necessary *get* and *set* methods. The constructors of each of the three shape classes should set the values of the private data members appropriately. There is no superclass from which to inherit default implementations of methods, so MyLine, MyOval and MyRectangle must each define their own *get* and *set* methods.

   Classes MyLine, MyOval and MyRectangle should implement the methods declared in the MyShape interface. Those methods are:

*   Set methods for each individual piece of data that allow the programmer to independently set any piece of data for a shape in the hierarchy (e.g., if you have an instance variable x1, you should have a method setX1).
*   Get methods for each individual piece of data that allow the programmer to independently retrieve any piece of data for a shape in the hierarchy (e.g., if you have an instance variable x1, you should have a method getX1).

Lab Exercises   Name:

Lab Exercise 2 — Using Interfaces

- The method

  ```
  public void draw( Graphics g );
  ```

- These classes should each contain a no-argument constructor that sets the coordinates to 0 and a constructor with arguments that sets the coordinates to the supplied values.

If implemented correctly, the shape classes and MyShape interface can be tested using the test program created in Lab Exercise 1 without any modifications.

Sample Output

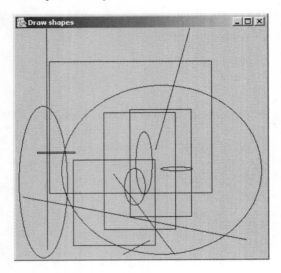

Program Template

```
1   // Lab 2: MyShape.java
2   // Declaration of interface MyShape.
3   import java.awt.Graphics;
4
5   /* Declare the header for interface MyShape. */
6
7      // method to draw the shape
8      /* Declare header for method draw. */
9
10     // set and get methods for each of the four private variables
11     /* Declare header for method setX1. */
12
13     /* Declare header for method setX2. */
14
15     /* Declare header for method setY1. */
16
17     /* Declare header for method setY2. */
18
19     /* Declare header for method getX1. */
20
21     /* Declare header for method getX2. */
```

Fig. L 10.7   MyShape.java. (Part 1 of 2.)

Lab Exercises   Name:

Lab Exercise 2 — Using Interfaces

```
22
23      /* Declare header for method getY1. */
24
25      /* Declare header for method getY2. */
26
27   } // end interface MyShape
```

Fig. L 10.7   MyShape.java. (Part 2 of 2.)

```
1    // Lab 2: MyLine.java
2    // Declaration of class MyLine.
3
4    /* Write a header for class MyLine that extends Object and implements MyShape. */
5
6        /* Declare any necessary instance variables. */
7
8        /* Declare a no-argument constructor for class MyLine. */
9
10       /* Declare a constructor with parameters representing the
11           coordinates of the line. */
12
13       // draw line
14       /* Implement method draw, that draws a line with the MyLine's coordinates. */
15
16       /* Implement the set and get methods for the private data members. */
17
18   } // end class MyLine
```

Fig. L 10.8   MyLine.java.

```
1    // Lab 2: MyOval.java
2    // Declaration of class MyOval.
3
4    /* Write a header for class MyOval that extends Object and implements MyShape. */
5
6        /* Declare any necessary instance variables. */
7
8        /* Declare a no-argument constructor for class MyOval. */
9
10       /* Declare a constructor with parameters representing the
11           coordinates of the oval. */
12
13       // draw oval
14       /* Implement method draw, that draws an oval with the MyOval's coordinates. */
15
16       /* Implement the set and get methods for the private data members. */
17
18   } // end class MyOval
```

Fig. L 10.9   MyOval.java.

```
1    // Lab 2: MyRectangle.java
2    // Declaration of class MyRectangle.
3
```

Fig. L 10.10   MyRectangle.java. (Part 1 of 2.)

Lab Exercises   Name:

Lab Exercise 2 — Using Interfaces

```
 4   /* Write a header for class MyRectangle that extends Object and implements MyShape. */
 5
 6       /* Declare any necessary instance variables. */
 7
 8       /* Declare a no-argument constructor for class MyRectangle. */
 9
10       /* Declare a constructor with parameters representing the
11          coordinates of the rectangle. */
12
13       // draw oval
14       /* Implement method draw, that draws an oval with the MyRectangle's coordinates. */
15
16       /* Implement the set and get methods for the private data members. */
17
18   } // end class MyRectangle
```

Fig. L 10.10   MyRectangle.java. (Part 2 of 2.)

Problem-Solving Tips

1. Note that class TestDrawWindow is not shown with the template code because it is identical to the version in Lab Exercise 1. You should simply reuse that version of the class.

2. Ensure that classes MyLine, MyOval and MyRectangle implement all the methods declared in the MyShape interface. Remember that the interfaces do not provide default implementations of methods, so you must implement the methods of the interface; otherwise, the new class must be an abstract class.

3. The default constructor of MyLine, MyOval and MyRectangle should set all of the coordinates to zero. The second constructor should receive x1, y1, x2 and y2 and use them to initialize the appropriate instance variables.

4. Validate the values in the set methods of the three shape classes.

5. If you have any questions as you proceed, ask your lab instructor for assistance.

Follow-Up Question and Activity

1. Compare Lab Exercise 1 and Lab Exercise 2. Discuss the benefits and disadvantages between extending a class called MyShape and implementing an interface called MyShape.

Lab Exercises　　　　　　　　　　Name:

Debugging

Name: _____　　　　　　Date: _____

Section: _____

The program in this section does not compile. Fix all the syntax errors so that the program will compile success-fully. Once the program compiles, execute the program, and compare the output with the sample output; then elim-inate any logic errors that may exist. The sample output demonstrates what the program's output should be once the program's code is corrected. The source code is available at www.deitel.com and at www.prenhall.com/deitel.

Sample Output

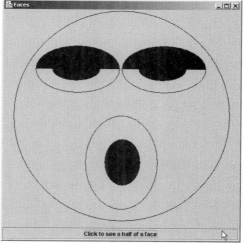

Lab Exercises   Name:

Debugging

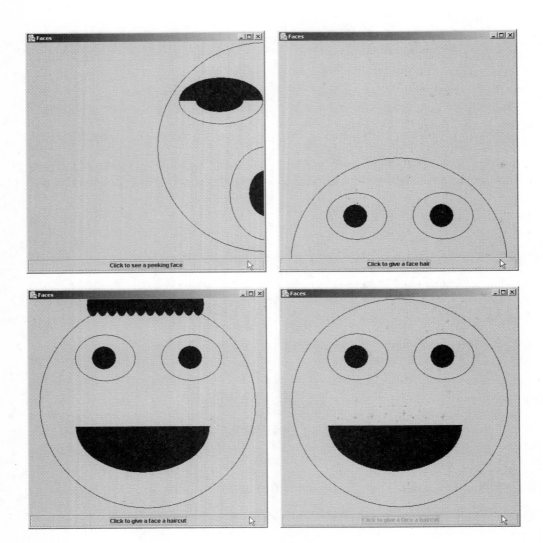

Broken Code

```
1    // Debugging Chapter 10: Face.java
2    // Declaration of class Face
3    import java.awt.*;
4
5    public class Face {
6
7        private int x = 25, y = 25;
8        private int width, height;
9
10       // all faces have same head
11       public Face()
12
13           width = 450;
```

Fig. L 10.11   Face.java. (Part 1 of 2.)

Lab Exercises   Name:

Debugging

```
14          height = 450;
15
16      public Face( int x, int y )
17
18          this();
19          x = x;
20          y = y;
21
22      public void drawHead( Graphics g )
23      {
24          g.drawOval( x, y, width, height );
25      }
26
27      public void drawEyes( Graphics g )
28      {
29          g.drawOval( x + 75, y + 75, 125, 100 );
30          g.drawOval( x + 255, y + 75, 125, 100 );
31          g.fillOval( x + 110, y + 100, 50, 50 );
32          g.fillOval( x + 290, y + 100, 50, 50 );
33      }
34
35      // abstract drawMouth method
36      public abstract void drawMouth( Graphics g );
37
38      // abstract draw method
39      public abstract void draw( Graphics g );
40
41  }   // end class Face
```

Fig. L 10.11 `Face.java`. (Part 2 of 2.)

```
1   // Debugging Chapter 10: HappyFace.java
2   // Declaration of class HappyFace
3   import java.awt.*;
4
5   public class HappyFace {
6       boolean hair = true;
7
8       // call default superclass constructor
9       public HappyFace()
10
11          width = 450;
12          height = 450;
13
14      public HappyFace( int x, int y )
15
16          Face( "x", "y" );
17
18
19      public HappyFace( boolean hair )
20      {
21          if ( hair )
22              this.hair = true;
23          Face();
24      }
25
```

Fig. L 10.12 `HappyFace.java`. (Part 1 of 2.)

Lab Exercises

Name:

Debugging

```
26      public void drawMouth( Graphics g )
27      {
28         g.drawLine( x + 75, y + 275, x + 355, y + 275 );
29         g.fillArc( x + 75, y + 175, 280, 200, 180, 180 );
30      }
31
32      public void drawHair( Graphics g )
33      {
34         for ( int i = x + 75, i <= x + 300, i += 20 );
35            g.fillOval( x + i, y - 15, 25, 50 );
36      }
37
38      private void drawHappy()
39      {
40         drawHead( g );
41         drawEyes( g );
42         drawMouth( g );
43
44         if ( hair )
45            drawHair( g );
46      }
47
48   } // end class HappyFace
```

Fig. L 10.12   `HappyFace.java`. (Part 2 of 2.)

```
1    // Debugging Chapter 10: SadFace.java
2    // Declaration of class SadFace
3    import java.awt.*;
4
5    public class SadFace {
6
7       // call default superclass constructor
8       public SadFace()
9
10         width = 450;
11         height = 450;
12
13      public SadFace( int x, int y)
14
15         Face( "x", "y" );
16
17      public void drawTear( Graphics g )
18      {
19         g.fillOval( x + 325, y + 180, 25, 50 );
20         g.fillOval( x + 325, y + 240, 25, 50 );
21      }
22
23      public void drawMouth( Graphics g )
24      {
25         g.drawLine( x + 75, y + 350, x + 355, y + 350 );
26         g.fillArc( x + 75, y + 250, 280, 200, 0, 180 );
27      }
28
29      private void drawSad()
30      {
```

Fig. L 10.13   `SadFace.java`. (Part 1 of 2.)

Lab Exercises

Name:

Debugging

```
31          drawHead( g );
32          drawEyes( g );
33          drawTear( g );
34          drawMouth( g );
35      }
36
37  } // end class SadFace
```

Fig. L 10.13　SadFace.java. (Part 2 of 2.)

```
1   // Debugging Chapter 10: AngryFace.java
2   // Declaration of class AngryFace
3   import java.awt.*;
4
5   public class AngryFace {
6
7       // call default superclass constructor
8       public AngryFace()
9
10          width = 450;
11          height = 450;
12
13      public AngryFace( int x, int y)
14
15          Face( "x", "y" );
16
17
18      public int drawEyes( Graphics g)
19      {
20          g.drawOval( x + 45, y + 75, 175, 100 );
21          g.drawOval( x + 225, y + 75, 175, 100 );
22          g.fillOval( x + 80, y + 100, 100, 50 );
23          g.fillOval( x + 260, y + 100, 100, 50 );
24          g.fillArc( x + 45, y + 75, 175, 100, 180, -180 );
25          g.fillArc( x + 225, y + 75, 175, 100, 180, -180 );
26      }
27
28      public void drawMouth( Graphics g )
29      {
30          g.drawOval( x + 150, y + 225, 150, 200 );
31          g.fillOval( x + 190, y + 275, 75, 100 );
32      }
33
34      private void drawAngry()
35      {
36          drawHead( g );
37          drawEyes( g );
38          drawMouth( g );
39      }
40
41  } // end class AngryFace
```

Fig. L 10.14　AngryFace.java.

Lab Exercises
Name:

Debugging

```
1   // Debugging Chapter 10: DrawFaces.java
2   // Program randomly draws shapes.
3   import java.awt.*;
4   import java.awt.event.*;
5   import javax.swing.*;
6
7   public class DrawFaces extends JFrame {
8      private Face faces = Face[ 7 ];
9      private int counter = 0;
10     private static String faceNames[ 7 ] = { " Happy", " Sad", "n Angry",
11        " half of a", " peeking", " hair", " a haircut" };
12     private JButton changeFace;
13     private boolean pressed = false;
14
15     // contructor
16     public DrawFaces()
17     {
18        JFrame( "Faces" );
19
20        faces[ 0 ] = HappyFace();
21        faces[ 1 ] = SadFace();
22        faces[ 2 ] = AngryFace();
23        faces[ 3 ] = AngryFace( 275, 25 );
24        faces[ 4 ] = HappyFace( 25, 275 );
25        faces[ 5 ] = HappyFace( true );
26        faces[ 6 ] = HappyFace();
27
28        changeFace = new JButton( "Click to see a " + faceNames[ 0 ] + " face" );
29        getContentPane().add( changeFace, BorderLayout.SOUTH );
30        changeFace.addActionListener(
31
32           new ActionListener() {
33
34              public void actionPerformed( ActionEvent e )
35              {
36                 pressed = true;
37                 repaint();
38              }
39           }
40
41        ); // end call to addActionListener
42     } // end constructor
43
44     // draw faces
45     public void paint( Graphics g )
46     {
47        super.paint( g );
48
49        if ( pressed )
50        {
51           faces[].draw( g );
52
53           if ( counter == 6 ) {
54              changeFace.setEnabled( false );
55           }
56           else if ( counter == 4 && counter == 5 ) {
```

Fig. L 10.15   DrawFaces.java. (Part 1 of 2.)

Lab Exercises   Name:

Debugging

```
57              changeFace.setText(
58                  "Click to give a face" + faceNames[ counter + 1 ] );
59          }
60          else {
61              changeFace.setText(
62                  "Click to see a" + faceNames[ counter + 1 ] + " face" );
63          }
64
65          ++counter;
66          pressed = false;
67      }
68
69   } // end method paint
70
71   public static void main( String args[] )
72   {
73      DrawFaces application = new DrawFaces();
74      application.setSize( 500, 520 );
75      application.setVisible( true );
76      application.setDefaultCloseOperation( JFrame.EXIT_ON_CLOSE );
77
78   } // end method main
79
80 } // end class DrawFaces
```

Fig. L 10.15   DrawFaces.java. (Part 2 of 2.)

Postlab Activities

Coding Exercises

Name: _____   Date:_____

Section: _____

These coding exercises reinforce the lessons learned in the lab and provide additional programming experience outside the classroom and laboratory environment. They serve as a review after you have successfully completed the *Prelab Activities* and *Lab Exercises*.

For each of the following problems, write a program or a program segment that performs the specified action.

1. Write a header for an abstract class called ShapeArea.

2. In the class of Coding Exercise 1, create a protected instance variable shapeName, of type String, and write an accessor method getShapeName for obtaining its value.

3. In the class of Coding Exercise 2, define an abstract method getArea that returns a double representation of a specific shape's area. Subclasses of this class must implement getArea to calculate a specific shape's area.

Postlab Activities   Name:

Coding Exercises

4. Define a class SquareArea that inherits from class ShapeArea from Coding Exercise 3; it should contain an instance variable side, which is a side of the square, and a constructor that takes one argument representing the side of the square and sets the side variable. The constructor should set the inherited shapeName variable to the string "Square".

5. The SquareArea class from Coding Exercise 4 should implement the getArea method of its abstract superclass; this implementation should compute the area of the square and return the result.

Postlab Activities   Name:

Coding Exercises

6. Define a class `RectangleArea` that inherits from class `ShapeArea` of Coding Exercise 3. The new class should contain instance variables `length` and `width`. This class should provide a constructor that takes two arguments representing the length and width of the rectangle, sets the two variables and sets the inherited `shapeName` variable to the string `"Rectangle"`.

7. The `RectangleArea` class from Coding Exercise 6 should also implement the `getArea` method of its abstract superclass; this implementation should compute the area of the rectangle and return the result.

Postlab Activities   Name:

Coding Exercises

8. Write a driver class that tests these classes by creating an array that holds an instance of `SquareArea` and an instance of `RectangleArea`. The program should compute and display the areas of both objects. The program should allow a user to enter the values for the side of the square and the length and width of the rectangle.

Postlab Activities   Name:

Programming Challenge

Name: _____   Date:_____

Section: _____

The *Programming Challenges* are more involved than the *Coding Exercises* and may require a significant amount of time to complete. Write a Java program for each of the problems in this section. The answers to these problems are available at www.deitel.com, www.prenhall.com/deitel and on the *Java Multimedia Cyber Classroom: Fifth Edition*. Pseudocode, hints or sample output are provided to aid you in your programming.

1. Implement the Shape hierarchy shown in Fig. 9.3 of *Java How to Program, Fifth Edition*. Each TwoDimensionalShape should contain method getArea to calculate the area of the two-dimensional shape. Each ThreeDimensionalShape should have methods getArea and getVolume to calculate the surface area and volume, respectively, of the three-dimensional shape. Create a program that uses an array of Shape references to objects of each concrete class in the hierarchy. The program should print the object to which each array element refers. Also, in the loop that processes all the shapes in the array, determine whether each shape is a TwoDimensionalShape or a ThreeDimensionalShape. If a shape is a TwoDimensionalShape, display its area. If a shape is a ThreeDimensionalShape, display its area and volume.

Hints:

*   Your output should appear as follows:

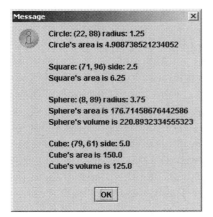

```
Message                               _ x

   i    Circle: (22, 88) radius: 1.25
        Circle's area is 4.908738521234052

        Square: (71, 96) side: 2.5
        Square's area is 6.25

        Sphere: (8, 89) radius: 3.75
        Sphere's area is 176.71458676442586
        Sphere's volume is 220.8932334555323

        Cube: (79, 61) side: 5.0
        Cube's area is 150.0
        Cube's volume is 125.0

                   [ OK ]
```

12

Graphics and Java2D

Objectives

- To understand graphics contexts and graphics objects.
- To understand and be able to manipulate colors.
- To understand and be able to manipulate fonts.
- To use `Graphics` methods to draw lines, rectangles, rectangles with rounded corners, three-dimensional rectangles, ovals, arcs and polygons.
- To use methods of class `Graphics2D` from the Java2D API to draw lines, rectangles, rectangles with rounded corners, ellipses, arcs and general paths.
- To be able to specify `Paint` and `Stroke` characteristics of shapes displayed with `Graphics2D`.

Assignment Checklist

Name: _____   Date:_____

Section: _____

Exercises	Assigned: Circle assignments		Date Due
Prelab Activities			
Matching	YES	NO	
Fill in the Blank	YES	NO	
Short Answer	YES	NO	
Programming Output	YES	NO	
Correct the Code	YES	NO	
Lab Exercises			
Exercise 1 — Concentric Circles	YES	NO	
Follow-Up Question and Activity	1		
Exercise 2 — Display Random Lines	YES	NO	
Follow-Up Question and Activity	1		
Exercise 3 — Drawing a Pyramid	YES	NO	
Follow-Up Questions and Activities	1, 2		
Debugging	YES	NO	
Postlab Activities			
Coding Exercises	1, 2, 3, 4, 5		
Programming Challenges	1, 2		

Assignment Checklist

Name:

Prelab Activities

Matching

Name: _____   Date:_____

Section: _____

After reading Chapter 12 of *Java How to Program: Fifth Edition*, answer the given questions. These questions are intended to test and reinforce your understanding of key Java concepts. You may answer these questions either before or during the lab.

For each term in the left column, write the letter for the description that best matches the term from the right column.

Term	Description
____ 1. `Component` class	a) Scheme for identifying every location on the screen.
____ 2. class `Color`	b) Passed to the `Color` constructor to specify the red, green and blue parts of a `Color`.
____ 3. pixel	c) Called to draw graphics on a `JFrame` or `JApplet`.
____ 4. method `paint`	d) Provides advanced two-dimensional graphics capabilities for processing line art, text and images.
____ 5. coordinate system	e) Display monitor's smallest unit of resolution.
____ 6. method `getHeight`	f) Indirect superclass of `JApplet`.
____ 7. `Serif`	g) Contains methods and constants for manipulating colors.
____ 8. Java2D API	h) Returns a value representing the height of a font in points.
____ 9. RGB value	i) A Java font name.
____ 10. `drawOval` method	j) Draws an arc relative to the bounding rectangle's top-left coordinates *(x, y)* with specified width and height.
____ 11. `drawArc` method	k) A subclass of class `Graphics`.
____ 12. `Graphics2D` class	l) Represents a shape constructed from straight lines and complex curves. ·
____ 13. `BufferedImage` class	m) Draws an oval with the specified width and height.
____ 14. `GeneralPath` class	n) Used to produce images in color and gray scale.

Prelab Activities   Name:

Fill in the Blank

Name: _____   **Date:**_____

Section: _____

Fill in the blanks for each of the following statements:

15. Java provides class _____ to display a dialog for selecting colors.

16. The _____ tab of the dialog for selecting colors allows you to select a color based on hue, saturation and brightness.

17. The _____ tab of the dialog for selecting colors allows you to select a color by using sliders to choose the red, green and blue components of the color.

18. Graphics methods _____ and _____ each require the same four arguments—the top-left *x-y* coordinate, the width and the height of a bounding rectangle—to draw (not fill) a shape.

19. A _____ object manages a graphics context.

20. Method setBackground of class _____ changes the background color of a GUI component.

21. The font style for a Font object can be set to _____, _____, _____ or _____.

22. To access the Java2D API capabilities, cast the Graphics reference to type _____ in the body of method paint.

23. Graphics2D method _____ sets the characteristics of the lines used to draw a shape.

24. Class Font's constructor takes three arguments—the font _____, the font _____ and the font _____.

25. Graphics2D method draw draws an object of any class that implements the interface _____.

Prelab Activities   Name:

Short Answer

Name: _____   Date:_____

Section: _____

Answer the following questions in the space provided. Your answers should be as concise as possible; aim for two or three sentences.

26. What is the basic process of drawing graphics on the screen?

27. What does the Java2D API provide? List at least three classes that define a variety of Java2D shapes.

28. What does RGB mean in the context of color? Approximately how many colors can be represented in the RGB color scheme?

Prelab Activities   Name:

Short Answer

29. How do you change a font? What happens if the specified font is not available on a system?

30. Describe the purpose of GeneralPath methods moveTo, lineTo and closePath.

Prelab Activities   Name:

Programming Output

Name: _____   Date:_____

Section: _____

For each of the given program segments, read the code and write the output in the space provided after each program. [*Note*: Do not execute these programs on a computer.]

31. What is output by the following program?

```
1   import java.awt.event.*;
2   import java.awt.*;
3   import javax.swing.*;
4
5   public class DrawPolygon extends JFrame {
6
7       // constructor
8       public DrawPolygon()
9       {
10          super( "Draw Polygon" );
11          setSize( 400, 400 );
12          setVisible( true );
13      }
14
15      public void paint( Graphics g )
16      {
17          super.paint( g );
18
19          int xCoordinates[] = { 100, 250, 300 };
20          int yCoordinates[] = { 100, 250, 300 };
21          Polygon polygon = new Polygon ( xCoordinates, yCoordinates, 3 );
22
23          g.drawPolygon( polygon );
24      }
25
26      // execute application
27      public static void main( String args[] )
28      {
29          DrawPolygon application = new DrawPolygon();
30          application.setDefaultCloseOperation( JFrame.EXIT_ON_CLOSE );
31      }
32
33  } // end class DrawPolygon
```

Prelab Activities   Name:

Programming Output

Draw your answer on the following grid:

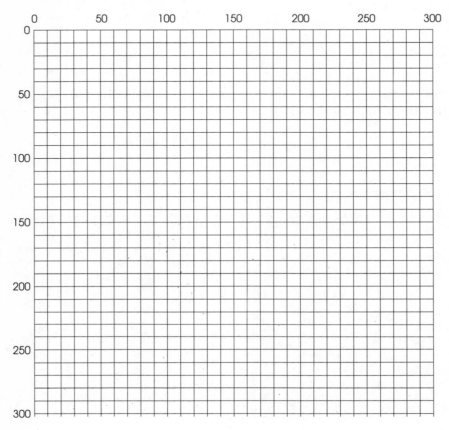

32. Assume that the following code is added at line 25 to the program in Programming Output Exercise 31. What is the output of the program?

```
1   for ( int k = 0; k < xCoordinates.length; k++ )
2      xCoordinates[ k ] = 200;
3
4   g.drawPolygon( xCoordinates, yCoordinates, 3 );
```

Prelab Activities

Name:

Programming Output

Draw your answer on the following grid:

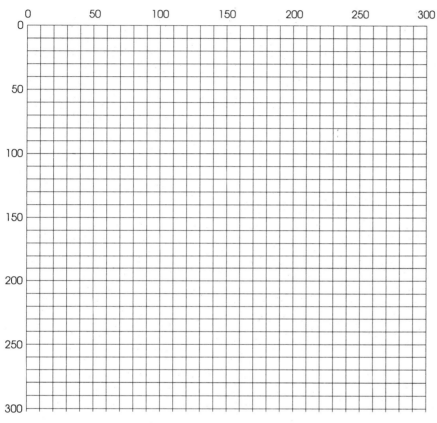

33. What is output by the following program?

```
1   import java.awt.event.*;
2   import java.awt.*;
3   import javax.swing.*;
4
5   public class DrawPicture extends JFrame {
6
7      // constructor
8      public DrawPicture()
9      {
10         super( "Draw Picture" );
11         setSize( 400, 400 );
12         setVisible( true );
13      }
14
15      public void paint( Graphics g )
16      {
17         super.paint( g );
18
19         g.setColor( Color.MAGENTA );
20         g.fillOval( 150, 140, 100, 110 );
```

(Part 1 of 2.)

Prelab Activities

Name:

Programming Output

```
21          g.setColor( Color.BLACK );
22
23          for ( int eyes = 180; eyes <= 210; eyes += 30 )
24             g.fillOval( eyes, 175, 10, 10 );
25
26          g.fillOval( 180, 210, 40, 5 );
27       }
28
29       // execute application
30       public static void main( String args[] )
31       {
32          DrawPicture application = new DrawPicture();
33          application.setDefaultCloseOperation( JFrame.EXIT_ON_CLOSE );
34       }
35
36    } // end class DrawPicture
```

(Part 2 of 2.)

Draw your answer on the following grid:

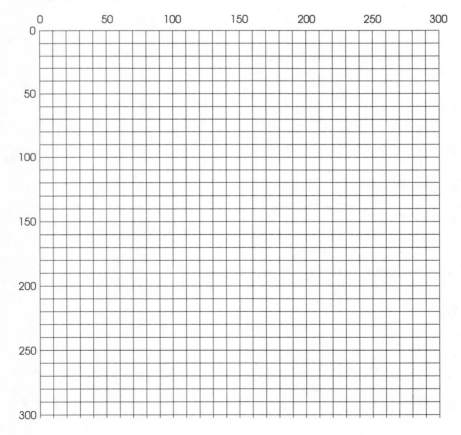

Prelab Activities   Name:

Correct the Code

Name: _____   Date: _____

Section: _____

Determine if there is an error in each of the following program segments. If there is an error, specify whether it is a logic error or a compilation error, circle the error in the program and write the corrected code in the space provided after each problem. If the code does not contain an error, write "no error." [*Note*: There may be more than one error in each program segment.]

Assume the following template definition of a class CorrectTheCode:

```
1   import java.awt.event.*;
2   import java.awt.*;
3   import javax.swing.*;
4
5   public class CorrectTheCode extends JFrame {
6
7       // constructor
8       public CorrectTheCode()
9       {
10          super( "Correct The Code" );
11          setSize( 400, 400 );
12          setVisible( true );
13      }
14
15      public void paint( Graphics g )
16      {
17          /* All the code segments below will be inserted here */
18      }
19
20      // execute application
21      public static void main( String args[] )
22      {
23          CorrectTheCode application = new CorrectTheCode();
24          application.setDefaultCloseOperation( JFrame.EXIT_ON_CLOSE );
25      }
26
27  } // end class CorrectTheCode
```

34. Insert the following code at line 17 in class CorrectTheCode. The code should display a cyan rectangle.

```
1   super.paint( g );
2   g.setColor( Color.Cyan );
3   g.drawRect( 150, 140, 100, 110 );
```

Your answer:

Prelab Activities   Name:

Correct the Code

35. Assume that the following code segment is added below the code from Correct the Code exercise 34. The following code should draw a filled rectangle in red.

```
1   g.setColor( Color ( 255, 0, 0 ) );
2   g.fillRect( 150, 140, 100, 110 );
```

Your answer:

36. Assume that the following code segment is added below the code from Correct the Code exercise 35. The following code should draw the point size of the font in black in the middle of the red square.

```
1   Font thisFont = new Font ( "Serif", Font.ITALIC, 18 );
2   FontMetrics traits = g.getFontMetrics( thisFont );
3
4   g.setColor( Color.BLACK );
5   g.setFont( thisFont );
6   g.drawString ( "Size: "  + ( trait.getHeight() - trait.getDescent() ), 170, 200 );
```

Your answer:

37. Assume that the following code segment is added below the code from Correct the Code exercise 36. The following code should draw a rectangle that surrounds the red filled rectangle created in Correct the Code exercise 35.

```
1   int xPoints = { 50, 350, 350, 50 };
2   int yPoints = { 50, 50, 350, 350 };
3   Polygon polyRect = new Polygon( xPoints, yPoints, 5 );
4
5   g.drawPolygon( polyRect );
```

Your answer:

Lab Exercises

Lab Exercise 1 — Concentric Circles

Name: _____   Date:_____

Section: _____

This problem is intended to be solved in a closed-lab session with a teaching assistant or instructor present. The problem is divided into six parts:

1. Lab Objectives

2. Description of the Problem

3. Sample Output

4. Program Template (Fig. L 12.1)

5. Problem-Solving Tips

6. Follow-Up Question and Activity

The program template represents a complete working Java program, with one or more key lines of code replaced with comments. Read the problem description and examine the sample output; then study the template code. Using the problem-solving tips as a guide, replace the /* */ comments with Java code. Compile and execute the program. Compare your output with the sample output provided. Then answer the follow-up question. The source code for the template is available at www.deitel.com and www.prenhall.com/deitel.

Lab Objectives

This lab was designed to reinforce programming concepts from Chapter 12 of *Java How to Program: Fifth Edition*. In this lab, you will practice:

- Using method drawArc.

The follow-up question and activity will also give you practice:

- Using method fillArc.

- Setting drawing colors.

Description of the Problem

Write a program that draws a series of eight concentric circles. The circles should be separated by 10 pixels. Use the drawArc method.

Sample Output

Lab Exercises

Name:

Lab Exercise 1 — Concentric Circles

Program Template

```
1    // Lab 1: Circles.java
2    // This program draws concentric circles
3    import java.awt.*;
4    import java.awt.event.*;
5    import javax.swing.*;
6
7    public class Circles extends JFrame {
8
9       // constructor
10      public Circles()
11      {
12         super( "Circles" );
13         setSize( 300, 300 );
14         setVisible( true );
15      }
16
17      // draw eight circles separated by 10 pixels
18      public void paint( Graphics g )
19      {
20         super.paint( g );
21
22         // create 8 concentric circles
23         /* Create a for loop that loops eight times. In the body of the loop,
24            calculate the side of the box bounding the arc and use drawArc to
25            display a circle. */
26      }
27
28      // execute application
29      public static void main( String args[] )
30      {
31         Circles application = new Circles();
32         application.setDefaultCloseOperation( JFrame.EXIT_ON_CLOSE );
33      }
34
35   } // end class Circles
```

Problem-Solving Tips

1. Create a `for` loop that draws a circle eight times. For each iteration, calculate the `side` of the box bounding the next inner circle.

2. As the `for` loop counter, use one variable that represents the *x*-and *y*-coordinates of the top-left corner of each arc's bounding rectangle. Increment this variable from zero to move the top-left corner closer to the center at a constant rate per iteration. The counter variable represents the value of both the x-and y-coordinates of the top-left corner of the bounding box.

3. Use 160 as the length of the sides for the box that bounds the largest of the eight circles. To calculate the size of the inner bounding boxes, use the following formula: `side = 160 - ( 2 * topLeft )`, where `topLeft` is the counter variable in the `for` loop.

Lab Exercises   Name:

Lab Exercise 1 — Concentric Circles

4. Use the drawArc method to display your output. To draw each circle with drawArc, pass the coordinates of the top-left corner of the arc's bounding box, pass side as the width and height of the arc, and sweep the arc from 0 to 360 degrees.

5. If you have any questions as you proceed, ask your lab instructor for assistance.

Follow-Up Question and Activity

1. Using method fillArc, modify the program so that when the variable topLeft is at 0, 20, 40 and so on, the circles would be filled with color cyan; otherwise, fill them with color gray.

Lab Exercises

Name:

Lab Exercise 2 — Display Random Lines

Name: _____

Date:_____

Section: _____

This problem is intended to be solved in a closed-lab session with a teaching assistant or instructor present. The problem is divided into six parts:

1. Lab Objectives
2. Description of the Problem
3. Sample Output
4. Program Template (Fig. L 12.2)
5. Problem-Solving Tips
6. Follow-Up Question and Activity

The program template represents a complete working Java program, with one or more key lines of code replaced with comments. Read the problem description and examine the sample output; then study the template code. Using the problem-solving tips as a guide, replace the /* */ comments with Java code. Compile and execute the program. Compare your output with the sample output provided. Then answer the follow-up question. The source code for the template is available at www.deitel.com and www.prenhall.com/deitel.

Lab Objectives

This lab was designed to reinforce programming concepts from Chapter 12 of *Java How to Program: Fifth Edition*. In this lab, you will practice:

- Using Java2D to draw lines in different thicknesses and colors.
- Using method draw from class Graphics2D.

The follow-up question and activity will also give you practice:

- Drawing.

Description of the Problem

Write a program that draws ten lines of random lengths in random colors and random thicknesses. Use class Line2D.Double objects and method draw of class Graphics2D to draw the lines. Set the size of the drawing area to 300 by 300.

Lab Exercises   Name:

Lab Exercise 2 — Display Random Lines

Sample Output

Program Template

```
1    // Lab 2: Lines2.java
2    // This program draws lines of different colors
3    import java.awt.*;
4    import java.awt.event.*;
5    import java.awt.geom.*;
6    import javax.swing.*;
7
8    public class Lines2 extends JFrame {
9       private Color colors[] = { Color.GREEN, Color.CYAN, Color.YELLOW,
10         Color.DARK_GRAY, Color.RED, Color.ORANGE, Color.GRAY, Color.PINK,
11         Color.MAGENTA };
12
13      // constructor
14      public Lines2()
15      {
16         super( "Lines" );
17
18         // set background to black to increase visibility
19         setBackground( Color.BLACK );
20
21         setSize( 300, 300 );
22         setVisible( true );
23      }
24
25      // create 10 lines
26      public void paint( Graphics g )
27      {
28         // create 2D by casting g to Graphics 2D
29         Graphics2D g2d = ( Graphics2D ) g;
30
31         for ( int y = 60; y < 250; y += 20 ) {
32
33            // choose a random color from array
34            /* Use Graphics2d method setColor to specify the drawing color as an
35               element of array colors */
36
```

Lab Exercises   Name:

Lab Exercise 2 — Display Random Lines

```
37                // choose a random thickness from 1-20
38                /* Use Graphics2d method setStroke to set the thickness of a line */
39
40                // choose a randon length and draw a line
41                /* Use Graphics2d method draw to set the length of each line */
42         }
43     }
44
45     // execute application
46     public static void main( String args[] )
47     {
48         Lines2 application = new Lines2();
49         application.setDefaultCloseOperation( JFrame.EXIT_ON_CLOSE );
50     }
51
52 } // end class Lines2
```

Problem-Solving Tips

1. This program requires you to create a line of code that picks a color at random from an array called `colors`. It also requires you to pick random numbers for the thickness and the length of each individual line.

2. Use `Math.random` to pick a number for the index into the array `colors`.

3. Use the same technique to pick a number between 1 and 20 for the thickness of each line. Use `Graphics2D` method `setStroke` to specify the thickness.

4. Pick random x-and y-coordinates for the endpoints of each line. Use these coordinates to initialize a `Line2D.Double` object; then display the object with `Graphics2D` method `draw`.

5. If you have any questions as you proceed, ask your lab instructor for assistance.

Follow-Up Question and Activity

1. Modify the program in Lab Exercise 2 so that after drawing ten random lines, the application clears itself and draws another batch of ten random lines. To allow the program to draw continuously, place a call to `repaint` as the last line in method `paint`. Place the following code segment in method `paint` before the `repaint` call to delay the execution time by 100 milliseconds:

```
1  // delays execution time for 100 milliseconds.
2  try {
3      Thread.sleep( 100 );
4  }
5
6  catch ( Exception exception ) {
7  }
```

Lab Exercises   Name:

Lab Exercise 3 — Drawing a Pyramid

Name: _____   Date:_____

Section: _____

This problem is intended to be solved in a closed-lab session with a teaching assistant or instructor present. The problem is divided into six parts:

1. Lab Objectives
2. Description of the Problem
3. Sample Output
4. Program Template (Fig. L 12.3)
5. Problem-Solving Tips
6. Follow-Up Questions and Activities

The program template represents a complete working Java program, with one or more key lines of code replaced with comments. Read the problem description and examine the sample output; then study the template code. Using the problem-solving tips as a guide, replace the /* */ comments with Java code. Compile and execute the program. Compare your output with the sample output provided. Then answer the follow-up questions. The source code for the template is available at www.deitel.com and www.prenhall.com/deitel.

Lab Objectives

This lab was designed to reinforce programming concepts from Chapter 12 of *Java How to Program: Fifth Edition*. In this lab, you will practice:

- Using class GeneralPath.
- Manipulating colors of shapes.

The follow-up questions and activities also will give you practice:

- Using method setColor.
- Understanding and manipulating coordinates to achieve desired results.

Description of the Problem

Write a program that draws a pyramid. Use class GeneralPath and method draw of class Graphics2D.

Sample Output

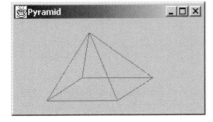

Lab Exercises   Name:

Lab Exercise 3 — Drawing a Pyramid

Program Template

```
1    // Lab 3: Pyramid.java
2    // Program draws a pyramid.
3    import java.awt.*;
4    import java.awt.geom.*;
5    import java.awt.event.*;
6    import javax.swing.*;
7
8    public class Pyramid extends JFrame {
9       /* Declare two arrays that contain x and y coordinates */
10
11      // constructor
12      public Pyramid()
13      {
14         super( "Pyramid" );
15         setSize( 275, 150 );
16         setVisible( true );
17      }
18
19      // draw pyramid
20      public void paint( Graphics g )
21      {
22         super.paint( g );
23
24         /* Cast the Graphics reference received by paint to a Graphics2D */
25
26         /* Define a GeneralPath object that represents a pyramid */
27
28         /* Set the color of pyramid using Graphics2D method setColor */
29
30         /* Use method moveTo to specify the first point in the pyramid */
31
32         /* Create a for loop that will access all the points in both arrays
33            to create the pyramid in the GeneralPath object */
34
35         /* Use method closePath to complete the pyramid */
36
37         /* Use Graphics2D method draw to display the pyramid. */
38      }
39
40      // execute application
41      public static void main( String args[] )
42      {
43         Pyramid application = new Pyramid();
44         application.setDefaultCloseOperation( JFrame.EXIT_ON_CLOSE );
45      }
46
47   } // end class Pyramid
```

Problem-Solving Tips

1. This program requires the programmer to instantiate two arrays that would hold the *x*- and *y*-coordinates representing the pyramid.

2. Write a line of code that will cast the Graphics reference received by paint to a Graphics2D reference and assign it to reference g2d to allow access to the Java2D features.

Lab Exercises   Name:

Lab Exercise 3 — Drawing a Pyramid

3. Method moveTo from class GeneralPath should specify the first point in the pyramid using the first element in each array.

4. Create a for loop that loops four times and uses lineTo and moveTo methods to create the pyramid from the given coordinates in the arrays.

5. Remember to use method closePath to draw a line from the last point to the point specified in the last call to moveTo.

6. Make sure that you also include method draw from Graphics2D to display the pyramid.

7. If you have any questions as you proceed, ask your lab instructor for assistance.

Follow-Up Questions and Activities

1. Modify Lab Exercise 3 so that it draws the same pyramid upside down.

2. Modify Lab Exercise 3 so that it draws a cube rather than a pyramid.

Lab Exercises   Name:

Debugging

Name: _____   Date:_____

Section: _____

The program in this section does not compile. Fix all the syntax errors so that the program will compile success-fully. Once the program compiles, execute the program, and compare the output with the sample output. Then eliminate any logic errors that may exist. The sample output demonstrates what the program's output should be once the program's code is corrected. The source code is available at the Web sites **www.deitel.com** and www.prenhall.com/deitel.

Sample Output

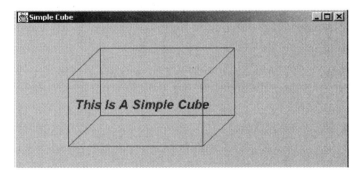

Broken Code

```java
1    // Debugging Problem: SimpleCube.java
2    // Chapter 12
3    import java.awt.event.*;
4    import java.awt.*;
5    import java.awt.geom.*;
6    import javax.swing.*;
7
8    public class SimpleCube extends JFrame {
9
10       // constructor
11       public SimpleCube()
12       {
13          super( "Simple Cube" );
14          setSize( 500, 500 );
15          setVisible( true );
16       }
17
18       public void paint( g )
19       {
20          super.paint( g );
21
22          int x = ( int ) ( Math.random() * 300 );
23          int y = ( int ) ( Math.random() * 300 );
```

Lab Exercises   Name:

Debugging

```
24
25          Graphics2D g2d = ( Graphics2D ) g;
26
27          g2d.setColor( new Color( Math.random(), Math.random(), Math.random() ) );
28          g2d.drawRect( x, y, 210, 110 );
29
30          // upper left line
31          g2d.drawLine( x, y , x + 50, y - 50 );
32
33          // upper right line
34          g2d.drawLine( x + 210, y, x + 260, y - 50  );
35
36          // lower right line
37          g2d.drawLine( x + 210, y + 110, x + 260, y + 60 );
38
39          // lower left line
40          g2d.drawLine( x, y + 110, x + 50, y + 60 );
41
42          int xUpperLeft = x + 50;
43          int yUpperLeft = y - 50;
44
45          int xUpperRight = x + 260;
46          int yUpperRight = y - 50;
47
48          int xLowerRight = x + 260;
49          int yLowerRight = y + 60;
50
51          int xLowerLeft = x + 50;
52          int yLowerleft = y + 60;
53
54          // close the rectangle
55          g2d.drawLine( xUpperLeft, yUpperLeft, xUpperRight, yUpperRight );
56          g2d.drawLine( xUpperRight, yUpperRight, xLowerRight, yLowerRight );
57          g2d.drawLine( xLowerRight, yLowerRight, xLowerLeft, yLowerleft );
58          g2d.drawLine( xLowerLeft, yLowerleft, xUpperLeft, yUpperLeft );
59
60          //draw the text
61          g2d.setFont( Font( "Font not specified", Font.BOLD, Font.ITALIC, 20 ) );
62          g2d.drawString( " This Is A Simple Cube ", x + 5, y + 50 );
63       }
64
65    // execute application
66    public static void main( String args[] )
67    {
68       SimpleCube application = new SimpleCube();
69       application.setDefaultCloseOperation();
70    }
71
72 } // end class SimpleCube
```

Postlab Activities

Coding Exercises

Name: _____   Date:_____

Section: _____

These coding exercises reinforce the lessons learned in the lab and provide additional programming experience outside the classroom and laboratory environment. They serve as a review after you have successfully completed the *Prelab Activities* and *Lab Exercises*.

For each of the following problems, write a program or a program segment that performs the specified action:

1. Declare four integer variables and assign each a random number in the range 0 to 299.

2. Use `Graphics` method `drawLine` to draw a line. Use the four variables you created in Coding Exercise 1 as arguments to `drawLine`.

3. Write a code segment that draws 16 randomly placed squares. Use `Graphics` method `drawRect` to draw each square. Each square should have a width and height of 30 pixels.

Postlab Activities   Name:

Coding Exercises

4. Cast the `Graphics` reference received by method `paint` to a `Graphics2D` reference and assign it to variable `graph2D`.

5. Rewrite the code segment from Coding Exercise 3 using the variable `graph2D` from Coding Exercise 4 and method `draw`. Use objects of class `Rectangle2D.Double` to create the 16 squares.

Postlab Activities   Name:

Programming Challenges

Name: _____   Date:_____

Section: _____

The *Programming Challenges* are more involved than the *Coding Exercises* and may require a significant amount of time to complete. Write a Java program for each of the problems in this section. The answers to these problems are available at www.deitel.com, www.prenhall.com/deitel and on the *Java Multimedia Cyber Classroom: Fifth Edition*. Pseudocode, hints or sample output are provided to aid you in your programming.

1. Write a program that draws a 10-by-10 grid. Create the grid by using instances of the Java 2D API class Rectangle2D.Double. Draw the grid with Graphics2D method draw.

Hints:
- Create a line of code that will cast the Graphics reference g received by method paint to a Graphics2D.
- Create nested for loops that will control the location of each square.
- Your output should appear as follows:

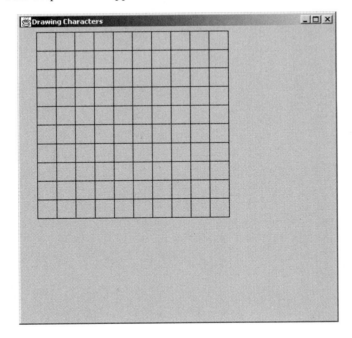

Postlab Activities

Name:

Programming Challenges

2. Write an application that randomly draws 100 lines using method `drawLine` of class `Graphics`.

Hints:

- Write code that will choose four random coordinates, and use them in a call to `Graphics` method `drawLine` to display a random line.

- Write lines of code that will choose three additional random numbers. Use `Graphics` method `setColor` to specify a random `Color` based on those values.

- Be sure to choose all the random numbers in a loop in method `paint` to ensure that new values are chosen for each of the 100 lines.

- Your output should appear as follows:

13

Graphical User Interface Components: Part 1

Objectives

- To be able to build graphical user interfaces (GUIs).
- To understand the packages containing GUI components, event-handling classes, and event-handling interfaces.
- To be able to create and manipulate buttons, labels, lists, textfields and panels.
- To understand mouse events and keyboard events.
- To understand and be able to use layout managers.

Assignment Checklist

Name: _____   **Date:** _____

Section: _____

Exercises	Assigned: Circle assignments	Date Due
Prelab Activities		
Matching	YES NO	
Fill in the Blank	YES NO	
Short Answer	YES NO	
Programming Output	YES NO	
Correct the Code	YES NO	
Lab Exercises		
Exercise 1 — Guess Game	YES NO	
Follow-Up Questions and Activities	1, 2	
Exercise 2 — Color GUI	YES NO	
Follow-Up Question and Activity	1	
Exercise 3 — Events	YES NO	
Follow-Up Question and Activity	1	
Debugging	YES NO	
PostLab Activities		
Coding Exercises	1, 2, 3, 4	
Programming Challenge	1	

Prelab Activities

Matching

Name: _____   Date: _____

Section: _____

After reading Chapter 13 of *Java How to Program: Fifth Edition*, answer the given questions. The questions are intended to reinforce your understanding of key concepts. You may answer the questions before or during the lab.

For each term in the left column, write the letter for the description from the right column that best matches the term.

Term	Description
____ 1. ImageIcon	a) A single-line area in which text can be entered by the user, but the text is hidden automatically.
____ 2. ItemListener	b) Handles key events that are generated when keys on the keyboard are pressed and released.
____ 3. JLabel	c) Displays a series of items from which the user may select one or more items.
____ 4. KeyEvent	d) Is used to load images of various formats, including Portable Network Graphics (PNG) format.
____ 5. JList	e) Layout manager that arranges components into five regions: North, South, East, West, and Center.
____ 6. KeyListener	f) Retrieves the Icon displayed on a JLabel or an AbstractButton.
____ 7. JRadioButton	g) Objects of subclasses of this type can have rollover icons that appear when the mouse moves over such components in a GUI.
____ 8. ActionEvent	h) Provides text instructions or information on a GUI.
____ 9. getIcon	i) Allows a JList user to select multiple items and those items are not required to be contiguous.
____ 10. AbstractButton	j) Must define method itemStateChanged.
____ 11. interface SwingConstants	k) Layout manager that divides the container into a grid of rows and columns.
____ 12. JComponent	l) A JButton generates this event type when the user presses the button.
____ 13. SINGLE_INTERVAL_SELECTION	m) Superclass to most Swing components.
____ 14. JPasswordField	n) Generates an ItemEvent when clicked.
____ 15. GridLayout	o) Layout manager that lays out components left to right in the order in which they are added to the container.
____ 16. MULTIPLE_INTERVAL_SELECTION	p) Allows JList user to select contiguous items.
____ 17. BorderLayout	q) Maintains a set of virtual key-code constants that represent every key on the keyboard.
____ 18. FlowLayout	r) Defines a set of common integer constants that are used with many Swing components.

Prelab Activities   Name: _____

Fill in the Blank

Name: _____   Date: _____

Section: _____

Fill in the blanks for each of the following statements:

19. JPasswordField method getPassword returns the password as an array of type _____.

20. A(n) _____ JList allows selection of a contiguous range of items by clicking the first item, then holding the *Shift* key and clicking the last item to select in the range.

21. By default, when a JLabel contains both text and an image, the text appears to the _____ of the image.

22. Swing GUI components are defined in package _____.

23. The Swing GUI components contain three state button types: _____, _____ and _____.

24. Method _____ specifies whether the user can modify the text in a JTextComponent.

25. The _____ layout manager arranges components from left to right in the order in which they are added to the container. When the edge of the container is reached, components are continued on the next line.

26. FlowLayout method _____ changes the alignment for the FlowLayout to FlowLayout.LEFT, FlowLayout.CENTER or FlowLayout.RIGHT.

27. Container method _____ recomputes the container's layout using the current layout manager for the Container and the current set of displayed GUI components.

28. When the user types data into a JTextField or JPasswordField and presses the *Enter* key, an event of type _____ occurs.

Prelab Activities   Name:

Short Answer

Name: _____   Date:_____

Section: _____

Answer the following questions in the space provided. Your answers should be as concise as possible; aim for two or three sentences.

29. What happens if the programmer does not add a GUI component to a container?

30. What happens if the programmer forgets to register an event handler for a GUI component?

31. What happens if the programmer does not specify a region in which a `Component` is to be placed in a `BorderLayout`?

Prelab Activities   Name:

Short Answer

32. What happens when more than one component is added to a particular region in a `BorderLayout`?

33. What happens if a programmer adds a component to a container that has not been instantiated?

Prelab Activities   Name:

Programming Output

Name: _____   Date:_____

Section: _____

For each of the given program segments, read the code and write the output in the space provided below each program. [*Note*: Do not execute these programs on a computer.] For the following exercises, draw the GUI that appears when the program executes.

34. What does the GUI look like in the following application?

```java
1    import java.awt.*;
2    import javax.swing.*;
3
4    public class Align extends JFrame {
5       private JButton okButton, cancelButton;
6       private JTextField inputName;
7       private JCheckBox fNameBox, lNameBox;
8       private JLabel nameLabel;
9       private JPanel checkPanel, buttonPanel, namePanel;
10
11      // constructor sets up GUI
12      public Align()
13      {
14         super( "Input Name" );
15
16         Container container = getContentPane();
17         container.setLayout( new FlowLayout( FlowLayout.CENTER, 10, 5 ) );
18
19         // build namePanel
20         nameLabel = new JLabel( "Type In Your Name" );
21         inputName = new JTextField( 20 );
22         namePanel = new JPanel();
23         namePanel.setLayout( new FlowLayout() );
24         namePanel.add( nameLabel );
25         namePanel.add( inputName );
26         container.add( namePanel );
27
28         setSize( 400, 150 );
29         setVisible( true );
30
31      } // end Align constructor
32
33      // execute application
34      public static void main( String args[] )
35      {
36         Align application = new Align();
37         application.setDefaultCloseOperation( JFrame.EXIT_ON_CLOSE );
38      }
39
40   } // end class Align
```

Prelab Activities   Name:

Programming Output

Your answer:

35. What does the GUI look like if the following code segment is added at line 27 of the program in Programming Output Exercise 34?

```
1    // build checkPanel
2    fNameBox = new JCheckBox( "First Name" );
3    lNameBox = new JCheckBox( "Last Name" );
4    checkPanel = new JPanel();
5    checkPanel.setLayout( new GridLayout( 1 , 2 ) );
6    checkPanel.add( fNameBox );
7    checkPanel.add( lNameBox );
8    container.add( checkPanel );
```

Your answer:

Prelab Activities   Name:

Programming Output

36. What does the GUI look like if the following code segment is added before the call to `setSize` in the constructor of the application in Programming Output Exercises 34–35?

```
1    // build button panel
2    okButton = new JButton( "Ok" );
3    cancelButton = new JButton( "Cancel" );
4    buttonPanel = new JPanel();
5    buttonPanel.setLayout( new GridLayout( 1, 2 ) );
6    buttonPanel.add( okButton );
7    buttonPanel.add( cancelButton );
8    container.add( buttonPanel );
```

Your answer:

37. What does the GUI look like if the following line of code replaced line 17 of the application in Programming Output Exercises 34–36?

```
1    container.setLayout( new FlowLayout( FlowLayout.LEFT, 10, 5 ) );
```

Your answer:

Prelab Activities

Name:

Programming Output

38. What does the GUI look like if the following line of code replaced line 17 of the application in Programming Output Exercises 34–36?

```
1   container.setLayout( new FlowLayout( FlowLayout.RIGHT, 10, 5 ) );
```

Your answer:

Prelab Activities   Name:

Correct the Code

Name: _____   Date:_____

Section: _____

Determine if there is an error in each of the following program segments. If there is an error, specify whether it is a logic error or a compilation error, circle the error in the program and write the corrected code in the space provided after each problem. If the code does not contain an error, write "no error." [*Note*: There may be more than one error in each program segment.]

Assume the following template definition of a class **Test1**:

```java
1    import java.awt.*;
2    import java.awt.event.*;
3
4    import javax.swing.*;
5
6    public class Test1 extends JFrame {
7       private JButton okay, clear;
8       private JTextArea content;
9       private String display = "";
10      private Container container;
11
12      public Test1()
13      {
14         super( " Test1 " );
15
16         container = getContentPane();
17
18         /* all the code segments below will be inserted here */
19
20         setSize( 200, 200 );
21         setVisible( true );
22      }
23
24      public static void main( String args[] )
25      {
26         Test1 application = new Test1();
27         application.setDefaultCloseOperation( JFrame.EXIT_ON_CLOSE );
28      }
29   } // end class Test1
```

Prelab Activities   Name:

Correct the Code

39. The following code should create a JButton with the value "Okay" and add it to the content pane referenced by container.

```
1   JButton okay;
2   okay = new JButton();
3   container.add( BorderLayout.CENTER );
```

Your answer:

40. The following code segment should create a JButton with the value "Clear" and a JTextArea in which the user is not allowed to type. Then, the code segment should add these components to the content pane referenced by container.

```
1   JButton clear;
2   clear = new JButton();
3   container.add( BorderLayout.SOUTH );
4
5   JTextArea content = new JTextArea( "Type or Click", 1, 4 );
6   content.setEditable();
7   container.add( BorderLayout.NORTH );
```

Your answer:

Prelab Activities

Name:

Correct the Code

41. The following code should add `ActionListener`s to the okay and clear buttons defined in Correct the Code Exercises 39–40 and specify how to handle each button's event.

```
1   okay.new ActionListener() {
2      public void actionPerformed( Actionevent e ) {
3         content.setText( "" );
4         display = "You clicked okay: ";
5         content.append( display );
6      }
7   }
8
9   clear.new ActionListener() {
10     public void actionPerformed( Actionevent e ) {
11        content.setText( "" );
12     }
13  }
```

Your answer:

Prelab Activities   Name:

Correct the Code

42. The following code should add a `KeyListener` to the `Test1` window.

```
1   addKeyListener(
2
3     new KeyAdapter() {
4
5        public void keyPressed( KeyEvent e ) {
6           switch ( e.getKeyChar() ) {
7
8              case 'c': case 'C':
9                 clear.doClick();
10                break;
11
12             case 'o':  case 'O':
13                okay.doClick();
14                break;
15          }
16       }
17    }
18  );
```

Your answer:

Lab Exercises

Lab Exercise 1 — Guess Game

Name: _____   Date:_____

Section: _____

This problem is intended to be solved in a closed-lab session with a teaching assistant or instructor present. The problem is divided into six parts:

1. Lab Objectives
2. Description of Problem
3. Sample Output
4. Program Template (Fig. L 13.1)
5. Problem-Solving Tips
6. Follow-Up Questions and Activities

The program template represents a complete working Java program, with one or more key lines of code replaced with comments. Read the problem description and examine the sample output; then study the template code. Using the problem-solving tips as a guide, replace the /* */ comments with Java code. Compile and execute the program. Compare your output with the sample output provided. Then answer the follow-up questions. The source code for the template is available at www.deitel.com and www.prenhall.com/deitel.

Lab Objectives

This lab was designed to reinforce programming concepts from Chapter 13 of *Java How to Program: Fifth Edition*. In this lab, you will practice:

*   Designing a GUI.
*   Processing events.
*   Creating and manipulating GUI components.

The follow-up questions and activities also will give you practice:

*   Using various GUI methods to manipulate components.
*   Adding additional components to a GUI.

Problem Description

Write a program that plays "guess the number" as follows: Your program chooses the number to be guessed by selecting an integer at random in the range 1–1000. The program then displays in a label:

```
I have a number between 1 and 1000.
Can you guess my number? Enter your guess:
```

A JTextField should be used to input the guess. As each guess is input the background color should change to either red or blue. Red indicates that the user is getting "warmer" and blue indicates that the user is getting "colder." A JLabel should display either "Too High" or "To Low" to help the user zero in on the correct answer. When the user gets the correct answer, "Correct!" should be displayed and the JTextField used for input should be changed to uneditable. A JButton should be provided to allow the user to play the game again. When the JButton is clicked, a new random number should be generated and the input JTextField changed to editable.

Lab Exercises   Name:

Lab Exercise 1 — Guess Game

Sample Output

 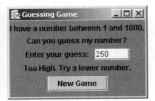

Program Template

```
1    // Lab 1: GuessGame.java
2    // Guess the number
3    import java.awt.*;
4    import java.awt.event.*;
5    import javax.swing.*;
6
7    public class GuessGame extends JFrame {
8       private int number, guessCount;
9       private int lastDistance;
10      private JTextField guessInput;
11      private JLabel prompt1, prompt2, prompt3, message;
12      private JButton newGame;
13      private Color background;
14      private Container container;
15
16      // set up GUI and initialize values
17      public GuessGame()
18      {
19         /* Write a line of code that calls the superclass constructor
20            and sets the title of this application to "Guessing Game" */
21
22         guessCount = 0;
23         background = Color.LIGHT_GRAY;
24
25         // create GUI components
26         prompt1 = new JLabel( "I have a number between 1 and 1000." );
27         prompt2 = new JLabel( "Can you guess my number?" );
28         prompt3 = new JLabel( "Enter your guess: " );
29
30         guessInput = new JTextField( 5 );
31         guessInput.addActionListener(
32
33            new ActionListener() {
34
35               public void actionPerformed( ActionEvent event )
36               {
37                  /* Write code that will obtain the guess, convert it to an int and
38                     pass that value to the react method */
39               }
40            }
41         );
42
43         message = new JLabel( "Guess result appears here." );
44
```

Fig. L 13.1   GuessGame.java (Part 1 of 3.)

Lab Exercises   Name:

Lab Exercise 1 — Guess Game

```
45      // button starts a new game
46      /* Write a statement that creates the "New Game" button */
47      newGame.addActionListener(
48
49         new ActionListener() {
50
51            public void actionPerformed( ActionEvent e )
52            {
53               /* Write code that resets the application to an appropriate state
54                  to start a new game. Reset the background color to light gray,
55                  set the JTextFields to their initial text, call
56                  generateRandomNumber number and repaint the GuessGame JFrame */
57            }
58         }
59      );
60
61      // add components to JFrame
62      container = getContentPane();
63      /* Write code that will set the layout of the container to a FlowLayout,
64         then add all the GUI components to the container */
65
66      setSize( 220, 150 );
67      setVisible( true );
68
69      generateRandomNumber(); // choose first random number
70   }
71
72   // choose a new random number
73   public void generateRandomNumber()
74   {
75      /* Write a statement that sets instance variable "number" to a
76         random number between 1 and 1000 */
77   }
78
79   // change background color
80   public void paint( Graphics g )
81   {
82      super.paint( g );
83      container.setBackground( background );
84   }
85
86   // react to new guess
87   public void react( int guess ) {
88      guessCount++;
89
90      /* Write code that sets instance variable currentDistance to 1000. This
91         variable's value will be used to determine if the background color
92         should be set to red or blue to indicate that the last guess was getting
93         closer to or further from the actual number. */
94
95      // first guess
96      if ( guessCount == 1 ) {
97         /* Write code to set instance variable lastDistance to the absolute value
98            of the difference between variables guess and number. This value will
99            be used with subsequent guesses to help set the background color. */
100
```

Fig. L 13.1   `GuessGame.java` (Part 2 of 3.)

Lab Exercises   Name:

Lab Exercise 1 — Guess Game

```
101            if ( guess > number )
102                message.setText( "Too High. Try a lower number." );
103            else
104                message.setText( "Too Low. Try a higher number." );
105        }
106        else {
107            /* Write code that sets instance variable currentDistance to the absolute
108               value of the difference between variables guess and number. This
109               variable's value will be compared with lastDistance to determine the
110               background color. */
111
112            // guess is too high
113            if ( guess > number ) {
114                message.setText( "Too High. Try a lower number." );
115
116                /* Write code that sets Color variable background to red if the
117                   currentDistance is less than or equal to lastDistance; otherwise,
118                   set background to blue. Then, assign currentDistance to
119                   lastDistance. */
120            }
121            else if ( guess < number ) { // guess is too low
122                message.setText( "Too Low. Try a higher number." );
123
124                /* Write code that sets Color variable background to red if the
125                   currentDistance is less than or equal to lastDistance; otherwise,
126                   set background to blue. Then, assign currentDistance to
127                   lastDistance. */
128            }
129            else { // guess is correct
130                message.setText( "              Correct!              " );
131                background = Color.LIGHT_GRAY;
132                guessInput.setEditable( false );
133                guessCount = 0; // prepare for next game
134            }
135
136            repaint();
137        } // end else
138
139    } // end method react
140
141    public static void main( String args[] )
142    {
143        GuessGame app = new GuessGame();
144        app.setDefaultCloseOperation( JFrame.EXIT_ON_CLOSE );
145    }
146
147 } // end class GuessGame
```

Fig. L 13.1   GuessGame.java (Part 3 of 3.)

Lab Exercises   Name:

Lab Exercise 1 — Guess Game

Problem-Solving Tips

1. Use methods from the `JTextField` class to manipulate all `JTextField` components. For instance, method `setText` will set the text of the text field, and method `setEditable` will set whether the text field can be edited or not.

2. Method `setBackground` from class `JFrame` sets the background color of the `JFrame`.

3. Use method `random` from the `Math` class to generate a random number from 1 to 1000. You will need to scale the range of values produced by `random` by 1000 and shift the range by 1.

4. Use variables `lastDistance` and `currentDistance` to determine the distance of the guess from the actual number. If this distance gets larger between guesses, set the background color of the `JFrame` to blue. If this distance gets smaller or stays the same, set the background color to red.

5. If you have any questions as you proceed, ask your lab instructor for assistance.

Follow-Up Questions and Activities

1. Modify the previous program to keep track of how many guesses the user has made, and display that number in another `JLabel` in the `JFrame`.

2. Now modify the previous program so that there is another `JLabel` in the `JFrame` that contains the number to be guessed, but does not become visible, until the user guesses the right number. In other words the `JLabel` is always there, the user just can't see it until the correct number is guessed. [Hint: use method `setVisible` to show and hide the `JLabel`.]

    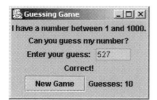

Lab Exercises   Name:

Lab Exercise 2 — Color GUI

Name: _____   Date:_____

Section: _____

This problem is intended to be solved in a closed-lab session with a teaching assistant or instructor present. The problem is divided into six parts:

1. Lab Objectives
2. Description of Problem
3. Sample Output
4. Program Template (Fig. L 13.2)
5. Problem-Solving Tips
6. Follow-Up Question and Activity

The program template represents a complete working Java program, with one or more key lines of code replaced with comments. Read the problem description and examine the sample output; then study the template code. Using the problem-solving tips as a guide, replace the /* */ comments with Java code. Compile and execute the program. Compare your output with the sample output provided. Then answer the follow-up question. The source code for the template is available at www.deitel.com and www.prenhall.com/deitel.

Lab Objectives

This lab was designed to reinforce programming concepts from Chapter 13 of *Java How to Program: Fifth Edition*. In this lab you will practice:

*   Adding event listeners to your GUIs to listen for events and react to them.
*   Defining private inner classes for handling events.
*   Using JPanels to layout your GUI.

The follow-up question and activity will also give you practice:

*   Modifying functionality of an existing GUI.

Problem Description

Design a GUI that allows a user to type into a JTextArea, and be able to choose the color of the background of that text area and choose the color of the foreground of that text area also. Your GUI should contain a JTextArea in which the user can type, a JComboBox that lists all the colors from which the user can choose, two mutually exclusive JRadioButtons for choosing either the background or foreground and a JButton that allows the user to apply the changes. [*Note:* Setting the foreground color of a JTextArea changes the color of the all the text that appears in the JTextArea.]

Lab Exercises   Name:

Lab Exercise 2 — Color GUI

Sample Output

Program Template

```
1   // Lab 2: ColorGUI.java
2   // Program that enables the user to change the foreground and
3   // background colors of a JTextArea.
4   import java.awt.*;
5   import java.awt.event.*;
6   import javax.swing.*;
7
8   public class ColorGUI extends JFrame {
9      private JPanel panel1, panel2, panel3;
10     private JTextArea area;
11     private JComboBox colorList;
12     private JRadioButton backBox, foreBox;
13     private ButtonGroup colorGroup;
14     private JButton apply;
15     private Color backColor, foreColor, selected;
16     private boolean background = false;
17     private Container container;
18
19     private String colorNames[] =
20        { "RED", "BLUE", "GREEN", "YELLOW", "MAGENTA", "CYAN" };
21     private Color colors[] = { Color.RED, Color.BLUE, Color.GREEN,
22        Color.YELLOW, Color.MAGENTA, Color.CYAN };
23
24     // set up GUI and initialize values
25     public ColorGUI()
26     {
27        /* Write a statement that calls the superclass constructor
28           and sets the title of this application to "Color GUI" */
29
30        /* Write a statement that sets Color member variable "selected" to red */
31
32        // create GUI components
33        area = new JTextArea( 3, 20 );
34        area.setFont( new Font( null, Font.ITALIC, 16 ) );
35        area.setText( "Type text here" );
36
37        // sets the area so that text will wrap to the next line
38        area.setLineWrap( true );
39        area.setEditable( true );
40
```

Fig. L 13.2   ColorGUI.java. (Part 1 of 3.)

Lab Exercises   Name:

Lab Exercise 2 — Color GUI

```
41        colorList = new JComboBox( colorNames );
42        colorList.setSelectedIndex( 0 );
43        colorList.addItemListener( new ListHandler() );
44
45        backBox = new JRadioButton( "background", false );
46        foreBox = new JRadioButton( "foreground", false );
47        backBox.addItemListener( new RadioButtonHandler() );
48        foreBox.addItemListener( new RadioButtonHandler() );
49
50        /* Write code that creates a new ButtonGroup and adds the
51           backBox and foreBox JRadioButtons to the ButtonGroup */
52
53        apply = new JButton( "Apply" );
54        apply.setEnabled( false );
55        apply.addActionListener( new ButtonHandler() );
56
57        // create panels and add components to the panels
58        /* Write code that creates three new JPanels (panel1, panel2 and panel3) */
59
60        /* Write code adds the GUI components to the JPanels as follows:
61           add area to panel1; add colorList, backBox, and foreBox to panel2;
62           and add apply to panel3 */
63
64        // add panels to container
65        container = getContentPane();
66        container.setLayout( new FlowLayout() );
67        /* Write code that adds the three JPanels to the container */
68
69        setSize( 300, 200 );
70        setVisible( true );
71    }
72
73    // inner class for button actions
74    private class ButtonHandler implements ActionListener
75    {
76        public void actionPerformed( ActionEvent event )
77        {
78            // set backColor or foreColor based on the value of
79            // instance variable "background"
80            /* Write code that determines whether boolean instance variable
81               "background" is true. If so, set instance variable backColor to the
82               selected Color and set the background color of the JTextArea.
83               Otherwise set foreColor to the selected Color and set the forground
84               color of the JTextArea */
85
86            /* Write a statement that repaints the JTextArea */
87        } // end actionPerformed method
88
89    } // end inner class ButtonHandler
90
91    // inner class for radio button actions
92    private class RadioButtonHandler implements ItemListener {
93
94        public void itemStateChanged( ItemEvent event )
95        {
96            /* Write code that sets instance variable "background" to true if
97               backBox is selected or false if foreBox is selected */
```

Fig. L 13.2   ColorGUI.java. (Part 2 of 3.)

Lab Exercises   Name:

Lab Exercise 2 — Color GUI

```
98
99            /* Write a statement that enables the apply Button */
100
101       } // end itemStateChanged method
102
103     } // end inner class RadioButtonHandler
104
105     // inner class for actions in colorList combo box
106     private class ListHandler implements ItemListener {
107
108        public void itemStateChanged( ItemEvent event )
109        {
110           selected = colors[ colorList.getSelectedIndex() ];
111
112        } // end itemStateChanged method
113
114     } // end inner class ListHandler
115
116
117     // execute application
118     public static void main( String args[] )
119     {
120        ColorGUI application = new ColorGUI();
121        application.setDefaultCloseOperation( JFrame.EXIT_ON_CLOSE );
122     }
123
124 } // end class ColorGUI
```

Fig. L 13.2   ColorGUI.java. (Part 3 of 3.)

Problem-Solving Tips

1. Use methods setForeground and setBackground from class JTextArea to set the foreground and background of the JTextArea in your GUI.

2. Be sure to add both JRadioButtons to the ButtonGroup. This will ensure that they are mutually exclusive.

3. Do not add the ButtonGroup to your GUI. Class ButtonGroup does not derive from class Component, so it cannot be attached to the GUI. Instead, add the radio buttons to the GUI.

4. If you have any questions as you proceed, ask your lab instructor for assistance.

Follow-Up Question and Activity

1. Modify the previous program so that the foreground color and the background color cannot be the same color. If the user attempts to set the background to the current foreground color, then the foreground should be set to black and the background to the color selected by the user. Similarly, if the user attempts to set the foreground to the current background color, then the background should be set to black and the foreground to the color selected by the user.

Lab Exercises   Name:

Lab Exercise 3 — Events

Name: _____   Date:_____

Section: _____

This problem is intended to be solved in a closed-lab session with a teaching assistant or instructor present. The problem is divided into six parts:

1. Lab Objectives
2. Description of Problem
3. Sample Output
4. Program Template (Fig. L 13.3)
5. Problem-Solving Tips
6. Follow-Up Question and Activity

The program template represents a complete working Java program, with one or more key lines of code replaced with comments. Read the problem description and examine the sample output; then study the template code. Using the problem-solving tips as a guide, replace the /* */ comments with Java code. Compile and execute the program. Compare your output with the sample output provided. Then answer the follow-up question. The source code for the template is available at www.deitel.com and www.prenhall.com/deitel.

Lab Objectives

This lab was designed to reinforce programming concepts from Chapter 13 of *Java How to Program: Fifth Edition*. In this lab you will practice:

*   Understanding when events occur and how they are generated.
*   Displaying information about different events.

The follow-up question and activity will also give you practice:

*   Using the methods provided by the event classes.

Problem Description

It is often useful to display the events that occur during the execution of a program to help understand when the events occur and how they are generated. Write a program that enables the user to generate and process various events discussed in this chapter. The program should provide methods from the ActionListener, ItemListener, MouseListener, MouseMotionListener, and KeyListener interfaces to display messages when the events occur. Use method toString to convert the event objects received in each event handler into a String that can be displayed. Method toString creates a String containing all the information in the event object. Create a GUI that will generate all the desired events and display all the event information in a scrollable JTextArea.

Lab Exercises   Name:

Lab Exercise 3 — Events

Sample Output

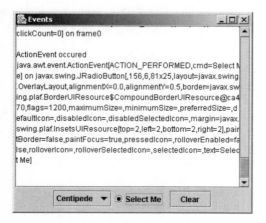

Program Template

```
1    // Lab 3: Events.java
2    // Display messages that contain information about each event that occurs.
3    import java.awt.*;
4    import java.awt.event.*;
5    import javax.swing.*;
6    import javax.swing.event.*;
7
8    public class Events extends JFrame implements ActionListener, ItemListener,
9       MouseListener, MouseMotionListener, KeyListener {
10
11      private JPanel panel1;
12      private JScrollPane scrollPane;
13      private JTextArea output;
14      private JComboBox comboBox;
15      private JRadioButton radioButton;
16      private JButton clearButton;
17      private Container container;
18
19      private String names[] = { "Anteater", "Caterpillar", "Centipede", "Fire Fly" };
20
21      // set up GUI and register event handlers
22      public Events()
23      {
24         super( "Events" );
25
26         // create GUI components
27         output = new JTextArea( 10, 30 );
28         output.setLineWrap( true );
29         output.setEditable( false );
30         output.setBackground( Color.WHITE );
31         output.setForeground( Color.BLACK );
32
33         // add the output area to a scroll pane so the user can scroll the output
34         /* Write a statement that attaches the output JTextArea to a JScrollPane */
35
```

Fig. L 13.3   Events.java. (Part 1 of 3.)

Lab Exercises   Name:

Lab Exercise 3 — Events

```
36        // comboBox listens for item events
37        comboBox = new JComboBox( names );
38        /* Write a statement that registers an ItemListener for this JComboBox */
39        /* Write a statement that registers a KeyListener for this JComboBox */
40
41        // radioButton listens for action events
42        radioButton = new JRadioButton( "Select Me", false );
43        /* Write a statement that registers an ActionListener for
44           this JRadioButton */
45
46        // clear button for clearing the output area
47        clearButton = new JButton( "Clear" );
48        clearButton.addActionListener(
49
50           // anonymous inner class for clearing the output area
51           /* Write code that defines an anonymous inner class that
52              will clear the output JTextArea when the clear button is clicked */
53
54        ); // end call to AddActionListener
55
56        // application listens to its own mouse events
57        /* Write code that registers a MouseListener
58           and a MouseMotionListener for the the Events JFrame */
59
60        panel1 = new JPanel();
61        panel1.add( comboBox );
62        panel1.add( radioButton );
63        panel1.add( clearButton );
64
65        // add components to container
66        container = getContentPane();
67        container.setLayout( new BorderLayout() );
68        container.add( scrollPane, BorderLayout.CENTER );
69        container.add( panel1, BorderLayout.SOUTH );
70
71        setSize( 375, 325 );
72        setVisible( true );
73
74     } // end constrcutor
75
76     // ActionListener event handlers
77
78     /* Implement the ActionListener interface. Display the string representation
79        of each event that occurs in the output JTextArea. */
80
81     // ItemListener event handlers
82
83     /* Implement the ItemListener interface. Display the string representation
84        of each event that occurs in the output JTextArea. */
85
86     // MouseListener event handlers
87
88     /* Implement the MouseListener interface. Display the string representation
89        of each event that occurs in the output JTextArea. */
90
91     // MouseMotionListener event handlers
```

Fig. L 13.3   Events.java. (Part 2 of 3.)

Lab Exercises   Name:

Lab Exercise 3 — Events

```
92
93      /* Implement the MouseMotionListener interface. Display the string representation
94         of each event that occurs in the output JTextArea. */
95
96      // KeyListener event handlers
97
98      /* Implement the KeyListener interface. Display the string representation
99         of each event that occurs in the output JTextArea. */
100
101     // execute application
102     public static void main( String args[] )
103     {
104        Events application = new Events();
105        application.setDefaultCloseOperation( JFrame.EXIT_ON_CLOSE );
106     }
107
108  } // end class Events
```

Fig. L 13.3   Events.java. (Part 3 of 3.)

Problem-Solving Tips

1. The application itself should listen for all events except the clear button's event. Register each listener with this as the listener.

2. Every method of an interface must be defined in a class that implements that interface or else a compilation error will occur. So, ensure that you define all the methods specified by the interfaces implemented in this application.

3. In each event-handling method, you should append a string containing information about the event to the output JTextArea.

4. Use method append from class JTextArea to display all the event information. Place newlines between each event string to make the output easier to read.

5. If you have any questions as you proceed, ask your lab instructor for assistance.

Lab Exercises   Name:

Lab Exercise 3 — Events

Follow-Up Question and Activity

1. There are many methods in each of the event classes that will return information regarding the event that occurred. One method that is common to all the events we generated in the previous program is method `param-String`. This method returns a much shorter informational string than the one returned by method `toString`, which will make the output text easier to read. Modify the `Events` program to use method `paramString` rather than method `toString` to output information about the events.

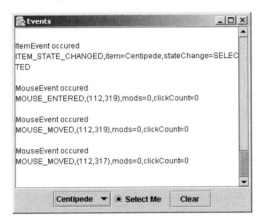

Lab Exercises　　　　　　　　　　　　　　　Name:

Debugging

Name: _____　　　　　　Date: _____

Section: _____

The program in this section does not compile. Fix all the syntax errors so that the program will compile success-fully. Once the program compiles, execute the program, and compare its output with the sample output; then elim-inate any logic errors that may exist. The sample output demonstrates what the program's output should be once the program's code is corrected. The source code is available at www.deitel.com and at www.prenhall.com/deitel.

Sample Output

Broken Code

```java
1    // Debugging problem Chapter 13: Phone.java
2    // Program creates a GUI that resembles a phone with functionality.
3    import java.awt.*;
4    import java.awt.event.*;
5    import javax.swing.*;
6
7    public class Phone extends JFrame {
8       private Jbutton keys[];
9       private JPanel keyPad, lcd;
10      private JTextArea lcdContent;
11      private String lcdOutput = "";
12      private int count;
13
14      // constructor sets up GUI
15      public Phone()
16      {
17         super( "Phone" );
18
19         lcdContent = new JTextArea( 4, 15 );
20         lcdContent.setEditable( false );
21         lcd.add( lcdContent );
```

Fig. 13.1　Phone.java. (Part 1 of 3.)

Lab Exercises   Name:

Debugging

```
22
23        keys = new Jbutton[ 15 ];
24
25        // initialize all digit key Buttons
26        for ( int i = 3; i <= 11; i++ )
27           keys[ i ] = new Jbutton( String.valueOf( i - 2 ) );
28
29        // initialize all non-digit key Buttons
30        keys[ 0 ] = new Jbutton( "Send" );
31        keys[ 1 ] = new Jbutton( "clr" );
32        keys[ 2 ] = new Jbutton( "End" );
33        keys[ 12 ] = new Jbutton( "*" );
34        keys[ 13 ] = new Jbutton( "0" );
35        keys[ 14 ] = new Jbutton( "#" );
36
37        keys[ 0 ].addActionListener(
38
39              public void actionPerformed( ActionEvent e )
40              {
41                 lcdContent.setText( " " );
42                 lcdOutput = "Calling...\n\n" + lcdOutput;
43                 lcdContent.append( lcdOutput );
44              } // end method actionPerformed
45
46           } // end new ActionListener
47
48        ) // end addActionListener call
49
50        keys[ 1 ].addActionListener(
51
52           new ActionListener() {
53
54              public void actionPerformed( ActionEvent e )
55              {
56                 if ( lcdOutput.length() == 0 ||
57                    lcdOutput.substring( 0, 1 ).equals( "C" ) )
58                    return;
59                 else {
60                    lcdOutput = lcdOutput.substring( 0, ( lcdOutput.length() - 1 ) );
61                    lcdContent.setText( " " );
62                    lcdContent.append( lcdOutput );
63                 } // end else
64
65              } // end method actionPerformed
66
67           } // end object ActionLstener
68
69        ) // end addActionListener call
70
71        keys[ 2 ].addActionListener(
72
73           new ActionListener() {
74
75              public void actionPerformed( ActionEvent e )
76              {
77                 lcdContent.setText( " " );
```

Fig. 13.1   Phone.java. (Part 2 of 3.)

Lab Exercises　　　　　　　　　　　　　　　　　Name:

Debugging

```
78              lcdOutput = "";
79
80          } // end method actionPerformed
81
82        } // end new ActionListener
83
84     ) // end ActionListener call
85
86     for ( int i = 3; i <= 14; i++ ) {
87        keys[ i ].addActionListener(
88
89          new ActionListener() {
90
91            public void actionPerformed( ActionEvent e )
92            {
93                lcdOutput += e.getActionCommand();
94
95                if ( lcdOutput.substring( 0, 1 ).equals( "C" ) )
96                    return;
97
98                lcdContent.append( e.getActionCommand() );
99            } // end method actionPerformed
100
101        } // end new ActionListener
102
103      ) // end addActionListener call
104
105    } // end for loop
106
107    // set keyPad layout to grid layout
108    keyPad = new JPanel();
109    keyPad.setLayout( new GridLayout( 5, 3 ) );
110
111    // add buttons to keyPad panel
112    for ( int i = 0; i <= 14; i++ )
113      keyPad.add( keys[ i ] );
114
115    // add components to container
116    Container container = getContentPane();
117    container.add( lcdOutput, BorderLayout.NORTH );
118
119    setSize( 200, 300 );
120    setVisible( true );
121
122  } // end Phone constructor
123
124  // execute application
125  public static void main( String args[] )
126  {
127    Phone application = new Phone();
128    application.setDefaultCloseOperation( JFrame.EXIT_ON_CLOSE );
129
130  } // end method main
131
132 } // end class Phone
```

Fig. 13.1　Phone.java. (Part 3 of 3.)

Postlab Activities

Coding Exercises

Name: _____   Date:_____

Section: _____

These coding exercises reinforce the lessons learned in the lab and provide additional programming experience outside the classroom and laboratory environment. They serve as a review after you have successfully completed the *Prelab Activities* and *Lab Exercises*.

For each of the following problems, write a program or a program segment that performs the specified action.

1. Create the following GUI (you will provide functionality later): The GUI consists of three JLists: two that contain the numbers 0–9, and one that contains three operations (+, – and *). The GUI should also contain a JButton with the label "Calculate" and a JTextField. Each JList should also be contained in a JScrollPane. The window shown is separated into two JPanels — the top one contains the three JScrollPanes in a GridLayout, and the bottom one contains the "Calculate" button and the JText-Field in a BorderLayout. You may space and size all the components as you like.

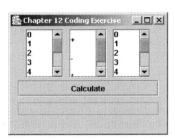

Postlab Activities   Name:

Coding Exercises

2. Modify the program from Coding Exercise 1 such that each JList is set to SINGLE_SELECTION.

3. Modify the program from Coding Exercise 2 by adding an ActionListener to the "Calculate" button. When the button is pressed, it should retrieve the values from the three lists and display the calculated value in the JTextField (e.g., if "1", "+" and "2" are selected in the lists, then the JTextField should display "1 + 2 = 3").

Postlab Activities   Name:

Coding Exercises

4. Modify the program from Coding Exercise 3 so that, when the user clicks the **"Calculate"** button, the program ensures that the user selected a value from each list. If not, the program should display a message telling the user that an item must be selected from each list.

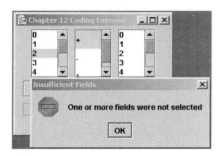

Postlab Activities   Name:

Programming Challenge

Name: _____   Date:_____

Section: _____

The *Programming Challenges* are more involved than the *Coding Exercises* and may require a significant amount of time to complete. Write a Java program for each of the problems in this section. The answers to these problems are available at www.deitel.com, www.prenhall.com/deitel and on the *Java Multimedia Cyber Classroom: Fifth Edition*. Pseudocode, hints or sample outputs are provided for each problem to aid you in your programming.

1. Create an application that enables the user to paint a picture by using the mouse to draw. The user should be able to choose the shape to draw, the color in which the shape should appear and whether the shape should be filled with color. Use the graphical user interface components discussed in this chapter, such as JCombo-Boxes, JRadioButtons and JCheckBoxes, to allow the user to select various options. The program should provide a JButton that allows the user to erase the contents of the window.

Hints:

*   Your application should use JPanels to arrange the GUI components as shown in the screen captures on the following page.

*   This is a large exercise. You should break the development process into smaller pieces.

*   First set up the layout with no functionality (i.e. just the look and feel of the application.)

*   Next add functionality to the application: Add listeners to all the tool components and a mouse listener for the window.

*   You may use any number of colors that you would like.

*   Enable the user to draw at least lines, rectangles and ovals.

*   Drawing should occur only when the user drags the mouse across the drawing area.

*   Place the JPanel containing the tools in the SOUTH region of your window's BorderLayout.

Postlab Activities   Name:

Programming Challenge

- Your application should appear as shown in the following screen captures:

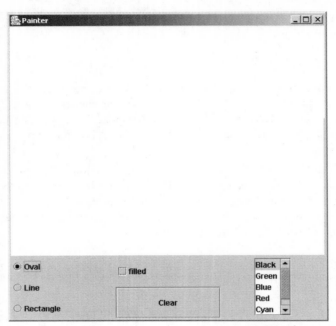

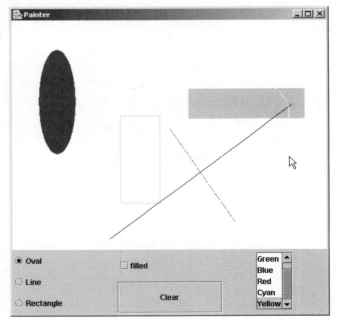

15

Exception Handling

Objectives

- To understand exception and error handling.
- To be able to use `try` blocks to test a segment of code for errors.
- To use `throw` statements to communicate information about an error.
- To use `catch` clauses to handle any exceptions that were thrown.

Assignment Checklist

Name: _____   Date:_____

Section: _____

Exercises	Assigned: Circle assignments		Date Due
Prelab Activities			
Matching	YES	NO	
Fill in the Blank	YES	NO	
Short Answer	YES	NO	
Programming Output	YES	NO	
Correct the Code	YES	NO	
Lab Exercises			
Exercise — Access Array	YES	NO	
Follow-Up Question and Activity	1		
Debugging	YES	NO	
Postlab Activities			
Coding Exercises	1, 2		

Prelab Activities

Matching

Name: _____   Date:_____

Section: _____

After reading Chapter 15 of *Java How to Program: Fifth Edition*, answer the given questions. These questions are intended to test and reinforce your understanding of key Java concepts. You may answer these questions either before or during the lab.

For each term in the column on the left, write the corresponding letter for the description that best matches it from the column on the right.

Term	Description
____ 1. `try`	a) A method uses this keyword to initiate an exception.
____ 2. `finally`	b) A method that displays the method-call stack at the time that an exception occurred.
____ 3. `Exception`	c) Thrown when a program attempts to divide by zero in integer arithmetic.
____ 4. `catch`	d) A block containing code that may generate exceptions.
____ 5. `throw`	e) Superclass from which all exceptions are derived.
____ 6. `ArithmeticException`	f) A serious problem from which most programs cannot recover.
____ 7. `NumberFormatException`	g) An exception that can occur at any point during the execution of the program and can usually be avoided by coding properly.
____ 8. `printStackTrace`	h) A method that returns an array of `StackTraceElement`s.
____ 9. stack unwinding	i) An exception handler.
____ 10. `getStackTrace`	j) The process by which an exception that is not caught is returned to a calling method in an attempt to locate an appropriate `catch` clause.
____ 11. `RuntimeException`	k) Thrown when an attempt is made to convert a `String` to a numeric value and the `String` does not represent a number.
____ 12. `Error`	l) A block of code that releases resources that might have been allocated in a corresponding `try` block.

Prelab Activities   Name:

Fill in the Blank

Name: _____   **Date:**_____

Section: _____

Fill in the blank for each of the following statements:

13. A(n) _____ is an indication that a problem occurred during the program's execution.

14. Each _____ specifies the type of exception it can handle.

15. Only _____ objects can be used with the exception-handling mechanism.

16. If no exception handler matches a particular thrown object, the search for a match continues in an enclosing _____.

17. Once an exception is thrown, program control cannot return directly to the _____.

18. The programmer encloses in a `try` block the _____ and any code that _____ if an exception occurs.

19. A `catch` clause for type _____ can handle exceptions of any type.

20. A `catch` clause for type _____ can catch any object that can be used with the exception-handling mechanism.

21. A(n) _____ always executes as long as program control enters its corresponding `try` block.

22. A(n) _____ lists the exceptions that a method might throw.

Prelab Activities

Name:

Short Answer

Name: _____   Date:_____

Section: _____

In the space provided, answer each of the given questions. Your answers should be as concise as possible; aim for two or three sentences.

23. Explain when exception handling should be used.

24. What is the difference between the termination model of exception handling, used in Java, and the resumption model of exception handling?

Prelab Activities

Name: _____

Short Answer

25. Describe the general flow of control through a `try...catch...finally` when an exception occurs and is caught.

26. Describe the general flow of control through a `try...catch...finally` when an exception occurs and is not caught. What happens to the exception object that was thrown?

27. Explain the restrictions on the `throws` clause of a subclass method that overrides a superclass method.

Prelab Activities   Name: _____

Short Answer

28. Explain the "catch or declare" requirement of Java exception handling. How does this affect exception types that are direct or indirect subclasses of `RuntimeException`?

29. Why would a `catch` clause rethrow an exception?

30. Explain the process of stack unwinding

Prelab Activities   Name:

Programming Output

Name: _____   Date:_____

Section: _____

For each of the given program segments, read the code and write the output in the space provided below each program. [*Note*: Do not execute these programs on a computer.]

31. What is output by the following application?

```java
 1    import javax.swing.*;
 2
 3    public class Test {
 4
 5       public static String lessThan100( int number ) throws Exception
 6       {
 7          if ( number >= 100 )
 8             throw new Exception( "Number too large." );
 9
10          return "The number " + number + " is less than 100";
11       }
12
13       public static void main( String args[] )
14       {
15          try {
16             System.out.println( lessThan100( 1 ) );
17             System.out.println( lessThan100( 22 ) );
18             System.out.println( lessThan100( 100 ) );
19             System.out.println( lessThan100( 11 ) );
20          }
21          catch( Exception exception ) {
22             System.out.println( exception.toString() );
23          }
24
25          System.exit( 0 );
26
27       } // end main method
28
29    } // end class Test
```

Your answer:

Programming Output

32. What is output by the following program?

```java
public class Test {

   public static void method3() throws RuntimeException
   {
      throw new RuntimeException( "RuntimeException occurred in method3" );
   }

   public static void method2() throws RuntimeException
   {
      try {
         method3();
      }

      catch ( RuntimeException exception ) {
         System.out.println( "The following exception occurred in method2\n" +
            exception.toString() );
         throw exception;
      }

   } // end method2

   public static void method1() throws RuntimeException
   {
      try {
         method2();
      }

      catch ( RuntimeException exception ) {
         System.out.println( "The following exception occurred in method1\n" +
            exception.toString() );
         throw exception;
      }

   } // end method1

   public static void main( String args[] )
   {
      try {
         method1();
      }
      catch ( RuntimeException exception ) {
         System.out.println( "The following exception occurred in main\n" +
            exception.toString() );
      }

      System.exit( 0 );

   } // end main

} // end class test
```

Prelab Activities   Name:

Programming Output

Your answer:

33. What is output by the following program?

```
1   import javax.swing.*;
2
3   public class Test {
4
5      public static String divide( int number1, int number2 )
6      {
7         return number1 + " divided by " + number2 + " is " + ( number1 / number2 );
8      }
9
10     public static void main( String args[] )
11     {
12        try {
13           System.out.println( divide( 4, 2 ) );
14           System.out.println( divide( 20, 5 ) );
15           System.out.println( divide( 100, 0 ) );
16        }
17        catch( Exception exception ) {
18           System.out.println( exception.toString() );
19        }
20
21        System.exit( 0 );
22
23     } // end main
24
25  } // end class Test
```

Your answer:

Prelab Activities   Name:

Programming Output

34. What is output by the following program if the user enters the values 3 and 4.7?

```java
 1    import javax.swing.*;
 2
 3    public class Test {
 4
 5       public static String sum( int num1, int num2 )
 6       {
 7          return num1 + " + " + num2 + " = " + ( num1 + num2 );
 8       }
 9
10       public static void main( String args[] )
11       {
12          int number1, number2;
13
14          try {
15             number1 =
16                Integer.parseInt( JOptionPane.showInputDialog( "Enter an integer: " ) );
17
18             number2 = Integer.parseInt( JOptionPane.showInputDialog(
19                "Enter another integer: " ) );
20
21             System.out.println( sum( number1, number2 ) );
22          }
23          catch ( NumberFormatException numberFormatException ) {
24             System.out.println( numberFormatException.toString() );
25          }
26
27          System.exit( 0 );
28
29       } // end main method
30
31    } // end class Test
```

Your answer:

Prelab Activities   Name:

Correct the Code

Name: _____   Date:_____

Section: _____

Determine if there is an error in each of the following program segments. If there is an error, specify whether it is a logic error or a compilation error, circle the error in the program and write the corrected code in the space provided after each problem. If the code does not contain an error, write "no error." [*Note*: There may be more than one error in each program segment.]

35. The following code segment should `catch` only `NumberFormatException`s and display an error message dialog if such an exception occurs:

```
1   catch ( Exception exception )
2      JOptionPane.showMessageDialog( this,
3         "A number format exception has occurred",
4         "Invalid Number Format", JOptionPane.ERROR_MESSAGE );
```

Your answer:

36. The following code segment should `catch` two exception types that could be thrown by `method1` and display an appropriate error message dialog in each case:

```
1   try
2      method1();
3
4   catch ( NumberFormatException n, ArithmeticException a ) {
5      JOptionPane.showMessageDialog( this,
6         "The following exception occurred \n" + n.toString() +
7         " \n" + a.toSting();
8         "Exception occurred", JOptionPane.ERROR_MESSAGE );
9   }
```

37. *Your answer:*

Prelab Activities

Name: _____

Correct the Code

38. The following code segment should display an error message dialog if the user does not enter two integers:

```
1  try {
2     int number1 =
3        Integer.parseInt( JOptionPane.showInputDialog( "Enter first integer:" ) );
4     int number2 =
5        Integer.parseInt( JOptionPane.showInputDialog( "Enter second integer:" ) );
6
7     JOptionPane.showMessageDialog( null, "The sum is: " + ( number1 + number2 ) );
8  }
```

Your answer:

Lab Exercises

Lab Exercise — Access Array

Name: _____   Date:_____

Section: _____

The following problem is intended to be solved in a closed-lab session with a teaching assistant or instructor present. The problem is divided into six parts:

1. Lab Objectives
2. Description of the Problem
3. Sample Output
4. Program Template (Fig. L 15.1 and Fig. L 15.2)
5. Problem-Solving Tips
6. Follow-Up Question and Activity

The program template represents a complete working Java program with one or more key lines of code replaced with comments. Read the problem description and examine the sample output, then study the template code. Using the problem-solving tips as a guide, replace the /* */ comments with Java code. Compile and execute the program. Compare your output with the sample output provided. Then answer the follow-up question. The source code for the template is available at www.deitel.com and www.prenhall.com/deitel.

Lab Objectives

This lab was designed to reinforce programming concepts from Chapter 15 of *Java How to Program: Fifth Edition*. In this lab, you will practice:

- Using exception handling to determine valid inputs.
- Using exception handling to write more robust and more fault-tolerant programs.

The follow-up question and activity also will give you practice:

- Creating your own exception type and throwing exceptions of that type.

Description of the Problem

Write a program that will allow a user to input integer values into an array of size 10. The program should allow for retrieving values from the array by index or by specifying a value greater than 0 to search for in the array. The program should handle any exceptions that might arise when inputting values into the array or accessing array elements. The program should also make use of the exception class NumberNotFoundException, defined below. If an attempt is made to access an element outside the array bounds, catch the ArrayIndexOutOfBounds exception and display an appropriate error message.

Lab Exercises   Name:

Lab Exercise — Access Array

Sample Output

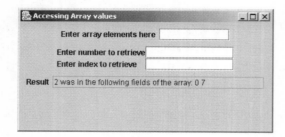

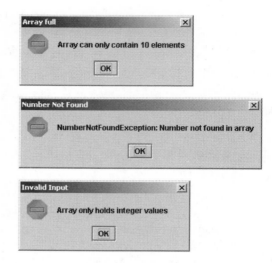

Program Template

```
1   // NumberNotFoundException.java
2   // Thrown when a number is not found during a search of an array
3
4   public class NumberNotFoundException extends Exception {
5
6      // no-argument constructor specifies default error message
7      public NumberNotFoundException()
8      {
9         super( "Number not found in array" );
10     }
11
12     // constructor to allow customized error message
13     public NumberNotFoundException( String message )
14     {
15        super( message );
16     }
17
18  }
```

Fig. L 15.1   NumberNotFoundException.java.

```
1   // Lab 1: ArrayAccess.java
2   // Program that allows user to insert items in an array or search
3   // for items in an array
4   import java.awt.*;
5   import java.awt.event.*;
6   import javax.swing.*;
7
8   public class ArrayAccess extends JFrame {
9      private JTextField inputField, retrieveValueField,
10        retrieveIndexField, outputField;
```

Fig. L 15.2   ArrayAccess.java. (Part 1 of 4.)

Lab Exercises   Name:

Lab Exercise — Access Array

```
11     private JPanel inputArea, retrievePanel, outputPanel;
12     private int num, index = 0, accessArray[];
13     private String result;
14
15     // set up GUI
16     public ArrayAccess()
17     {
18        super( "Accessing Array values" );
19
20        accessArray = new int[ 10 ];
21
22        // get content pane and set its layout
23        Container container = getContentPane();
24        container.setLayout( new FlowLayout() );
25
26        // set up input Panel
27        inputPanel = new JPanel();
28        inputPanel.add( new JLabel( "Enter array elements here" ) );
29        inputField = new JTextField( 10 );
30        inputField.addActionListener(
31
32           new ActionListener() {
33
34              public void actionPerformed( ActionEvent e )
35              {
36                 /* Write a try block in which the application reads the number
37                    entered in the inputField and assigns it to the next index
38                    in the array, then increments instance variable index. */
39
40                 /* Write catch clauses that catch the two types of exceptions
41                    that the previous try block might throw (NumberFormatException
42                    and ArrayIndexOutOfBoundsException), and display appropriate
43                    messages in error message dialogs. */
44
45                 inputField.setText( "" );
46
47              } // end method actionPerformed
48
49           } // end anonymous inner class
50
51        ); // end call to addActionListener
52
53        inputPanel.add( inputField );
54        container.add( inputPanel );
55
56        // set up retrieve Panel
57        retrievePanel = new JPanel( new GridLayout( 2, 2 ) );
58        retrievePanel.add( new JLabel( "Enter number to retrieve" ) );
59        retrieveValueField = new JTextField( 10 );
60        retrieveValueField.addActionListener(
61
62           new ActionListener() {
63
64              public void actionPerformed( ActionEvent event )
65              {
66                 /* Write code for a try block in which the application reads from
67                    retrieveValueField the number the user wants to find in the
```

Fig. L 15.2   ArrayAccess.java. (Part 2 of 4.)

Lab Exercises   Name:

Lab Exercise — Access Array

```
68              array, then searches the current array contents for the number.
69              If the number is found, the outputField should display all the
70              indices in which the number was found. If the number is not
71              found, a NumberNotFoundException should be thrown. */
72
73          /* Write catch clauses that catch the two types of exceptions that
74              the try block might throw (NumberFormatException and
75              NumberNotFoundException), and display appropriate messages
76              in error message dialogs. */
77
78          retrieveValueField.setText( "" );
79
80        } // end method actionPerformed
81
82      } // end anonymous inner class
83
84   ); // end call to addActionListener
85
86   retrievePanel.add( retrieveValueField );
87   retrievePanel.add( new JLabel( "Enter index to retrieve" ) );
88   retrieveIndexField = new JTextField( 10 );
89   retrieveIndexField.addActionListener(
90
91      new ActionListener() {
92
93        public void actionPerformed( ActionEvent event )
94        {
95          /* Write code for a try block in which the application reads from
96              retrieveIndexField the index of a value in the array, then
97              displays the value at that index in the outputField. If the index
98              input by the user is not a number a NumberFormatException should
99              be thrown. If the number input by the user is outside the array
100             bounds or represents an element in which the application has not
101             stored a value, an ArrayIndexOutOfBoundsException should
102             be thrown. */
103
104         /* Write catch clauses that catch the two types of exceptions that
105             the try block might throw (NumberFormatException and
106             ArrayIndexOutOfBoundsException), and display appropriate
107             messages in error message dialogs. */
108
109         retrieveIndexField.setText( "" );
110
111       } // end method actionPerformed
112
113     } // end anonymous inner class
114
115   ); // end call to addActionListener
116
117   retrievePanel.add( retrieveIndexField );
118   container.add( retrievePanel );
119
120   // set up output Panel
121   outputPanel = new JPanel();
122   outputPanel.add( new JLabel( "Result" ) );
123   outputField = new JTextField( 30 );
124   outputField.setEditable( false );
```

Fig. L 15.2   ArrayAccess.java. (Part 3 of 4.)

Lab Exercises   Name:

Lab Exercise — Access Array

```
125        outputPanel.add( outputField );
126        container.add( outputPanel );
127
128        setSize( 400, 200 );
129        setVisible( true );
130
131    } // end constructor
132
133    // execute application
134    public static void main( String args[] )
135    {
136        ArrayAccess application = new ArrayAccess();
137        application.setDefaultCloseOperation( JFrame.EXIT_ON_CLOSE );
138    }
139
140 } // end class ArrayAccess
```

Fig. L 15.2   `ArrayAccess.java`. (Part 4 of 4.)

Problem-Solving Tips

1. When you search the array for the value, you should define a `boolean` value at the beginning of the `try` block and initialize it to `false`. If the value is found in the array, set the `boolean` value to `true`. This will help you determine whether you need to `throw` an exception.

2. Refer to the sample output to decide what messages to display in the error dialogs.

3. Each of the three event handlers will have its own `try...catch` statement.

4. If you have any questions as you proceed, ask your lab instructor for assistance.

Follow-Up Question and Activity

1. Modify the previous program by creating another exception class called `DuplicateValueException` for detecting whether the user inputs a duplicate number. A `DuplicateValueException` should be thrown if the user inputs a value that already resides in the array. Also, display an appropriate error message. The program should continue normal execution after handling the exception.

Lab Exercises   Name:

Debugging

Name: _____   Date:_____

Section: _____

The program in this section does not compile. Fix all the syntax errors, so that the program will compile successfully. Once the program compiles, execute the program, and compare the output with the sample output. Then eliminate any logic errors that may exist. The sample output demonstrates what the program's output should be once the program's code is corrected. The source code is available at the Web sites www.deitel.com and www.prenhall.com/deitel.

Sample Output

```
SpecialIoException: Special IO Exception Occurred
```

Fig. L 15.3   Output for DebugException.java.

Broken Code

```
1   import java.io.*;
2
3   public class SpecialIoException throws IOException {
4
5      public SpecialIoException()
6      {
7         super( "Special IO Exception Occurred" );
8      }
9
10     public SpecialIoException( String message )
11     {
12        this( message );
13     }
14
15  }  // end class SpecialIoException
```

Fig. L 15.4   SpecialIoException.java.

```
1   // Debugging Chapter 15: DebugException.java
2
3   import java.io.*;
4
5   public class DebugException {
6
7      public static void main( String args[] )
8      {
9         try {
10           throw new SpecialIoException();
11        }
```

Fig. L 15.5   DebugException.java. (Part 1 of 2.)

Lab Exercises

Name:

Debugging

```
12          catch ( Exception exception ) {
13              System.err.println( exception.toString() );
14          }
15          catch ( IOException ioException ) {
16              System.err.println( ioException.toString() );
17          }
18          catch ( SpecialIoException sIoException ) {
19              sIoException.toString();
20          }
21
22      }  // end method main
23
24  }  // end class DebugException
```

Fig. L 15.5   `DebugException.java`. (Part 2 of 2.)

Postlab Activities

Coding Exercises

Name: _____   Date:_____

Section: _____

These coding exercises reinforce the lessons learned in the lab and provide additional programming experience outside the classroom and laboratory environment. They serve as a review after you have successfully completed the *Prelab Activities* and *Lab Exercises*.

For each of the following problems, write a program or a program segment that performs the specified action:

1. Define a class `InvalidInputException`. This class should be a direct subclass of `Exception`. It should specify the default message `"Your input was invalid."`, but should also enable the programmer to specify a custom message as well.

2. Define a class `ExceptionTest` based on class `DivideByZeroTest` of Fig. 15.1 of *Java How To Program: Fifth Edition*. Not only should `ExceptionTest` check for division by zero and valid integer input, it should also ensure that the integers being input are positive. If they are not, it should throw an `InvalidInputException` with the message `"You must enter positive numbers."`. The program should catch this exception and display an error message dialog

17

Files and Streams

Objectives

- To become familiar with sequential-access file processing.
- To be able to create, read, write and update files.

Assignment Checklist

Name: _____   Date:_____

Section: _____

Exercises	Assigned: Circle assignments		Date Due
Prelab Activities			
Matching	YES	NO	
Fill in the Blank	YES	NO	
Short Answer	YES	NO	
Correct the Code	YES	NO	
Lab Exercises			
Exercise — Shapes	YES	NO	
Debugging	YES	NO	
Postlab Activities			
Coding Exercises	1, 2		
Programming Challenge	1		

Prelab Activities

Matching

Name: _____   Date:_____

Section: _____

After reading Chapter 17 of *Java How to Program: Fifth Edition*, answer the given questions. These questions are intended to test and reinforce your understanding of key Java concepts. You may answer these questions either before or during the lab.

For each term in the left column, write the letter for the description that best matches the term from the right column.

Term	Description
____ 1. sequential-access file	a) Group of eight bits.
____ 2. field	b) An indication that there are no more contents to read from a file.
____ 3. record	c) File in which records are stored in order by the record-key field.
____ 4. file	d) This class enables programs to obtain information about a file or directory.
____ 5. InputStream	e) Group of related records.
____ 6. byte	f) An abstract class that defines methods for performing input.
____ 7. OutputStream	g) Group of related fields.
____ 8. FileWriter	h) This class implements interface ObjectInput.
____ 9. File class	i) A tagging interface that allows objects to be used with object streams.
____ 10. end-of-file marker	j) This class implements interface ObjectOutput.
____ 11. ObjectInputSream	k) Composed of characters or bytes that convey meaning for one part of a record.
____ 12. ObjectOutputStream	l) A class that writes characters to a file.
____ 13. Serializable	m) An abstract class that defines methods for performing output.

Prelab Activities   Name:

Fill in the Blank

Name: _____   Date:_____

Section: _____

Fill in the blank for each of the following statements:

14. Programs use classes from package _____ to perform Java file I/O.

15. Streams provide _____ between programs and files, memory or other programs across a network.

16. A collection of programs designed to create and manage databases is called a(n) _____.

17. Java creates three stream objects that are associated with devices when a Java program begins executing. These three objects are _____, _____ and _____.

18. _____ is an I/O-performance-enhancement technique.

19. Java views each file as a(n) _____.

20. To write objects into a file, use stream objects of types _____ and _____.

21. To read objects from a file, use stream objects of types _____ and _____.

22. Each file ends in some machine-dependent form of _____ marker.

23. `System.out` and `System.err` are objects of class _____ (for text-based output).

24. Stream objects can be _____ to create stream objects with combined functionality, such as writing objects to a file.

25. The set of all characters used to write programs and represent data items on a particular computer is called that computer's _____.

Prelab Activities   Name:

Short Answer

Name: _____   Date:_____

Section: _____

In the space provided, answer each of the given questions. Your answers should be as concise as possible; aim for two or three sentences.

26. Why is file processing useful for storing data?

27. What is the purpose of implementing interface `Serializable` in a new class?

Prelab Activities

Name:

Short Answer

28. Describe the characteristics of a sequential-access file.

29. What are the three predefined stream objects that you can use in a program and what is the purpose of each?

30. Describe how you would read lines of text from a text file. Specify the class(es) you would use to accomplish this task.

Prelab Activities

Name:

Correct the Code

Name: _____   Date:_____

Section: _____

Determine if there is an error in each of the following program segments. If there is an error, specify whether it is a logic error or a compilation error, circle the error in the program and write the corrected code in the space provided after each problem. If the code does not contain an error, write "no error." [*Note*: There may be more than one error in each program segment.]

31. The following code segment should open a file for object output:

```
1  ObjectOutputStream output = new ObjectOutputStream( new FileOutput( "file.dat" ) );
```

Your answer:

32. The following code segment should open a file for object input:

```
1  FileInputStream input = new FileInputStream( "file.dat" );
```

Your answer:

Prelab Activities   Name:

Correct the Code

33. The following code segment should write the object named `record` into a file. Assume that `output` is a properly defined object of class `ObjectOutputStream`.

```
1    output.write( record );
```

Your answer:

34. The following code segment should catch each of the exceptions that can occur when reading `Account-Record` objects from a file of serialized `AccountRecord`s. Assume that `input` is a properly defined object of class `ObjectInputStream`.

```
1    try {
2        record = ( AccountRecord ) input.readObject();
3    }
4    catch ( IOException exception ) {
5
6    }
```

Your answer:

Lab Exercises

Lab Exercise — Shapes

Name: _____   Date:_____

Section: _____

This problem is intended to be solved in a closed-lab session with a teaching assistant or instructor present. The problem is divided into five parts:

1. Lab Objectives
2. Description of the Problem
3. Sample Output
4. Program Template (Fig. L 17.1)
5. Problem-Solving Tips

The program template represents a complete working Java program with one or more key lines of code replaced with comments. Read the problem description and examine the sample output; then study the template code. Using the problem-solving tips as a guide, replace the /* */ comments with Java code. Compile and execute the program. Compare your output with the sample output provided. The source code for the template is available at www.deitel.com and www.prenhall.com/deitel.

Lab Objectives

This lab was designed to reinforce programming concepts from Chapter 17 of *Java How to Program: Fifth Edition*. In this lab you will practice:

- Opening files for input and output.
- Reading and writing objects to a file.

Problem Description

Modify the MyShape hierarchy of classes for drawing shapes (created in the Chapter 10 *Lab Exercises*) so that the user can store a random shape drawing in a file and subsequently load that drawing and display it. Modify class TestDrawWindow so that the window contains three buttons in the South region of the window's BorderLayout. The buttons allow the user to generate a random drawing, store a random drawing to a file and load a random drawing from a file, respectively. When the user loads an existing drawing from a file, the program should display the drawing.

Lab Exercises   Name:

Lab Exercise — Shapes

Sample Output

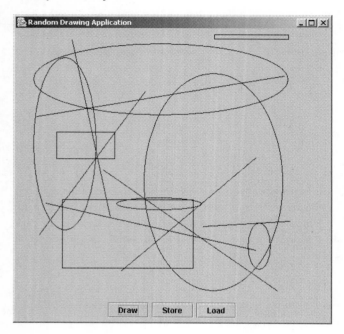

Template

```
1    // MyShape.java
2    // Definition of class MyShape.
3    import java.io.Serializable;
4
5    /* Write a header for public abstract class MyShape. Implement the interface that
6       allows MyShape objects to be read from and written to files as objects. */
7
8       private int x1, x2, y1, y2;
9
10      // default constructor initializes values with 0
11      public MyShape()
12      {
13         this( 0, 0, 0, 0 );
14      }
15
16      // constructor
17      public MyShape( int x1, int y1, int x2, int y2 )
18      {
19         setX1( x1 );
20         setX2( x2 );
21         setY1( y1 );
22         setY2( y2 );
23      }
24
25      // abstract draw method
26      public abstract void draw( java.awt.Graphics g );
```

Fig. L 17.1   `MyShape.java`. (Part 1 of 2.)

Lab Exercises   Name:

Lab Exercise — Shapes

```
27
28      // accessor and mutator methods for each of the
29      // four private variables:
30      public void setX1( int x )
31      {
32          x1 = ( x < 0 ? 0 : x );
33      }
34
35      public void setX2( int x )
36      {
37          x2 = ( x < 0 ? 0 : x );
38      }
39
40      public void setY1( int y )
41      {
42          y1 = ( y < 0 ? 0 : y );
43      }
44
45      public void setY2( int y )
46      {
47          y2 = ( y < 0 ? 0 : y );
48      }
49
50      public int getX1()
51      {
52          return x1;
53      }
54
55      public int getX2()
56      {
57          return x2;
58      }
59
60      public int getY1()
61      {
62          return y1;
63      }
64
65      public int getY2()
66      {
67          return y2;
68      }
69
70  } // end class MyShape
```

Fig. L 17.1   MyShape.java. (Part 2 of 2.)

```
1   // MyOval.java
2   // Definition of class MyOval.
3
4   public class MyOval extends MyShape {
5
6       // call default superclass constructor
7       public MyOval()
8       {
9           super();
```

Fig. L 17.2   MyOval.java. (Part 1 of 2.)

Lab Exercises   Name:

Lab Exercise — Shapes

```
10      } // end no-argument constructor
11
12      // call superclass constructor passing parameters
13      public MyOval( int x1, int y1, int x2, int y2 )
14      {
15         super( x1, y1, x2, y2 );
16      }
17
18      // draw oval
19      public void draw( java.awt.Graphics g )
20      {
21         g.drawOval( Math.min( getX1(), getX2() ), Math.min( getY1(), getY2() ),
22            Math.abs( getX2() - getX1() ), Math.abs( getY2() - getY1() ) );
23      }
24
25   } // end class MyOval
```

Fig. L 17.2   `MyOval.java`. (Part 2 of 2.)

```
1    // MyRectangle.java
2    // Definition of class MyRectangle.
3
4    public class MyRectangle extends MyShape {
5
6       // call default superclass constructor
7       public MyRectangle()
8       {
9          super();
10      }
11
12      // call superclass constructor passing parameters
13      public MyRectangle( int x1, int y1, int x2, int y2 )
14      {
15         super( x1, y1, x2, y2 );
16      }
17
18      // draw rectangle
19      public void draw( java.awt.Graphics g )
20      {
21         g.drawRect( Math.min( getX1(), getX2() ), Math.min( getY1(), getY2() ),
22            Math.abs( getX2() - getX1() ), Math.abs( getY2() - getY1() ) );
23      }
24
25   } // end class MyRectangle
```

Fig. L 17.3   `MyRectangle.java`.

```
1    // MyLine.java
2    // Definition of class MyLine.
3
4    public class MyLine extends MyShape {
5
6       // call default superclass constructor
7       public MyLine()
8       {
```

Fig. L 17.4   `MyLine.java`. (Part 1 of 2.)

Lab Exercises   Name:

Lab Exercise — Shapes

```
 9        super();
10    } // end no-argument constructor
11
12    // call superclass constructor passing parameters
13    public MyLine( int x1, int y1, int x2, int y2 )
14    {
15        super( x1, y1, x2, y2 );
16    }
17
18    // draw line
19    public void draw( java.awt.Graphics g )
20    {
21        g.drawLine( getX1(), getY1(), getX2(), getY2() );
22    }
23
24 } // end class MyLine
```

Fig. L 17.4   MyLine.java. (Part 2 of 2.)

```
 1    // Lab 1: TestDrawWindow.java
 2    // Program draws a random drawing of shapes, can store a drawing of
 3    // random shapes and can load a drawing of random shapes.
 4    import java.awt.*;
 5    import java.lang.*;
 6    import java.awt.event.*;
 7    import java.io.*;
 8    import javax.swing.*;
 9
10    public class TestDrawWindow extends JFrame {
11
12        private MyShape shape[];
13
14        private ObjectOutputStream output;
15        private ObjectInputStream input;
16
17        private JPanel buttonPanel;
18        private JButton drawButton, storeButton, loadButton;
19        private Container container;
20
21        // contructor
22        public TestDrawWindow()
23        {
24            super( "Random Drawing Application" );
25
26            drawButton = new JButton( "Draw" );
27            /* Write code that registers an ActionListener for drawButton.
28               The event handler should call method drawRandom. */
29
30            storeButton = new JButton( "Store" );
31            storeButton.setEnabled( false );
32            /* Write code that registers an ActionListener for storeButton.
33               The event handler should call method storeDrawing. */
34
35            loadButton = new JButton( "Load" );
36            /* Write code that registers an ActionListener for loadButton.
37               The event handler should call method loadDrawing. */
```

Fig. L 17.5   TestDrawWindow.java. (Part 1 of 4.)

Lab Exercises   Name:

Lab Exercise — Shapes

```
38
39          buttonPanel = new JPanel();
40          buttonPanel.add( drawButton );
41          buttonPanel.add( storeButton );
42          buttonPanel.add( loadButton );
43
44          container = getContentPane();
45          container.add( buttonPanel, BorderLayout.SOUTH );
46
47          setSize( 500, 500 );
48          setVisible( true );
49       } // end constructor
50
51       // method to draw random shapes
52       private void drawRandom()
53       {
54          int shapeType, x1, x2, y1, y2;
55
56          shape = new MyShape[ 15 ];
57
58          for ( int i = 0; i < shape.length; i++ ) {
59
60             x1 = ( int ) ( Math.random() * 425 + 25 );
61             x2 = ( int ) ( Math.random() * 425 + 25 );
62             y1 = ( int ) ( Math.random() * 425 + 25 );
63             y2 = ( int ) ( Math.random() * 425 + 25 );
64
65             shapeType = ( int ) ( Math.random() * 3 ) + 1;
66
67             switch ( shapeType ) {
68
69                case 1:
70                   shape[ i ] = new MyLine( x1, y1, x2, y2 );
71                   break;
72
73                case 2:
74                   shape[ i ] = new MyOval( x1, y1, x2, y2 );
75                   break;
76
77                case 3:
78                   shape[ i ] = new MyRectangle( x1, y1, x2, y2 );
79                   break;
80             }
81          }
82
83          /* Write statements that enable the storeButton and repaint the window. */
84
85       } // end method drawRandom
86
87       // method to store a drawing of random shapes
88       private void storeDrawing()
89       {
90          JFileChooser fileChooser = new JFileChooser();
91          fileChooser.setFileSelectionMode( JFileChooser.FILES_ONLY );
92
93          int result = fileChooser.showSaveDialog( this );
```

Fig. L 17.5   TestDrawWindow.java. (Part 2 of 4.)

Lab Exercises   Name:

Lab Exercise — Shapes

```
94
95        // if the user clicked the Cancel button on dialog, return
96        /* Write code that will return from this method if the user
97           selects Cancel from the JFileChooser dialog. */
98
99        File fileName = fileChooser.getSelectedFile();
100
101       // display an error if file name is invalid
102       /* Write code that determines whether the file name is null or an empty
103          string. If the file name is invalid display an error message dialog. */
104       else {
105          try {
106             /* Write code that creates a new ObjectOutputStream for the file
107                selected by the user, then write the contents of array shape to the
108                file, flush the output stream and close the output stream. */
109          }
110          /* Write code that catches any exceptions that might occur
111             in the try block above */
112       } // end else
113
114    } // end method storeDrawing
115
116    // method to load a drawing of random shapes
117    private void loadDrawing()
118    {
119       JFileChooser fileChooser = new JFileChooser();
120       fileChooser.setFileSelectionMode( JFileChooser.FILES_ONLY );
121
122       int result = fileChooser.showOpenDialog( this );
123
124       // if the user clicked the Cancel button on dialog, return
125       /* Write code that will return from this method if the user
126          selects Cancel from the JFileChooser dialog. */
127
128       File fileName = fileChooser.getSelectedFile();
129
130       // display an error if file name is invalid
131       /* Write code that determines whether the file name is null or an empty
132          string. If the file name is invalid display an error message dialog. */
133       else {
134          try {
135             /* Write code that creates a new ObjectInputStream for the file
136                selected by the user, then assign array variable "shape" the
137                object read from the file and close the input stream. */
138          }
139          /* Write code that catches any exceptions that might occur
140             in the try block above */
141
142          /* Write statements that enable the storeButton and repaint the window */
143       } // end else
144
145    } // end method loadDrawing
146
147    // draw shapes
148    public void paint( Graphics g )
149    {
```

Fig. L 17.5   TestDrawWindow.java. (Part 3 of 4.)

Lab Exercises   Name:

Lab Exercise — Shapes

```
150          super.paint( g );
151
152          if ( shape != null ) {
153              for ( int i = 0; i < shape.length; i++ )
154                  shape[ i ].draw( g );
155          }
156      }
157
158      // create a TestDrawWindow object
159      public static void main( String args[] )
160      {
161          TestDrawWindow application = new TestDrawWindow();
162          application.setDefaultCloseOperation( JFrame.EXIT_ON_CLOSE );
163      }
164
165  } // end class TestDrawWindow
```

Fig. L 17.5   TestDrawWindow.java. (Part 4 of 4.)

Problem-Solving Tips

1. To write objects with an ObjectOutputStream and read objects with an ObjectInputStream, the objects' class(es) must implement interface Serializable.

1. Once interface Serializable is implemented in a superclass, all subclasses of that superclass are considered to implement interface Serializable as well.

2. Use method repaint to repaint the window whenever a new drawing needs to be displayed.

3. When reading an object in from a file, you must cast the object to its appropriate type.

4. Code related to processing object streams might throw exceptions for many reasons. All IOExceptions are checked exceptions, so these exceptions must be caught or your program will not compile.

5. Test the file processing functionality as follows: Create a random drawing, then click the **Store** button to store the drawing in a file and terminate the application. Execute the application again and click the **Load** button to load the previously saved image from the file so the application can draw it.

Lab Exercises   Name:

Debugging

Name: _____   Date: _____

Section: _____

The program in this section does not compile. Fix all the syntax errors, so that the program will compile success-fully. Once the program compiles, execute the program, and compare the output with the sample output. Then eliminate any logic errors that may exist. The sample output demonstrates what the program's output should be once the program's code is corrected. The source code is available at the Web sites www.deitel.com and www.prenhall.com/deitel.

Sample Output

Broken Code

```
1   // Debugging Exercise: CreateSequentialFile.java
2   // Writing objects sequentially to a file with class ObjectOutputStream.
3   import java.io.*;
4   import java.awt.*;
5   import java.awt.event.*;
6   import javax.swing.*;
7
8   import com.deitel.jhtp5.ch17.BankUI;
9   import com.deitel.jhtp5.ch17.AccountRecord;
10
11  public class CreateSequentialFile extends JFrame {
12     private ObjectInputStream input;
13     private BankUI userInterface;
14     private JButton enterButton, openButton;
15
16     // set up GUI
17     public CreateSequentialFile()
18     {
19        super( "Creating a Sequential File of Objects" );
20
21        // create instance of reusable user interface
22        userInterface = new BankUI( 4 );  // four textfields
23        getContentPane().add( userInterface, BorderLayout.CENTER );
24
25        // configure button doTask1 for use in this program
26        openButton = userInterface.getDoTask1Button();
27        openButton.setText( "Save into File ..." );
```

Fig. L 17.6   CreateSequentialFile.java. (Part 1 of 4.)

Lab Exercises

Name:

Debugging

```
28
29          // register listener to call openFile when button pressed
30          openButton.addActionListener(
31
32             // anonymous inner class to handle openButton event
33             new ActionListener() {
34
35                // call openFile when button pressed
36                public void actionPerformed( ActionEvent event )
37                {
38                   openFile();
39                }
40
41             } // end anonymous inner class
42
43          ); // end call to addActionListener
44
45          // configure button doTask2 for use in this program
46          enterButton = userInterface.getDoTask2Button();
47          enterButton.setText( "Enter" );
48          enterButton.setEnabled( false );   // disable button
49
50          // register listener to call addRecord when button pressed
51          enterButton.addActionListener(
52
53             // anonymous inner class to handle enterButton event
54             new ActionListener() {
55
56                // call addRecord when button pressed
57                public void actionPerformed( ActionEvent event )
58                {
59                   addRecord();
60                }
61
62             } // end anonymous inner class
63
64          ); // end call to addActionListener
65
66          // register window listener to handle window closing event
67          addWindowListener(
68
69             // anonymous inner class to handle windowClosing event
70             new WindowAdapter() {
71
72                // add current record in GUI to file, then close file
73                public void windowClosing( WindowEvent event )
74                {
75                   if ( output != null )
76                      addRecord();
77
78                   closeFile();
79                }
80
81             } // end anonymous inner class
82
83          ); // end call to addWindowListener
```

Fig. L 17.6   CreateSequentialFile.java. (Part 2 of 4.)

Lab Exercises   Name:

Debugging

```
84
85          setSize( 300, 200 );
86          setVisible( true );
87
88      } // end CreateSequentialFile constructor
89
90      // allow user to specify file name
91      private void openFile()
92      {
93          File fileName = new File( "sequential.dat" );
94
95          // open file
96          try {
97              output = new ObjectOutputStream( fileName.open() );
98
99              openButton.setEnabled( false );
100             enterButton.setEnabled( true );
101         }
102
103         // process exceptions from opening file
104         catch ( FileOpenException fileOpenException ) {
105             JOptionPane.showMessageDialog( this, "Error Opening File", "Error",
106                 JOptionPane.ERROR_MESSAGE );
107         }
108     } // end method openFile
109
110     // close file and terminate application
111     private void closeFile()
112     {
113         // close file
114         try {
115             System.exit( 0 );
116             output.close();
117         }
118
119         // process exceptions from closing file
120         catch( IOException ioException ) {
121             JOptionPane.showMessageDialog( this, "Error closing file",
122                 "Error", JOptionPane.ERROR_MESSAGE );
123             System.exit( 1 );
124         }
125     }
126
127     // add record to file
128     public void addRecord()
129     {
130         int accountNumber = 0;
131         AccountRecord record;
132         String fieldValues[] = userInterface.getFieldValues();
133
134         // if account field value is not empty
135         if ( ! fieldValues[ BankUI.ACCOUNT ].equals( "" ) ) {
136
137             // output values to file
138             try {
139                 accountNumber = Integer.parseInt( fieldValues[ BankUI.ACCOUNT ] );
```

Fig. L 17.6   CreateSequentialFile.java. (Part 3 of 4.)

Lab Exercises

Name:

Debugging

```
140
141              if ( accountNumber > 0 ) {
142
143                  // create new record
144                  record = new AccountRecord( accountNumber,
145                     fieldValues[ BankUI.FIRSTNAME ],
146                     fieldValues[ BankUI.LASTNAME ],
147                     Double.parseDouble( fieldValues[ BankUI.BALANCE ] ) );
148
149                  // output record and flush buffer
150                  record.writeObject( fileName );
151                  output.flushBuffer();
152              }
153              else {
154                  JOptionPane.showMessageDialog( this,
155                     "Account number must be greater than 0", "Bad account number",
156                     JOptionPane.ERROR_MESSAGE );
157              }
158
159              // clear textfields
160              userInterface.clearFields();
161
162          } // end try
163
164          // process invalid account number or balance format
165          catch ( AccountNumberException accountNumberException ) {
166              JOptionPane.showMessageDialog( this, "Bad account number or balance",
167                 "Invalid Number Format", JOptionPane.ERROR_MESSAGE );
168          }
169
170          // process exceptions from file output
171          catch ( IOException ioException ) {
172              JOptionPane.showMessageDialog( this, "Error writing to file",
173                 "IO Exception", JOptionPane.ERROR_MESSAGE );
174              closeFile();
175          }
176
177      } // end if
178
179   } // end method addRecord
180
181   // execute application
182   public static void main( String args[] )
183   {
184      new CreateSequentialFile();
185   }
186
187 } // end class CreateSequentialFile
```

Fig. L 17.6   CreateSequentialFile.java. (Part 4 of 4.)

Postlab Activities

Coding Exercises

Name: _____   Date:_____

Section: _____

These coding exercises reinforce the lessons learned in the lab and provide additional programming experience outside the classroom and laboratory environment. They serve as a review after you have successfully completed the *Prelab Activities* and *Lab Exercises*.

For each of the following problems, write a program or a program segment that performs the specified action:

1. Create a simple sequential-access file-processing program that might be used by professors to help manage their student records. For each student, the program should obtain an ID number, the student's first name, the student's last name and the student's grade. The data obtained for each student constitutes a record for the student and should be stored in an object of a class called `Student`. The program should save the record in a file specified by the user.

Postlab Activities

Name:

Coding Exercises

2. Create a simple sequential-access file-processing program to complement the program in Coding Exercise 1. This program should open a file created by the Coding Exercise 1 program and read and display the grade information for each student. A general summary of the total number of A's, B's, etc., should also be provided.

Postlab Activities   Name:

Programming Challenges

Name: _____   Date:_____

Section: _____

The *Programming Challenges* are more involved than the *Coding Exercises* and may require a significant amount of time to complete. Write a Java program for the problem in this section. The answer to this problem is available at www.deitel.com, www.prenhall.com/deitel and on the *Java Multimedia Cyber Classroom: Fifth Edition*. Pseudocode, hints or sample outputs are provided for the problem to aid you in your programming.

1. *(Telephone-Number Word Generator)* Standard telephone keypads contain the digits zero through nine. The numbers two through nine each have three letters associated with them. (See Fig. L 17.7.) Many people find it difficult to memorize phone numbers, so they use the correspondence between digits and letters to develop seven-letter words that correspond to their phone numbers. For example, a person whose telephone number is 686-2377 might use the correspondence indicated in Fig. L 17.7 to develop the seven-letter word "NUM-BERS." Each seven-letter word corresponds to exactly one seven-digit telephone number. The restaurant wishing to increase its takeout business could surely do so with the number 825-3688 (i.e., "TAKEOUT").

    Each seven-letter phone number corresponds to many separate seven-letter words. Unfortunately, most of these words represent unrecognizable juxtapositions of letters. It is possible, however, that the owner of a barbershop would be pleased to know that the shop's telephone number, 424-7288, corresponds to "HAIR-CUT." The owner of a liquor store would, no doubt, be delighted to find that the store's number, 233-7226, corresponds to "BEERCAN." A veterinarian with the phone number 738-2273 would be pleased to know that the number corresponds to the letters "PETCARE." An automotive dealership would be pleased to know that the dealership number, 639-2277, corresponds to "NEWCARS."

    Write a program that, given a seven-digit number, uses a `PrintWriter` object to write to a file every possible seven-letter word combination corresponding to that number. There are 2187 (3^7) such combinations. Avoid phone numbers with the digits 0 and 1.

Digit	Letters
2	A B C
3	D E F
4	G H I
5	J K L
6	M N O
7	P R S
8	T U V
9	W X Y

Fig. L 17.7   Telephone keypad digits and letters.

Hints:

*   You can create the `PrintWriter` object as follows:

    ```
    PrintWriter writer = new PrintWriter( new FileWriter( "phonenumbers.txt" ) );
    ```

*   Class `PrintWriter` provides methods `print` and `println`. Method `print` outputs its argument as text. Method `println` outputs its argument as text followed by a newline.

Index

The DEITEL® Suite of Products...

Getting Started with Microsoft® Visual C++™ 6 with an Introduction to MFC

BOOK / CD-ROM

©2000, 163 pp., paper
(0-13-016147-0)

Visual C++ .NET How To Program

BOOK / CD-ROM

©2004, 1400 pp., paper
(0-13-437377-4)

Written by the authors of the world's best-selling introductory/intermediate C and C++ textbooks, this comprehensive book thoroughly examines Visual C++® .NET. *Visual C++® .NET How to Program* begins with a strong foundation in the introductory and intermediate programming principles students will need in industry, including fundamental topics such as arrays, functions and control structures. Readers learn the concepts of object-oriented programming, including how to create reusable software components with classes and assemblies. The text then explores such essential topics as networking, databases, XML and multimedia. Graphical user interfaces are also extensively covered, giving students the tools to build compelling and fully interactive programs using the "drag-and-drop" techniques provided by the latest version of Visual Studio .NET, Visual Studio .NET 2003.

Advanced Java™ 2 Platform How to Program

BOOK / CD-ROM

©2002, 1811 pp., paper
(0-13-089560-1)

Expanding on the world's best-selling Java textbook—*Java™ How to Program*— *Advanced Java™ 2 Platform How To Program* presents advanced Java topics for developing sophisticated, user-friendly GUIs; significant, scalable enterprise applications; wireless applications and distributed systems. Primarily based on Java 2 Enterprise Edition (J2EE), this textbook integrates technologies such as XML, JavaBeans, security, JDBC™, JavaServer Pages (JSP™), servlets, Remote Method Invocation (RMI), Enterprise JavaBeans™ (EJB) and design patterns into a production-quality system that allows developers to benefit from the leverage and platform independence Java 2 Enterprise Edition provides. The book also features the development of a complete, end-to-end e-business solution using advanced Java technologies. Additional topics include Swing, Java 2D and 3D, XML, design patterns,

CORBA, Jini™, JavaSpaces™, Jiro™, Java Management Extensions (JMX) and Peer-to-Peer networking with an introduction to JXTA. This textbook also introduces the Java 2 Micro Edition (J2ME™) for building applications for handheld and wireless devices using MIDP and MIDlets. Wireless technologies covered include WAP, WML and i-mode.

C# How to Program

BOOK / CD-ROM

©2002, 1568 pp., paper
(0-13-062221-4)

An exciting addition to the *How to Program Series*, *C# How to Program* provides a comprehensive introduction to Microsoft's new object-oriented language. C# builds on the skills already mastered by countless C++ and Java programmers, enabling them to create powerful Web applications and components—ranging from XML-based Web services on Microsoft's .NET platform to middle-tier business objects and system-level applications. *C# How to Program* begins with a strong foundation in the introductory- and intermediate-programming principles students will need in industry. It then explores such essential topics as object-oriented programming and exception handling. Graphical user interfaces are extensively covered, giving readers the tools to build compelling and fully interactive programs. Internet technologies such as XML, ADO .NET and Web services are covered as well as topics including regular expressions, multithreading, networking, databases, files and data structures.

Visual Basic® .NET How to Program Second Edition

BOOK / CD-ROM

©2002, 1400 pp., paper
(0-13-029363-6)

Learn Visual Basic .NET programming from the ground up! The introduction of Microsoft's .NET Framework marks the beginning of major revisions to all of Microsoft's programming languages. This book provides a comprehensive introduction to the next version of Visual Basic—Visual Basic .NET—featuring extensive updates and increased functionality. *Visual Basic .NET How to Program, Second Edition* covers introductory programming techniques as well as more advanced topics, featuring enhanced treatment of developing Web-based applications. Other topics discussed include an extensive treatment of XML and wireless applications, databases, SQL and ADO .NET, Web forms, Web services and ASP .NET.

nd many other fields. Concise introductions to Java, JavaServer Pages, VBScript, Active Server Pages and Perl/CGI provide readers with the essentials of these programming languages and server-side development technologies to enable them to work effectively with XML. The book also covers cutting-edge topics such as XSL, DOM™ and SAX, plus a real-d e-commerce case study and a complete chapter on Web accessibility that addresses Voice XML. It includes tips such as Common Programming Errors, Software Engineering Observations, Portability Tips and Debugging Hints. Other topics covered include XHTML, CSS, DTD, schema, parsers, XPath, XLink, namespaces, XBase, XInclude, XPointer, XSLT, XSL Formatting Objects, JavaServer Pages, XForms, topic maps, X3D, MathML, OpenMath, CML, BML, CDF, RDF, SVG, Cocoon, WML, XBRL and BizTalk™ and SOAP™ Web resources.

Perl How to Program

`BOOK / CD-ROM`

©2001, 1057 pp., paper (0-13-028418-1)

This comprehensive guide to Perl programming emphasizes the use of the Common Gateway Interface (CGI) with Perl to create powerful, dynamic multi-tier Web-based client/server applications. The book begins with a clear and careful introduction to programming concepts at a level suitable for beginners, and proceeds through advanced topics such as references and complex data structures. Key Perl topics such as regular expressions and string manipulation are covered in detail. The authors address important and topical issues such as object-oriented programming, the Perl database interface (DBI), graphics and security. Also included is a treatment of XML, a bonus chapter introducing the Python programming language, supplemental material on career resources and a complete chapter on Web accessibility. The text includes tips such as Common Programming Errors, Software Engineering Observations, Portability Tips and Debugging Hints.

e-Business & e-Commerce How to Program

`BOOK / CD-ROM`

©2001, 1254 pp., paper (0-13-028419-X)

This innovative book explores programming technologies for developing Web-based e-business and e-commerce solutions, and covers e-business and e-commerce models and business issues. Readers learn a full range of options, from "build-your-own" to turnkey solutions. The book examines scores of the top e-businesses (examples include Amazon, eBay, Priceline, Travelocity, etc.), explaining the technical details of building successful e-business and e-commerce sites and their underlying business premises. Learn how to implement the dominant e-commerce models—shopping carts, auctions, name-your-own-price, comparison shopping and bots/ intelligent agents—by using markup languages (HTML, Dynamic HTML and XML), scripting languages (JavaScript, VBScript and Perl), server-side technologies (Active Server Pages and Perl/CGI) and database (SQL and ADO), security and online payment technologies. Updates are regularly posted to **www.deitel.com** and the book includes a CD-ROM with software tools, source code and live links.

Visual Basic® 6 How to Program

`BOOK / CD-ROM`

©1999, 1015 pp., paper (0-13-456955-5)

Visual Basic® 6 How to Program was developed in cooperation with Microsoft to cover important topics such as graphical user interfaces (GUIs), multimedia, object-oriented programming, networking, database programming, VBScript®, COM/DCOM and ActiveX®.

ORDER INFORMATION

SINGLE COPY SALES:
Visa, Master Card, American Express, Checks, or Money Orders only
Toll-Free: 800-643-5506; Fax: 800-835-5327

GOVERNMENT AGENCIES:
Prentice Hall Customer Service
(#GS-02F-8023A)
Phone: 201-767-5994; Fax: 800-445-6991

COLLEGE PROFESSORS:
For desk or review copies, please visit us on the World Wide Web at www.prenhall.com

CORPORATE ACCOUNTS:
Quantity, Bulk Orders totaling 10 or more books. Purchase orders only — No credit cards.
Tel: 201-236-7156; Fax: 201-236-7141
Toll-Free: 800-382-3419

CANADA:
Pearson Technology Group Canada
10 Alcorn Avenue, suite #300
Toronto, Ontario, Canada M4V 3B2
Tel.: 416-925-2249; Fax: 416-925-0068
E-mail: phcinfo.pubcanada@pearsoned.com

UK/IRELAND:
Pearson Education
Edinburgh Gate
Harlow, Essex CM20 2JE UK
Tel: 01279 623928; Fax: 01279 414130
E-mail: enq.orders@pearsoned-ema.com

EUROPE, MIDDLE EAST & AFRICA:
Pearson Education
P.O. Box 75598
1070 AN Amsterdam, The Netherlands
Tel: 31 20 5755 800; Fax: 31 20 664 5334
E-mail: amsterdam@pearsoned-ema.com

ASIA:
Pearson Education Asia
317 Alexandra Road #04-01
IKEA Building
Singapore 159965
Tel: 65 476 4688; Fax: 65 378 0370

JAPAN:
Pearson Education
Nishi-Shinjuku, KF Building 101
8-14-24 Nishi-Shinjuku, Shinjuku-ku
Tokyo, Japan 160-0023
Tel: 81 3 3365 9001; Fax: 81 3 3365 9009

INDIA:
Pearson Education Indian Liaison Office
90 New Raidhani Enclave, Ground Floor
Delhi 110 092, India
Tel: 91 11 2059850 & 2059851
Fax: 91 11 2059852

AUSTRALIA:
Pearson Education Australia
Unit 4, Level 2
14 Aquatic Drive
Frenchs Forest, NSW 2086, Australia
Tel: 61 2 9454 2200; Fax: 61 2 9453 0089
E-mail: marketing@pearsoned.com.au

NEW ZEALAND/FIJI:
Pearson Education
46 Hillside Road
Auckland 10, New Zealand
Tel: 649 444 4968; Fax: 649 444 4957
E-mail: sales@pearsoned.co.nz

SOUTH AFRICA:
Pearson Education
P.O. Box 12122
Mill Street
Cape Town 8010 South Africa
Tel: 27 21 686 6356; Fax: 27 21 686 4590

LATIN AMERICA:
Pearson Education Latinoamerica
815 NW 57th Street Suite 484
Miami, FL 33158
Tel: 305 264 8344; Fax: 305 264 7933

Introducing the <u>new</u> SIMPLY SERIES!

The Deitels are pleased to announce the new *Simply Series*. These books take an engaging new approach to teaching programming languages from the ground up. The pedagogy of this series combines the DEITEL® signature *LIVE-CODE™ Approach* with an *APPLICATION-DRIVEN™ Tutorial Approach* to teaching programming with outstanding pedagogical features that help students learn.

Simply Visual Basic® .NET An APPLICATION-DRIVEN™ Tutorial Approach

Visual Studio .NET 2002 Version:
©2004, 830 pp., paper
(0-13-140553-5)

Visual Studio .NET 2003 Version:
©2004, 830 pp., paper
(0-13-142640-0)

Simply Visual Basic® .NET An APPLICATION-DRIVEN™ Tutorial Approach guides readers through building real-world applications that incorporate Visual Basic .NET programming fundamentals. Using a step-by-step tutorial approach, readers begin learning the basics of programming and each successive tutorial builds on the readers' previously learned concepts while introducing new programming features. Learn GUI design, controls, methods, functions, data types, control structures, procedures, arrays, object-oriented programming, strings and characters, sequential files and more in this comprehensive introduction to Visual Basic .NET. We also include higher-end topics such as database programming, multimedia and graphics and Web applications development. If you're using Visual Studio® .NET 2002, choose the Visual Studio .NET 2002 version; or, if you're moving to Visual Studio .NET 2003, you can use the updated edition with updated screen captures and line numbers.

Simply C# An APPLICATION-DRIVEN™ Tutorial Approach

©2004, 850 pp., paper
(0-13-142641-9)

Simply C# An APPLICATION-DRIVEN™ Tutorial Approach guides readers through building real-world applications that incorporate C# programming fundamentals. Using a step-by-step tutorial approach, readers begin learning the basics of programming and each successive tutorial builds on the readers' previously learned concepts while introducing new programming features. Learn GUI design, controls, methods, functions, data types, control structures, procedures, arrays, object-oriented programming, strings and characters, sequential files and more in this comprehensive introduction to C#. We also include higher-end topics such as database programming, multimedia and graphics and Web applications development.

Simply Java™ Programming An APPLICATION-DRIVEN™ Tutorial Approach

©2004, 950 pp.,
paper
(0-13-142648-6)

Simply Java™ Programming An APPLICATION-DRIVEN™ Tutorial Approach guides readers through building real-world applications that incorporate Java programming fundamentals. Using a step-by-step tutorial approach, readers begin learning the basics of programming and each successive tutorial builds on the readers' previously learned concepts while introducing new programming features. Learn GUI design, components, methods, event-handling, types, control statements, arrays, object-oriented programming, exception-handling, strings and characters, sequential files and more in this comprehensive introduction to Java. We also include higher-end topics such as database programming, multimedia, graphics and Web applications development.

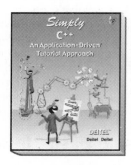

Simply C++ An APPLICATION-DRIVEN™ Tutorial Approach

©2004, 800 pp.,
paper
(0-13-142660-5)

For information about *Simply C++ An APPLICATION-DRIVEN™ Tutorial Approach* and other *Simply Series* books under development, visit **www.deitel.com**. You may also sign up for the DEITEL® Buzz Online at **www.deitel.com/newsletter/subscribe.html** for monthly updates on the entire DEITEL® publishing program.

Deitel & Associates is recognized worldwide for its best-selling *How to Program Series* of books for college and university students and its signature LIVE-CODE™ approach to teaching programming languages. Now, for the first time, Deitel & Associates brings its proven teaching methods to a new series of books specifically designed for professionals.

THREE TYPES OF BOOKS FOR THREE DISTINCT AUDIENCES:

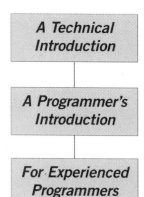

A Technical Introduction

A Programmer's Introduction

For Experienced Programmers

A Technical Introduction books provide programmers, technical managers, project managers and other technical professionals with introductions to broad new technology areas.

A Programmer's Introduction books offer focused treatments of programming fundamentals for practicing programmers. These books are also appropriate for novices.

For Experienced Programmers books are for experienced programmers who want a detailed treatment of a programming language or technology. These books contain condensed introductions to programming language fundamentals and provide extensive intermediate level coverage of high-end topics.

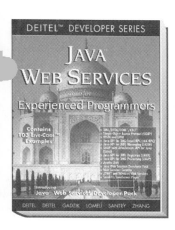

Java™ Web Services for Experienced Programmers

© 2003, 700 pp., paper (0-13-046134-2)

Java™ Web Services for Experienced Programmers from the DEITEL™ Developer Series provides the experienced Java programmer with 103 LIVE-CODE™ examples and covers industry standards including XML, SOAP, WSDL and UDDI. Learn how to build and integrate Web services using the Java API for XML RPC, the Java API for XML Messaging, Apache Axis and the Java Web Services Developer Pack. Develop and deploy Web services on several major Web services platforms. Register and discover Web services through public registries and the Java API for XML Registries. Build Web Services clients for several platforms, including J2ME. Significant Web Services case studies also are included.

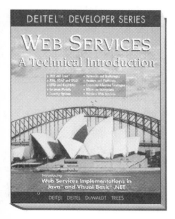

Web Services: A Technical Introduction

© 2003, 400 pp., paper (0-13-046135-0)

Web Services: A Technical Introduction from the DEITEL™ Developer Series familiarizes programmers, technical managers and project managers with key Web services concepts, including what Web services are and why they are revolutionary. The book covers the business case for Web services—the underlying technologies, ways in which Web services can provide competitive advantages and opportunities for Web services-related lines of business. Readers learn the latest Web-services standards, including XML, SOAP, WSDL and UDDI; learn about Web services implementations in .NET and Java; benefit from an extensive comparison of Web services products and vendors; and read about Web services security options. Although this is not a programming book, the appendices show .NET and Java code examples to demonstrate the structure of Web services applications and documents. In addition, the book includes numerous case studies describing ways in which organizations are implementing Web services to increase efficiency, simplify business processes, create new revenue streams and interact better with partners and customers.

Complete Training Courses

Each complete package includes the corresponding *How to Program Series* textbook and interactive multimedia Windows-based CD-ROM Cyber Classroom. *Complete Training Courses* are perfect for anyone interested in Web and e-commerce programming. They are affordable resources for college students and professionals learning programming for the first time or reinforcing their knowledge.

Intuitive Browser-Based Interface

You'll love the *Complete Training Courses'* new browser-based interface, designed to be easy and accessible to anyone who's ever used a Web browser. Every *Complete Training Course* features the full text, illustrations and program listings of its corresponding *How to Program* book—all in full color—with full-text searching and hyperlinking.

Further Enhancements to the Deitels' Signature LIVE-CODE™ Approach

Every code sample from the main text can be found in the interactive, multimedia, CD-ROM-based *Cyber Classrooms* included in the *Complete Training Courses*. Syntax coloring of code is included for the *How to Program* books that are published in full color. Even the recent two-color and one-color books use effective syntax shading. The *Cyber Classroom* products are always in full color.

Audio Annotations

Hours of detailed, expert audio descriptions of thousands of lines of code help reinforce concepts.

Easily Executable Code

With one click of the mouse, you can execute the code or save it to your hard drive to manipulate using the programming environment of your choice. With selected *Complete Training Courses*, you can also load all of the code into a development environment such as Microsoft® Visual C++™, enabling you to modify and execute the programs with ease.

Abundant Self-Assessment Material

Practice exams test your understanding of key concepts with hundreds of test questions and answers in addition to those found in the main text. The textbook includes hundreds of programming exercises, while the *Cyber Classrooms* include answers to about half the exercises.

www.phptr.com/phptrinteractive

The Complete C++ Training Course, Fourth Edition

(0-13-100252-X)

The Complete Java™ Training Course, Fifth Edition

(0-13-101766-7)

The Complete Visual Basic® .NET Training Course, Second Edition

(0-13-042530-3)

The Complete C# Training Course

(0-13-064584-2)

The Complete Internet & World Wide Web Programming Training Course, Second Edition

(0-13-089550-4)

The Complete XML Programming Training Course

(0-13-089557-1)

The Complete e-Business & e-Commerce Programming Training Course

(0-13-089549-0)

The Complete Perl Training Course

(0-13-089552-0)

The Complete Visual Basic® 6 Training Course

(0-13-082929-3)

The Complete Python Training Course

(0-13-067374-9)

The Complete Wireless Internet & Mobile Business Programming Training Course

(0-13-062335-0)

All of these ISBNs are retail ISBNs. College and university instructors should contact your local Prentice Hall representative or write to cs@prenhall.com for the corresponding student edition ISBNs.

If you would like to purchase the Cyber Classrooms separately...

Prentice Hall offers Multimedia Cyber Classroom CD-ROMs to accompany the *How to Program Series* texts for the topics listed at right. If you have already purchased one of these books and would like to purchase a stand-alone copy of the corresponding *Multimedia Cyber Classroom,* you can make your purchase at the following Web site:

www.informit.com/cyberclassrooms

C++ Multimedia Cyber Classroom, 4/E, ISBN # 0-13-100253-8

C# Multimedia Cyber Classroom, ask for product number 0-13-064587-7

e-Business & e-Commerce Cyber Classroom, ISBN # 0-13-089540-7

Internet & World Wide Web Cyber Classroom, 2/E, ISBN # 0-13-089559-8

Java Multimedia Cyber Classroom, 5/E, ISBN # 0-13-101769-1

Perl Multimedia Cyber Classroom, ISBN # 0-13-089553-9

Python Multimedia Cyber Classroom, ISBN # 0-13-067375-7

Visual Basic 6 Multimedia Cyber Classroom, ISBN # 0-13-083116-6

Visual Basic .NET Multimedia Cyber Classroom, 2/E, ISBN # 0-13-065193-1

XML Multimedia Cyber Classroom, ISBN # 0-13-089555-5

Wireless Internet & Mobile Business Programming Multimedia Cyber Classroom, ISBN # 0-13-062337-7

e-LEARNING • from Deitel & Associates, Inc.

Cyber Classrooms, Web-Based Training and Course Management Systems

DEITEL is committed to continuous research and development in e-Learning.

We are pleased to announce that we have incorporated examples of Web-based training, including a five-way Macromedia® Flash™ animation of a for loop in Java™, into the *Java 2 Multimedia Cyber Classroom, 5/e* (which is included in *The Complete Java 2 Training Course, 5/e*). Our instruc-

tional designers and Flash animation team are developing additional simulations that demonstrate key programming concepts.

We are enhancing the Multimedia *Cyber Classroom* products to include more audio, pre- and post-assessment questions and Web-based labs with solutions for the benefit of professors and students alike. In addition, our Multimedia *Cyber Classroom* products, currently available in CD-ROM format, are being ported to Pearson's CourseCompass course-management system—*a powerful e-platform for teaching and learning*. Many DEITEL® materials are available in WebCT, Blackboard and CourseCompass formats for colleges, and will soon be available for various corporate learning management systems. For more information on course management systems, please visit us on the Web at www.prenhall.com/cms.

WHAT'S COMING FROM THE DEITELS

Future Publications

Here are some new books we are considering for 2003/2004 release:

Simply Series: *Simply C++, Simply C#.*

Computer Science Series: *Java Software Design, C++ Software Design.*

Internet and Web Programming Series: *Internet and World Wide Web How to Program 3/e; Open Source Software Development: Linux, Apache, MySQL, Perl and PHP.*

DEITEL® Developer Series: *ASP .NET with Visual Basic .NET, ASP .NET with C#.*

Object Technology Series: *OOAD with the UML, Design Patterns, Java and XML.*

Java Series: *Advanced Java™ 2 Platform How to Program 2/e.*

Operating Systems, Third Edition

This fall we will wrap up the first book in our new *Computer Science Series, Operating Systems, Third Edition.* This book will be entirely updated to reflect current core operating system concepts and design considerations. Using Java™ code to illustrate key points, *Operating Systems* will introduce processes, concurrent programming, deadlock and indefinite postponement, mutual exclusion, physical and virtual memory, file systems, disk performance, distributed systems, security and more. To complement the discussion of operating system concepts, the book will feature extensive case studies on the latest operating systems, including the soon-to-be-released Linux kernel version 2.4 and the Windows XP operating system. This book covers all of the core topics and many elective topics recommended by the Joint Task Force on Computing Curricula 2001 developed by the IEEE Computer Society and ACM, making it an ideal textbook for undergraduate operating systems courses.

ur official e-mail newsletter, the DEITEL® BUZZ ONLINE, is a free publication designed to keep you updated on our publishing program, instructor-led corporate training courses, hottest industry trends and topics and more.

Issues of our newsletter include:

- **Technology Spotlights** that feature articles and information on the hottest industry topics drawn directly from our publications or written during the research and development process.

- **Anecdotes** and/or **challenges** that allow our readers to interact with our newsletter and with us. We always welcome and appreciate your comments, answers and feedback. We will summarize all responses we receive in future issues.

- **Announcements** on what's happening at Deitel as well as updated information on our publishing plans.

- **Highlights** and **Announcements** on current and upcoming products that are of interest to professionals, students and instructors.

  Information on our **instructor-led corporate training courses delivered at organizations worldwide**. Complete course listings and special course highlights provide readers with additional details on DEITEL™ training offerings.

- Our newsletter is available in both **full-color HTML** or **plain-text** formats depending on your viewing preferences and e-mail client capabilities.

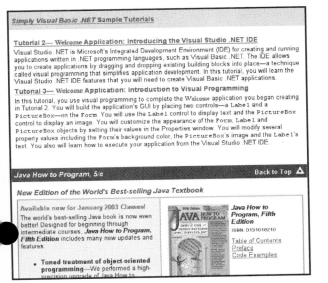

- Learn about the history of Deitel & Associates, our brands, the bugs and more in the **Lore and Legends** section of the newsletter.

- **Hyperlinked Table of Contents** allows readers to navigate quickly through the newsletter by jumping directly to specific topics of interest.

To sign up for the DEITEL® BUZZ ONLINE newsletter, visit `www.deitel.com/newsletter/subscribe.html`.

Turn the page to find out more about Deitel & Associates!

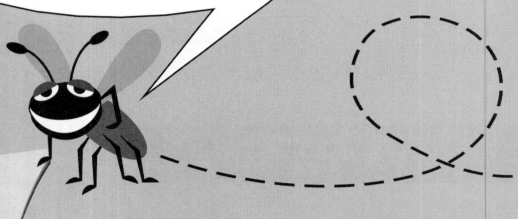